Literature at the Barricades

The American Writer in the 1930s

Photograph courtesy
Dorothea Lange Collection,
The Oakland Museum

Literature at the Barricades

The American Writer
in the 1930s

EDITED BY
RALPH F. BOGARDUS and FRED HOBSON

The University of Alabama Press
University, Alabama

Library of Congress Cataloging in Publication Data

Main entry under title:

Literature at the barricades.

Essays presented at the Fifth Alabama Symposium on English and American Literature, Tuscaloosa, Ala., Oct. 19–21, 1978.
Includes bibliographies and index.
1. American literature—20th century—History and criticism—Congresses. 2. Authors, American—20th century—Political and social views—Congresses.
3. Literature and society—United States—Congresses.
4. Depressions—1929—United States—Congresses.
I. Bogardus, Ralph F., 1938–   II. Hobson, Fred C., 1943–
PS223.L5   810'.9'0052   81-3015
ISBN 0-8173-0078-3   AACR2
ISBN 0-8173-0079-1 (pbk.)

TO THE MEMORY OF

James T. Farrell

(1904–1979)

Contents

Acknowledgments

This book of essays originated in the Fifth Alabama Symposium on English and American Literature, "The American Writer in the 1930s," which took place in Tuscaloosa, Alabama, on 19–21 October 1978. The conference itself (and, thus, this book) was made possible by a grant from the Research Development Program of the National Endowment for the Humanities and funding from The University of Alabama. The editors wish to thank both for their support.

In particular, we acknowledge help from The Presidential Venture Fund, the Office of Academic Affairs, the College of Arts and Sciences, and the College of Continuing Education, all of The University of Alabama.

The following persons at the University deserve special mention, because their support was moral as well as financial: Douglas E. Jones, dean of the College of Arts and Sciences; George Wolfe, associate professor, Department of English, and originator of the Alabama Symposia on English and American Literature; and Charles E. Adams, director of conference activities, and John H. Burton, associate director of conference activities, both of the Division of Continuing Education.

In addition, the following acknowledgments are due: Townsend Ludington and E. P. Dutton Publishers for permission to use "Friendship Won't Stand That," which, though originally presented at the conference, appeared in revised, different form in *John Dos Passos: A Twentieth Century Odyssey* (New York: Dutton, 1980); the Alderman Library of the University of Virginia, Charlottesville, for permission to use materials from the John Dos Passos papers; the Special Collections, Southern Illinois University Library, for permission to use materials from the John Howard Lawson Papers; and Amanda Lawson, Elizabeth Dos Passos, and the late Susan Edward Lawson, for permission to quote from these materials.

The University of Kentucky Library, Lexington, for permission to use quotations from materials in the Harriette Arnow Special Collection.

Hilton Kramer, literary executor for the estate of Josephine Herbst, and Georges Borchardt, Incorporated, Herbst's literary agent, for permission to use "Yesterday's Road," which originally appeared in *New American Review* 3 (1968).

Alan Wald and *Occident* for permission to use "Revolutionary Intellectuals: *Partisan Review* in the 1930s," which originally appeared in *Occident* 8 (Spring 1974) and has been revised and expanded for inclusion in this volume.

James T. Farrell and the *American Mercury* for graciously allowing us to reprint Farrell's perceptive essay "The End of a Literary Decade," originally published in the *American Mercury* 48 (1939).

Special thanks are due Elinor Langer, who originally appeared in the symposium, subsequently urged us to use the Herbst memoir in this volume, and helped us secure permission to include it. We wish also to thank Jan Wilson for her intelligent, patient, and tireless efforts expended in completing the original typescript of this book, and Cynthia Graff Hobson for editorial assistance.

Literature at the Barricades

The American Writer in the 1930s

Introduction

Few disagree that the decade of the 1930s embodied one of the major experiences ever to be thrust upon American life and the American mind. The Great Depression was an unprecedented material failure; yet it was more than just material in its consequences and implications. It permeated America's collective consciousness. Life's tone changed radically, values took on new perspective, and a reexamination of both seemed inescapable. Initially, as Alfred Kazin puts it, "the impact of the crisis on culture was far more violent than its transformation of the social order . . . it was an education by shock."[1] It was also an education by ordeal. The damage was so widespread that a check was placed on the prevailing optimism. The American dream was seriously questioned as never before, and communism for a time looked good to people who would never have considered it earlier. It was the only decade—other than the 1860s, and perhaps the late 1960s and 1970s—when it became disquietingly clear to Americans that things do not always work, that human designs have limits.

The American writer of the 1930s reported and reflected the age. There was no need to announce, as T. S. Eliot had in the 1920s, that a wasteland was with us. Because Americans had long been basically materialistic, they tended to lose hope when they lost things. And since people did indeed lose jobs, homes, farms, fortunes or modest savings, and—most tellingly—their self-respect and hope, they did not have to be reminded by their writers that times were bad. They felt the harsh facts daily even though they might not have comprehended fully why these things were happening. Still, no one sensed the ordeal of depression any more deeply or intensely than did artists and intellectuals; it was they who faced the experience most questioningly and sought to understand and to articulate its cultural meanings most clearly and forcefully.

An important and highly visible aspect of the cultural crisis was the crisis in literature. As never before, the intellectuals' questions led them to become politically conscious and, ultimately, engaged. Their involvement was, for the most part, with the left, and it was widespread and often deep. "In any view," Lionel Trilling reminds us, "the importance of the radical movement of the Thirties cannot be overestimated. It may be said to have created the American intellectual class as we now know it in its great size and influence. It fixed the character of this class as being, through all mutations of opinion, predominantly of the left." And the style of that class—its "moral urgency . . . sense of crisis . . . concern with personal salvation"—was, in Trilling's view, also shaped by the decade's politics.[2] Kazin would seem to agree—at least in part. There emerged, he argues, "a new generation [of writers] armed with fresh purpose" who "personified a transformation of sensibility, of style, of the very nature of the American literary character, that seemed unprecedented. . . . Writing was no longer an exercise of personality testing the range of the writer's strategy and powers; it was an expression of belief" that resulted in a kind of literary sociology containing a raw, authentic, naturalistic force at its best and a crude, false, polemical fizzle at its worst.[3] Yet where Kazin and Trilling see the period somewhat positively, as one that inexorably demanded intense response from writers and produced a few notable works among innumerable failures, Leslie Fiedler offers a more negative view. While agreeing that the period was enormously influential, he believes that the decade's experience was almost wholly disastrous to good American writing, because it forced writers "to distort their values and betray the myths which informed their authentic work in pursuit of shifting critical acclaim and an audience that had radically changed its allegiances."[4] That or risk being dismissed and ignored.

These views suggest that the 1930s was a problematic period for American writers. They also suggest some of the prevailing conventions that tend to dominate literary thinking about the 1930s. First, it is fairly common to see the decade's experience as one that stimulated and promoted the rebirth of American literary naturalism, a mode that along with realism ("proletarian fiction" became the catchword) dominated the literary scene. Second, it is thought to have been a time when writers—and by implication, their art—became subservient to the radical politics of the day (usually Communist), either giving up art altogether for political action or turning their talents toward the illustration and service of an ever-shifting political line. Of course, the first phenomenon is generally believed to have flowed in large part from the second. In any event, the most damaging consequences of the period's existential imperatives are thought to have been the pervasive lapse of critical-mindedness and intellectual honesty and the widespread betrayal of the modernist literary tradition. Modernist experimentation, it is assumed, was jettisoned voluntarily by politically born-again writers, or its practice was successfully discredited, impeded, and corrupted by literary "commissars" like Mike Gold, Joseph Freeman, and Granville Hicks. It is this presumed hiatus of modernism that some post-1930s critics subsequently lamented almost more than they decried the artists' supposed willingness to march vacant-eyed to the tune of the Stalinist drummer.

But did artists and critics mindlessly don red uniforms for the long march, did naturalism and realism dominate the 1930s literary scene, and did modernism disappear only to be saved from obscurity by the New Critics? A closer look, a more analytical study suggests a restrained but solid no, leavened by a faint, diminished yes.

"How to reconcile Rimbaud's *la Vraie Vie* with the commune." So queries Josephine Herbst in her memoir "Yesterday's Road," reprinted in this volume. Her words imply something of the dilemma that indeed faced writers who were impressed by modern art but could not ignore depression realities; and her phrasing of that dilemma is, if not exactly apocalyptic, at least apt. Most of the writers who turned left during the 1930s were molded in a different age. Their thinking and sensibilities were forged during the 1920s and earlier, and many of them were deeply influenced by the modernist writers and experience as well as by the breakdown of Victorian values and assumptions.

1922 is, of course, the important date to recall: a watershed year that symbolizes the birthing-time of literary modernism. It was then that Eliot's *Waste Land* and Joyce's *Ulysses* were published, thereby setting the course most young writers would seek to travel for the rest of that decade. Realism and naturalism were not summarily banished as a consequence. Sinclair Lewis wrote some of his best work during the 1920s, and Theodore Dreiser's masterpiece, *An American Tragedy*, appeared in 1925. And younger writers dazzled by modernism's sensibility and style—Hemingway and Fitzgerald, for example—still owed something to the older tradition of realism.[5] But modernist experimentation was in the air; it was a new force that writers and critics began to acknowledge, tried to understand, and turned into practice. Once again, it seemed, American artists were looking to Europe; for other influences did not really count—that is, not before the crash.

Modernism did not just die, however, when the bottom fell out of the stock market in 1929. The 1930s must be seen as an extension of the literary teens and the 1920s. "I was formed more in the Twenties than the Thirties," protests James T. Farrell, a major American writer mainly viewed as the quintessentially 1930s figure. "By the start of the Thirties, I was committed to what can best be called realism in literature. . . . I was affected and influenced in and during the Thirties. But I was decidedly formed and ready before the Thirties started. And I had read and been influenced by many, Ben Hecht, Maxwell Bodenheim, George Moore, James Joyce, Hemingway, Sherwood Anderson, Nietzsche, Red Lewis, etc., and not solely and simply by Teddy Dreiser."[6] Farrell was not just a realist; he was, as Donald Pizer argues in this volume, also a modernist. His prose method owed more to James Joyce than it did to Dreiser or the realists. So did the writing of others in the 1930s: Henry Roth's *Call It Sleep*, Dos Passos's *U.S.A.* (begun in the 1920s), and Faulkner's books (the best of which were written during the late 1920s and early 1930s).[7] And while it is certainly true, as Walter B. Rideout notes in *The Radical Novel in the United States, 1900–1954*, that more so-called radical novels were written in the 1930s than in any of the individual decades between 1900 and 1950, it does not follow that modernism was dead.[8]

American intellectuals were aware of the modernist achievement as they faced depression America and sought to determine what their place and role ought to be in that grim environment. But equally obvious to most of them was the fact that they could not exist outside politics; they knew that, as Stephen Spender puts it, "in a crisis of a whole society every work takes on a political look in either being symptomatic of that crisis (which is itself, of course, political) or in avoiding it."[9] The crisis challenged modernism, creating a paradox shrewdly defined by Spender in his memoirs: "the essence of the modern movement was that it was centered on itself and not on anything outside it; neither on ideology or theology nor on the expression of the poet's feelings and personality. One might say that the moment Thirties writing became illustrative of Marxist texts or reaction to 'history'—and to the extent to which it did those things—it ceased to be a part of the modern movement." Yet, he continues, modernism was crucial because it presented writers possessing a 1930s political point of view

> with a medium in which it was possible for us to write about modern life, say whatever we chose, without taking thought as to whether language and form were "poetic." In writing about politics, we were using the instrument of language provided for us by our predecessors to express that which they avoided in their work, an overt subject matter. We were putting the subject back into poetry. We were taking the medium of poetry, which to them was an end in itself, and using it as an instrument for realizing our felt ideas about the time in which we were living. Yet members of my generation continued to think that poetry should be judged by standards which were not ideological.[10]

While Spender's experience and generation were British, his point seems appropriate to the 1930s American experience. Like their English counterparts, American writers and critics fellow-traveled or even became Communists for a time. But the best of them never gave up the idea that art was to be judged not according to correct ideological standards but according to aesthetic ones.

Nowhere is this idea more clearly evidenced than in the literary battles of the 1930s. As Daniel Aaron shows in his definitive *Writers on the Left*, these skirmishes occurred not long after intellectuals started becoming involved in left-wing politics, and they grew in frequency and heatedness as the 1930s ground on.[11] The *New Masses* began to court important, potentially sympathetic writers as early as 1927, and none other than Mike Gold himself urged that a link existed between the new art and political radicalism: both were antibourgeois, and therefore antibourgeois modernists ought to be potential allies in the left's cause since their consciousness was so close to that of the political radicals'. Political radicalism offered an end to alienation to intellectuals and artists for whom there was no real audience in bourgeois culture. Marxism, Gold believed, stimulated hopes that out of radical change would come an advanced culture, one that would correspond in seriousness and inventiveness to modernist art and appeal to a wide audience which, undiverted by commercial glitter and false promise, could respond appreciatively.[12] There was certainly some perspicacity in Gold's observations, for many American writers did find communism appealing for those reasons during the late 1920s and early 1930s.[13] Yet, in spite of its attraction, very few actually joined the party.

Notwithstanding its early promise, the love affair between literature and Communist politics could not last. Writers retained just as much critical distance from the party as sympathy with the more generalized radical critique of America. This attitude manifested itself fairly early, centering on the issue that Gold may have consciously tried to defuse at the outset of the courtship: the question of the integrity and independence of art and the artist. The experience of one of the courted, Edmund Wilson, is illustrative of this state of affairs. Though a supporter of literary modernism, Wilson had repudiated aestheticism, pure art, and the detached artist in a 1927 essay in the *New Republic*. He thereby seemed to be responding to Gold's flirtation. After completing *Axel's Castle* in 1929, Wilson moved on to political and cultural reportage, giving up his seat as the *New Republic*'s literary editor. Yet he never rejected the modernist achievements, nor did he judge writers' literary merit by their politics. His attitude surfaced vigorously soon after the first of the notorious literary battles took place—the Gold-Wilder debate that appeared in several issues of the *New Republic* during 1930. Thornton Wilder had been attacked by Gold for the effete, reactionary humanist tendencies that allegedly pervaded his books. Wilson, after a detour that took him to Harlan County, Scottsboro, and *The American Jitters*, felt it necessary to respond to Gold. In Wilson's view—set down in "The Literary Class War" and published in 1932—Gold's attack denoted "the eruption of the Marxist issues out of the literary circles of the radicals into the field of general criticism. It has now become plain that the economic crisis is to be accompanied by a literary one."[14] The danger was clear to Wilson: Gold's repudiation "was an attempt to arraign Mr. Wilder at the bar of the Communist ideology."[15] Though Wilson partly agreed with certain of Gold's criticisms of Wilder (and said so in print during the controversy), he was disturbed by what he saw as an "atmosphere of intellectual confusion—an atmosphere which had not yet cleared up."[16] Wilson, by his own admission, did not devote nearly as much time in the 1930s to writing about literary events as he had in the 1920s or would in the 1940s, but he still continued to defend writers like Eliot, the technique of modernism, and numerous American writers of the past who did not seem to fit the left's profile of artists in uniform. And, of course, Wilson was not alone in his efforts.

The battle begun by Gold and others was to continue throughout the 1930s. This fact underlines the truth that the best writers and most thoughtful critics refused to follow the party line—something that at best was confused and shifting throughout the period.[17] At the First Writers' Congress in 1935, for instance, there were open defenses of writing that did not fit the Communist view by writers such as James T. Farrell, John Dos Passos, and Kenneth Burke. As time passed and the issue of literature's integrity became more embattled, the fights became fiercer and more bitter. And even though the controversy over "leftism" vigorously took place in the pages of the *New Masses* as well as those of the *New Republic* and *Partisan Review,* such openness and apparent unity were disappearing rapidly. The respective positions of the contending critics and writers were becoming irreconcilable. The year 1936 seems to have been decisive in these debates: James T. Farrell's *A Note on Literary Criticism* appeared and signaled the beginning of the irreparable split in the literary left. The book was attacked in the *New Masses* by Granville Hicks and defended in *Partisan Review and Anvil* by Alan Calmer and in the *Nation* by Edmund Wilson. That same year, the old *Partisan Review* (having become briefly *Partisan Review and Anvil*) folded, and its editors began their move toward an independent literary Marxism. This move became obvious when Rahv, Phillips, and other young literary intellectuals brashly spoke out at the Second Writers' Congress in June 1937. Then, as if to add insult to injury, this group resuscitated *Partisan Review* in December 1937 and made it the intellectual home for independent literary radicals such as Dwight Macdonald, James T. Farrell, F. W. Dupee, Lionel Trilling, and Mary McCarthy. Without question, this group was committed to good literature as well as radical, usually Marxist, thinking. Among their efforts—perhaps best exemplified by Philip Rahv—was the attempt to reconcile literary modernism and Marxism. And though that merger may not have been successfully achieved, modernism received support and explication from these independent radicals that was as intelligent and forceful as that coming from the pens of the New Critics.[18]

Despite this literary independence, many would still insist that the fiction and poetry of the 1930s prove that art and politics cannot mix without the former being diminished or destroyed by the latter. However, in the light of literary history, this view also seems shortsighted. "The 'literary intelligentsia,'" Walter Lacqueur reminds us, "has been prominent in all political movements of the past two hundred years; they have played a decisive role in revolutions even if their function usually extended no further than blazing the trail."[19] Moreover, artists' works have always reflected, overtly or covertly, sociopolitical worldviews precisely because artists have always been creatures existing in a world made up of social and political phenomena.[20] Jane Austen's fiction reflects her age's social and cultural milieux; Balzac replicates his world of the emerging French middle classes amidst the chaos of an old order being replaced by a new one; and Dickens gives us a vivid, harsh look at an urbanizing, industrializing England.

Of course, as Irving Howe argues in *Politics and the Novel*, political content in a work does not automatically make it "political" literature. Dealing specifically with the novel, Howe suggests that the most useful measure for deciding that question is whether the writing's political aspect is central or necessary to a cogent analysis of the book itself.[21] Then he proceeds to discuss a number of political novels, assessing their artistic qualities and judging some excellent, some flawed. Like Howe, we cannot fail to recognize that much good literature is political. Zola's *Germinal*, with its partly Marxist, partly Darwinist consciousness, is; and so are Henry James's *The Princess Casamassima* and *The Bostonians*, with their respective treatments of London anarchists and Boston reformers. Works by some of the greatest Russian writers—Gogol (*Dead Souls*), Turgenev (*Fathers and Sons*), Tolstoy (*War and Peace*), and Dostoevsky (*The Possessed*)—are political, too. Indeed, Dostoevsky's *Notes from Underground*, a protomodernist classic, is aggressively political in its antipolitical stance and in its calculated attack on Chernyshevsky's utopian political novel, *What Is to Be Done?* At random, one can list so many other good or great writers whose art is enhanced or given its central power by political content: Nathaniel Hawthorne, James Fenimore Cooper, Joseph Conrad, Ignazio Silone, Doris Lessing, and V. S. Naipaul.

The question to be asked in each instance is whether the writer has absorbed the political subject matter and transformed it so that it serves rather than submerges his or her own imaginative purposes. So long as artists have the gifts—the imaginative intelligence and the sense of craft— to make art, they can use politics just as they are able to use any other subject: to probe the human condition, to get at what it is to be human, and to unfold truths and beauties that reside in these things. On the other hand, if they allow—for whatever reasons—their art to be shaped by a party line or other nonartistic considerations rather than their own creative judgments, they court disaster.

It was just such a corruption—an ideological and aesthetic authoritarianism—that the best 1930s writers and critics avoided and opposed. Many fine works of art emerged during the period. Some were political in Howe's sense of the term, others were not. But most were suffused with some sense of the political and economic crisis.

What follows is a series of essays that captures the sense—largely a struggle—of the 1930s literary experience. Though by no means exhaustive in their coverage, these essays deal in depth with the issues and problems alluded to in this impressionistic introduction. A special attempt has been made by the essayists to individualize the experience of being a writer in a time of overwhelming economic depression and political upheaval and thereby throw into relief the social, political, intellectual, and artistic problems and pressures that characterized the times and influenced the work.

The problematic temper and tone of the decade are poignantly and sharply evoked in Irving Howe's lead essay, providing the volume with a reflective overview. Following this are pieces that seek to convey the quality and temper of the period's experience from a close-up view— Herbst's memoir, Townsend Ludington's essay on the political dialogue between Dos Passos and John Howard Lawson, and James T. Farrell's pungent instant replay of the decade's wins and losses. Other essays analyze the period's meanings from a more distant stance: Daniel Aaron's discussion of Edmund Wilson, Louis Rubin's reflections on the literary South during the depression era, Alan Wald's history of the *Partisan Review* editors' journey toward independence, and Sylvia Cook's reassessment of John Steinbeck's literary relation to communism. Still other essayists deal more with the writers' products, the works themselves: Donald Pizer gives us a close reading of Farrell's *Studs Lonigan* in order to clarify its modernist roots; Hugh Kenner evocatively introduces us to two utterly neglected poets who began writing in the 1930s, George Oppen and Louis Zukofsky; Victor Kramer sensitively examines James Agee's prose method in *Let Us Now Praise Famous Men*; Jack Moore reestablishes Richard Wright as a southern as well as politically conscious writer; and Glenda Hobbs offers us her carefully researched, freshly intelligent reassessment of the much-ignored Harriette Arnow.

Obviously, many writers who might have been discussed are missing. One can reel off names like Nathanael West, Muriel Rukeyser, Tillie

Olson, Daniel Fuchs, Robert Cantwell, or Langston Hughes. Or the imaginative critic Kenneth Burke. Our only excuse for these omissions is that there was simply not time enough in the original symposium or sufficient space in the present volume. However, it is the editors' hope that this book will contribute to and stimulate the reassessment of 1930s writers in order to reestablish the importance of those deserving but often forgotten ones—and in doing so, clarify further the period's literary importance.

Part I

WRITERS AND POLITICS:
THE CHALLENGE OF THE
SOCIAL MUSE

The revolution must not be
understood as simply a revolt against the economic
chaos of today. It is an
immediate organ of cre-
ation. We believe that
in imaginative works, in
philosophic thought, in
concrete activities and
groups, the nucleus and
the framework of the new
society must be created
now.

Edmund Wilson,
Lewis Mumford,
Waldo Frank,
John Dos Passos,
and Sherwood
Anderson,
"Manifesto,"
1932

CHAPTER 1

IRVING HOWE

The Thirties in Retrospect

Once we brush aside the trivial notion that each decade in America must have its own cultural signature, what could we mean when speaking about "the thirties"? The thirties, that is, as more than a convention of the calendar; the thirties as a distinct, perhaps unique moment in our history.

Only one thing: that there occurred in the five or six years following 1929 a deep rift in American life, a rift in that benign continuity Americans had supposed to be their particular blessing. The assumption was destroyed that we lived under the sign of a providential destiny, one that would shelter us from the violence and blood of Europe. Or so it seemed to many people, though in fact only for a time, since the assumption of a providential destiny has regained its force among us, as an all but indestructible vanity of the American spirit.

There were intellectuals in the early thirties who welcomed this rift in our national life. They were sick of the smugness that the claim to a unique destiny had bred in the American character. They were sick of that narrowness of spirit that had been fostered by the crossing of a decadent Emersonianism with a gross social Darwinism. "To the writers and artists of my generation," wrote Edmund Wilson, the depression years were "not depressing but stimulating. One couldn't help being exhilarated at the sudden unexpected collapse of that stupid gigantic fraud" that celebrated Big Business.

Wilson may have been exaggerating a little, for together with relief at the collapse of fraud went fear, even terror, regarding the consequences. It's true, nevertheless, that a good many writers, especially those of Wilson's bent, thought that America was finally coming of age. Finally we were to enter the vestibule of historical maturity, perhaps tragedy.

The assumption of the "Americanness of America" speaks for a sense of national destiny that precludes harsh conflicts of class; speaks for an America unburdened by feudal heritage and only a little marred by capitalist excess; speaks for a historical passage, with but a few intervening bumps, from small landowner to comfortable suburbanite. Once before this vision had been brought into question, and that of course by the Civil War, when our capacity for blood in action and extremism of mind was sufficiently demonstrated. It might today also seem that a third such historical rift occurred in the sixties, though we cannot be sure—it may only have been a little fissure. But the thirties: they did represent a profound rift in a national experience supposedly marked out for smoothness and ease.

The thirties raised to a new seriousness what a fraction of left-wing intellectuals and immigrant workers had previously been able to assert only at the margin of our society: the possibility that American capitalism would share the fate of world capitalism. Marxist thinkers had long spoken of world capitalism as an integral system, the parts of which would necessarily stand or, better yet, fall together; this truism took on a new acuteness when the newspaper headlines told of millions thrown out of work, bankruptcies piling up, stock market speculators jumping out of windows. The heritage of Emersonianism, which had steadily dominated American culture for a century, now seemed to shrink to the paltriness of a "rugged individualism" bewildered by the twentieth century, and the heritage of Thoreau to the impotence of a president worshipping the sublimities of "the free market." The law of supply and demand, the right of the laborer to sell his labor at as low a price as the buyer could impose, the classical American wisdom of Henry Ford that "history is bunk"—all collapsed in the junkyard of depression America.

The mere facts are known, I suppose, to every literate person. What is hard, perhaps impossible, to convey is the sense of utter social breakdown, the coming apart of those tacit convictions that keep a society together. The historical imagination is at best a fragile gift, and I doubt that anyone under the age of forty-five can really grasp what it means to have lived through the depression, just as those now being born may never be able to grasp what it means to have lived through the Vietnam years. Perhaps it will make things a bit more vivid if I quote a few lines from an unpublished memoir summoning remembrances of years past as the child of immigrant Jewish workers in New York:

> It was a time profoundly disorganizing in its effects upon the young; there was no longer that intuitive transmission of cues by means of which social existence is regulated. We were still dutifully going to high school and college, partly because we knew of nothing else to do, partly because we liked to read books, and partly because our parents clung to the dream of education.
>
> All the time there were voices of anxiety at home, worried about "slack," the season without work, or complaining about reductions in the piece-work rates in the shops. One terrible day in the early thirties we heard that the Bank of the

United States had failed, and I sat in our apartment listening to my aunt and grandmother wailing over the loss of the few hundred dollars they had scraped together. . . .

Things had gone profoundly wrong. No later discounting of the excesses or fecklessness of the radicalism of the thirties can wipe away this simple truth.

Things had gone wrong not only in America but still more in Europe. Whatever the provincialism of immigrant Jewish life, it was far less provincial than most other segments of America in responding to the tragedies of Europe in the thirties. Even the least political among us knew that the rise of Hitler would soon tear our lives apart. When the Socialists of Vienna tried vainly in 1934 to put up a military resistance against the repressions of the Dollfuss government, I would hover around the newsstands—that was an important part of life in the thirties, people hovering around newsstands—to read the headlines with a grief I could barely have explained. Later I would feel the same way as the fascists approached Madrid. European society was breaking up, and the conclusion we drew from this fact, too simple no doubt, was that all possibility of mending or patching was done with, the time of apocalypse had come, everything would now depend on whether socialism could, in one last victorious upsurge, repel the barbarians. We saw no other choices, and the time did not encourage any.

At such a moment conservatism seemed either an intellectual joke or a mere reflex of privilege; liberalism seemed tired, pusillanimous, given to small repairs where an entire new structure was needed. That the society would partly right itself, through the welfare state created by Franklin Roosevelt, was not a possibility to be taken seriously.

Shaken loose from traditional opinions, frequently forced to accept a sharp drop of income, sometimes pushed into the ranks of the jobless, some American writers broke away from the routines of literary work in order to travel across the country, measuring the human costs of the depression. Edmund Wilson, Erskine Caldwell, Sherwood Anderson talked to hungry men in New York, listened to desperate strikers in North Carolina. The vision of the United States that began to emerge in their minds was notably similar to that of John Dos Passos's *U.S.A..* "We are two nations." Once a mere phrase, the class struggle now came to be the flesh and pain of daily life.

A considerable number of American writers turned left—and, as they made a point of pointing out, sharply left. Asked by the *Modern Quarterly* to discuss the relative merits of the socialist and communist movements, some of these writers gave wonderfully revealing answers. "Becoming a Socialist right now," said John Dos Passos, "would have just the same effect on anybody as drinking a bottle of near-beer."

A bit later Sherwood Anderson wrote in the *New Masses*: "Among these fighting young Communists [he had been watching them make speeches on New York street corners] I found poverty, youth, and no gloom. . . . If it be necessary, in order to bring about the end of a money civilization . . .

that we of the so-called artist class be submerged, let us be submerged. Down with us!" And at a New York meeting where Anderson asked himself, What is the difference between Socialists and Communists?, he answered with all the candor of his ingenuousness: "I guess the Communists mean it."

Why so many twentieth-century writers have yielded themselves to authoritarian ideas of both left and right is a problem allowing for no single or simple answer, but surely Anderson's sentence must rank high among the items of crucial evidence: *The Communists mean it!*

The belief in some ultimate reality, some total strategy for conquering history, which the Communists alone possessed; the notion that radicalism is a quantity improvable by addition and raised to glory by multiplication; the suspicion that politics is rendered authentic by the quota of violence attached to it; the impulse to self-abasement that intellectuals felt in the presence of the working class—no, not the working class, about which they knew little, but a caricature of it in the person of some party functionary— all these were central to the experience of the literary left in the thirties. Not many writers were careful in thinking through their new allegiance, and fewer still read deeply or critically in the Marx from whom it became fashionable to quote.

The whole sad story of the leftward-moving writers in the thirties—the yielding to a total ideology and an authoritarian party machine; the discarding of literary autonomy in behalf of crudely political ends; the pathetic effort of middle-class writers to create a "proletarian literature" never seriously defined or criticized; the unseemly gyrations of literary people in obedience to political dictate—this story is documented in Daniel Aaron's *Writers on the Left,* and there is no point in my repeating it here. But let me, if I can, rescue the experience of the thirties from two kinds of retrospective simplification: that of the neoconservative ideologues who would attribute it all to foolishness or knavery or rationalist heresy and that of younger, quasi-Marxist academics who grow sentimental about the fiascos of their elders. No; the leftward turn of American writers in the thirties was a complicated phenomenon, at once debasing and idealistic, submissive and rebellious, a break from corrupt traditional authority and a surrender to corrupt untried authority.

Perhaps the most troubling aspect of it was the need that serious and gifted people had for a ritual abandonment of their intellectual independence. I quote a few lines from a letter written in 1932 to Granville Hicks by a friend of his. I believe I know who this friend was, a critic of great refinement, and that makes his document all the more chilling as evidence for the psychology of totalitarian affiliation:

> It is a bad world in which we live, and so even the revolutionary movement is anything but what . . . it "ought" to be: God knows, I realize this, as you do, and

God knows it makes my heart sick at times: from one angle it seems nothing but grime and stink and sweat and obscene noises, and the language of the beasts. But surely this is what *history* is. It is not made by gentlemen and scholars . . . Lenin must have been (from a conceivable point of view) a dreadful man; so must John Brown, and Cromwell, and Marat. . . . I believe we can spare ourselves a great deal of pain and disenchantment and even worse (treachery to ourselves) if we discipline ourselves to accept the proletarian and revolutionary leaders . . . for what they are and must be: grim fighters in about the most dreadful and desperate struggle in all history—*not* reasonable and "critically-minded."

But, in behalf of complication, we must now turn about. There was more than abasement, there was also genuine idealism—indeed, precisely the mixture of the two was what made the experience of the thirties so terrible. So much has happened since the early thirties, so many expectations have turned sour and bitter, it is necessary to recall that in the midst of their moral and intellectual self-betrayals many of the writers who turned toward communism acted out of a valid sense of social despair, a yearning for social betterment. Wilson's gripping report of the Kentucky mining towns, Caldwell's heart-breaking account of the misery he found among southern sharecroppers, Hemingway's description of terrorized veterans in Florida—these were truthful testimony. A great deal in the experience of the left-wing writers during the thirties cannot survive the glare of criticism, but this judgment takes on significance—it takes on full rigor—only if one recognizes that behind the mistakes and the foolishness lay authentic strivings.

To suppose that our literary life in the thirties consisted of no more than a turn to radicalism by novelists and poets would be a gross distortion, the kind of distortion encouraged by popular history. There were in reality other, linked developments, less dramatic but at least as important.

The seeming dislodgment of the "exceptionalist" idea—the idea that America had been endowed with a special destiny exempting it from the woes of Europe—was due in good measure to the rising influence of Marxism. But this dislodgment had begun a good many years before 1930, and it had deeper causes in American cultural history.

All through that history one can detect an alternation of response to Europe. There is the effort simply to take over intact its high culture, mostly a Boston project. There is the wish, stronger on the prairies, that we cut ourselves off from the European past, its sophistication and corruptions, above all its sheer weightedness. The oscillation between these extremes had as their ostensible issue the idea of a total break.

But I doubt that any serious person could ever take that literally; certainly Emerson never did. We know that a total break, or even the desire for it, could end only in ignorance, know-nothingism, and counter-culture. The debate about the cultural relation between America and

Europe was really about the problem of how America might accept and bear the European past without sinking beneath its weight.

In the thirties, as perhaps never before, it seemed to many writers that we had no choice but to yield ourselves—Isaac before the knife—to the "Europeanization" of our culture. The left favored this view because it recognized tacitly that much of its ideology found provenance and justification in Europe. The critics setting themselves up as spokesmen for literary modernism felt that our culture had become too parochial, its regional and nationalist biases small-spirited. In the modern era a literature could only be cosmopolitan if it proposed to be serious. Even the group of conservative Fugitives in Nashville came under the sign of Europe, for their "agrarian vision," though drawn intellectually from Jeffersonianism, had as a point of kinship with northern radicalism that it repudiated the premise of an ever-mounting flow of commercial progress sponsored, in ascending order, by God, nature, and the free market.

Fundamentally, the exceptionalist idea is both source and sustenance of American liberalism. And as that liberalism seemed helpless in the thirties before the breakdown of society, so cultural exceptionalism also came to seem enfeebled and outmoded.

The Europeanization of American culture, begun at about the time of the First World War, was sharply quickened. Modernism triumphed—perhaps too much so, since modernism can flourish only when it has not yet triumphed. The welfare state, previously supposed a bad dream of European socialists, was grudgingly accepted, by some as a social device rescuing American liberalism, by others as a social device rescuing American capitalism, and by a small sophisticated minority as both. Hardly anyone, except such scorned elders as Van Wyck Brooks, would now have argued against the claim that American culture was inextricably part of an international culture. And you could see this not just in literature but still more in art, where in a few years the abstract expressionists would create a brilliant new style that could be cultivated in Tokyo or Bucharest, Rio de Janeiro or Paris quite as well as in New York.

What was happening was that the traditional authority, indeed the sovereignty, of Emersonianism was being challenged. It had not happened before. Historically regarded, Emerson haunts the American premises. He is both influence accepted and influence denied. Our wicked lamb, he has left his mark on every major American writer with the exception of Edith Wharton. Over and over again one hears echoes of Emerson's call for the self-reliant man, follower of instinct and conscience (the two, implausibly, not very distinct in his writing)—over and over again, echoes of his romanticism asserting the godly blessedness of human reach. Imagine the outrage of this idea, possibly only to America, that a relentless infinitude of will, emerging from a direct tie with Godhead, should appear in our writing as a

category of innocence! Captain Ahab is Emerson's dark nephew, unacknowledged but looming, and Jay Gatsby is his descendant along a bastard
line, grandson of an illicit union between the Faustian romanticism of the
New England philosopher and the acquisitiveness of the American
bourgeoisie.

And now in the early thirties it seemed as if Emersonians were finally
being dethroned in American culture.

The central tenets of Emersonianism—a quasi-religious celebration of
the individual, who, by virtue of his individuality, shares in a universal
current of divinity (or what Emerson calls "the infinitude of the private
man"); the extreme sundering of self from society, so that unlike most other
peoples we tend to see the two in total disjunction; the spiritualization of
nature, as surrogate for a "missing All"; the stress upon life as "unconditioned," a realm of freedom allowing vast maneuvers to the human
will—all of these seemed hard to credit in the thirties.

"Infinitude of private man"—a bad joke when one saw millions of private
men foundering and lost. Life as "unconditioned"—already deeply challenged by Melville and James, Wharton and Dreiser, and now it made
little sense to writers breaking their teeth on a new vocabulary of "forces of
production," "historical necessity," "social relations." The imagination as
autonomous and self-generating—a mere delusion to writers overwhelmed
by a malignant external reality. For there *was* a social world out there; it
existed in its own right, with its own forms, laws, and pressures; and it
made the human will seem pretty feeble if pitted individually against its
powers. Though the naturalistic novel had its roots in the work of such
earlier figures as Dreiser and Crane, it came in the thirties as an authentic
response, shadowing human existence as more recalcitrant, certainly more
"conditioned" than Emersonianism usually allowed. And thereby as more
European too. That some shoots of Emersonianism would nevertheless cut
their way through even this rocky soil, to survive and flourish in the
decades ahead, we know today. But how was anyone to know it in the
thirties?

Europe as idea, Europe as historical force, Europe as the past accumulated. Our major writers felt Europe as a hand of darkness writing messages
of shared trouble, tragic loss. Europe came to us with the new social fiction
of the twenties and thirties; it came with Hemingway's *The Sun Also Rises*,
Faulkner's *The Sound and the Fury*, James T. Farrell's *Studs Lonigan*, and
John Dos Passos's *U.S.A.* And thereby the American novel moved beyond
the idyll and the epic, both of which had dominated our prose fiction in the
nineteenth century—moved into the bloodied substance of the modern
world.

Fitzgerald's greatest novel, *Tender Is the Night*, is a book in which
Europe breaks open his consciousness. It figures there as a shaken aware-

ness of how severe are the limits of human will, and how quite beyond visible remedy are the stigmata of psychic disturbance and moral dislocation. The characters of this novel are distinctly American, yet we are not tempted to think of them, in the way we do about those of *The Great Gatsby*, as "representing" American experience in some high, mythic way. They are neither overblown for epic nor reduced for comedy; they are lifelike versions of men and women in a familiar society. Fitzgerald has matured into a man for whom suffering is as familiar as water; and there are passages that can be accounted for only by suggesting that, now beyond his inherited American sensibility, he has absorbed the idea of Europe: "One writes of scars healed, a loose parallel to the pathology of the skin, but there is no such thing in the life of the individual. There are open wounds, shrunk sometimes to the size of a pinprick, but wounds still. The marks of suffering are more comparable to the loss of a finger, or of the sight of an eye. We may not miss them, either, for one minute in a year, but if we should there is nothing to be done about it."

Much grief and time were needed before an American novelist could write that last sentence. Still more so to invent the exchange between Dick Diver and the Swiss psychiatrist Franz. Dick, with his swarming innocence, says that he plans "maybe to be the greatest psychologist that ever lived," and Franz answers, as if the voice of history: "That's very good—and very American. . . . It's more difficult for us."

With Hemingway, too, as he partly abandons that code of individual stoicism which had for him served as a sort of private soldier's Emersonianism, there comes a new sense of Europe. Europe in the thirties brings intimations of solidarity, inklings of collective being and fraternity. Spain shook Hemingway, not quite enough to make him really think, but it shook him. He would in fact never quite find a place of rest, a secure point of vision again, but would have to flounder both as man and writer in a limbo between worldviews.

So apparently native a writer as Faulkner also shows the heavy imprint of Europe. His first novel, perhaps through the shadowing of Dos Passos, is an explicit recognition that Europe can cripple the life of a provincial southern boy, though that boy may never know why or how it happened. In the Yoknapatawpha chronicle, seemingly a pure emanation from southern history and myth, there are signs of European consciousness. *The Sound and the Fury* registers the style of modernism, and its view of the human condition breaks sharply from the main lines of American sensibility. *Light in August*, for all its American setting, shares many of the characteristics of the European social novel, far more so than most earlier American fiction: it tells us how profoundly men are the creatures of their society, how crushing is the weight of the historical past.

There is another major writer, Wallace Stevens, in whom I see a saturation of the consciousness that I here abbreviate as European. One side of Stevens has recently been evoked by Harold Bloom, who declares him the progeny of "the inescapable father of the American Sublime," Ralph Waldo Emerson. But there is another Stevens, he who acknowledges that the grandeur and expansiveness of the "American Sublime" are now beyond his reach. As a trained connoisseur in chaos, he calmly accepts the disorder that provides the foreground of modern culture and then measures the losses that a secular imagination must suffer from the exhaustion of religious and historical myths. "The earth for us is flat and bare. / There are no shadows. Poetry / Exceeding music must take the place of empty heaven and its hymns, / Ourselves in poetry must take their place. . . . ." If the leftward-moving writers of the thirties had read Stevens with care, they would have found in his poetry, despite his hard conservative opinions, a voice proclaiming in a language partly derived from Emerson at least a partial dispossession of the Emersonian heritage.

In the literary culture of the thirties, the idea of Europe reaches us not only through the overwhelming sweep of modernism. It also comes through ethnic assertion, the entry of a generation of immigrant Jewish writers, or more accurately, writers who are the children of immigrant Jews.

Over the decades, by now stretching into centuries, American literature has drawn fresh energies from regions, subcultures, and ethnic and racial groups. At least until the twenties one could hardly speak of a national literature in America as something above or apart from the gatherings of talent that appear in these regions, subcultures, and ethnic and racial groups. The masterpieces of the nineteenth century emerge from the regions but also break past them, shaking off provincial self-centeredness yet retaining pungencies of local speech and the strength of local settings. By the twentieth century, it is southern writing that seems to be the one still-vital regional expression; in Faulkner's work local myth rises to art through a sensibility stimulated by European modernism.

A somewhat similar development, starting mostly in the thirties, occurs among the American Jewish writers: figures like Henry Roth, Daniel Fuchs, Delmore Schwartz, and then a bit later Saul Bellow, Bernard Malamud, Tillie Olson, and Philip Roth. They don't, to be sure, all come from the same part of the country, though most come from a few of the larger northern cities with heavy Jewish populations; yet, in a loose metaphorical sense, they constitute a "regional culture." Probably it is one of the last this country is going to have.

Their work, as it first emerges in a great novel like Henry Roth's *Call It Sleep* and in Daniel Fuchs's charming and melancholy trilogy of Brooklyn Jewish life during the depression, is regional in that it derives from and deals overwhelmingly with one locale; regional in that it offers curious local customs for the inspection of native readers; and regional in that it comes to us as an outburst of literary consciousness resulting from an encounter between an immigrant group and the host American culture. Yet this "regionalism" of Jewish American writing is itself shaped by the character of immigrant Yiddish culture, which by the twenties and thirties is mostly secular, radical, and universalist, carrying strong residues of European, especially Russian, culture that the more literate Jewish immigrants had brought across with them. We thus have the intriguing situation of a group of writers emerging from the constrictions of an ethnic subculture, some of them still betraying the accents and inflections of immigrant speech, but who nevertheless serve as conduits for both traditional nineteenth-century Russian literature and for the problematic dazzlements of such modernist European masters as Kafka, Babel, and Brecht. And here too there is a valuable friction—a friction characteristic of the thirties at their best— between native tradition and assaulting import.

For such a new generation of writers, just starting to find its way in the thirties, the main figures of American literature, as well as the main legends and myths carried in their fictions, were not immediately available. What could Emerson mean to a boy or girl growing up on the Lower East Side of New York? You will perhaps forgive me if I again quote from my own memoir about this experience:

> With American literature we were uneasy. It spoke in tones that seemed strange and discordant. Its romanticism was of a kind we could not really find the key to.
>
> Romanticism came to us not so much through the "American Renaissance" as through the eager appropriations that East European Jewish culture had made in the late nineteenth century from Turgenev and Chernyshevsky, Tolstoy and Chekhov. The dominant outlook of the immigrant Jewish culture was probably a shy, idealistic, ethicized, "Russian" romanticism, a romanticism directed more toward social justice than personal fulfillment. The sons and daughters of this immigrant milieu were insulated from American romanticism by their own inherited romanticism, with the differences magnified and the similarities, for a time, all but suppressed.
>
> American romanticism was more likely to reach us through the streets than the schools, through the enticements of popular songs than the austere demands of sacred texts. We absorbed, to be sure, fragments of Emerson, but an Emerson denatured and turned into a spiritual godfather of Herbert Hoover. This American sage seemed frigid and bland, distant in his New England village— and how could we, of all generations, give our hearts to a writer who had lived all his life "in the country"? Getting in touch with the real Emerson, whoever *that* might be, was not for us a natural process of discovering an ancestor or even removing the crusts of misconstruction which had been piled up by the generations. It was a task of rediscovering what we had never really discovered and

then of getting past the barriers of sensibility that separated Concord, Massachusetts, from the immigrant streets of New York.

These were real barriers, significant differences of taste and value. What could we make of all the talk, both from and about Emerson, which elevated individualism to a credo of life? Nothing in our tradition, little in our experience, prepared us for this, and if we were growing up in the 'thirties, when it seemed appropriate to feel estranged from whatever was "officially" American, we could hardly take that credo with much seriousness. The whole complex of Emersonian individualism seemed either a device of the Christians to lure us into a gentility that could only leave us helpless in the worldly struggles ahead, or a bit later, when we entered the phase of teen-age Marxism, it seemed a mere reflex of bourgeois ideology, especially that distinctive American form which posited an "exceptionalist" destiny for the New World.

For most of us, individualism seemed a luxury or deception of the gentile world. Immigrant Jewish culture had been rich in eccentrics, cranks, and individualist display. But the idea of an individual covenant with God, each man responsible for his own salvation; the claim that each man is captain of his soul (picture those immigrant kids, in white shirts and middy blouses, bawling out, "O Captain, My Captain"); the notion that you not only have one but more than one chance in life, which constitutes the American version of grace; and the belief that you rise or fall in accord with your own merits rather than the will of alien despots—these residues of Emersonianism seemed not only strange but sometimes even a version of that brutality which our parents had warned was intrinsic to gentile life. Perhaps our exposure to this warmed-over Emersonianism prompted us to become socialists, as if thereby to make clear our distaste for these American delusions and to affirm, instead, a heritage of communal affections and responsibilities.

Then, too, the Jewish would-be writers found the classical Americans, especially Emerson and Thoreau, a little wan and frail, deficient in those historical entanglements we felt to be essential to literature because inescapable in life. If we did not yet know we surely would have agreed with Henry James's judgment that Emerson leaves "a singular impression of paleness" and lacks "personal avidity." Born, as we liked to flatter ourselves, with the bruises of history livid on our souls, and soon to be in the clutch of new-world "avidities" that would make us seem distasteful or at least comic to other, more secure, Americans, we wanted a literature in which experience overflowed, engulfed, drenched. So we abandoned Emerson even before encountering him, and in later years some of us would never draw closer than to establish amiable diplomatic relations.

Hardest of all to take at face value was the Emersonian celebration of nature. Nature was something about which poets wrote and therefore it merited esteem, but we could not really suppose it was as estimable as reality—the reality which we knew to be social. Americans were said to love Nature, though there wasn't much evidence of this that our eyes could take in. Our own tradition, long rutted in *shtetl* mud and urban smoke, made little allowance for nature as presence or refreshment. Yiddish literature has a few pieces, such as Mendele's "The Calf," that wistfully suggest it might be good for Jewish children to get out of the *heder* (school) and into the sun; but this seems more a hygienic recommendation than a metaphysical commitment. If the talk about nature seemed a little unreal, it became still more so when capitalized as Nature; and once we reached college age and heard that Nature was an opening to God, perhaps even his phenomenal mask, it seemed quite as far-fetched as the Christian mystification about three gods collapsed into one. Nothing in our upbringing could prepare us to take seriously the view that God made his home in the woods. By now we rather doubted that He was to be found anywhere, or that we would care to meet Him if He were found, but we felt pretty certain that wherever He might keep himself, it was not in a tree, or even leaves of grass.

What linked man and God in our tradition was not nature but the commandment. Once some of us no longer cared to make such a linkage, either because we doubted the presence of God or the capacity of man, we still clung to the commandment, or at least to the shadow of its severities, for even in our defilements it lay heavily upon us.

Our appetites for transcendence had been secularized, and our messianic hungers brought into the noisy streets, so that often we found it hard to respond to, even to hear, the vocabulary of philosophical idealism which dominates American literature. Sometimes this earthboundedness of ours was a source of strength, the strength of a Delmore Schwartz or a Daniel Fuchs handling the grit of their experience. Sometimes it could sour into mere candy-store realism or sadden into park-bench resignation. If the imagination soared in the immigrant slums, it was rarely to a Protestant heaven.

There is more to be said on this theme, but I may have said enough already to suggest that one crucial aspect of literary culture in the thirties was the emergence of Jewish voices, both in tension and seeking accommodation with native traditions. From this encounter, neither would ever again be the same.

We can now complete our circle, turning back to the leftward-moving writers of the thirties—perhaps we have never really left them. Fervent as the left-wing literary atmosphere was, in the United States—even in New York, sometimes acknowledged as part of the United States—it could never become as thoroughly secure as its equivalents in certain European countries. The whole experience lasted perhaps eight or nine years, and while many famous names were involved (more than later cared to acknowledge), few stayed for very long or plunged in very deeply. There was a rapid turnover, and one reason for this was the susceptibility of intellectuals to criticism from the anti-Stalinist left. In no other Western country did the anti-Stalinist left play so prominent, if brief, a role as in America, steadily breaking away the most distinguished of the writers who had come within the cultural orbit of the Communist party.

When an intellectual in Germany during the late twenties or in France during the middle thirties attached himself to the Communist movement, he was at least choosing "the real thing." He found himself caught up with and in some respect sustained by a powerful movement containing hundreds of thousands of people—a movement so brilliantly organized and providing its followers with a life so nearly self-contained that it could guard its intellectuals from the stabs of independent left-wing criticism. But in America the Communist movement could provide no such "protective custody." And since all Marxist discussion in America had a way of seeming academic, it followed that some of the writers who had been drawn to Stalinism as an ideology might also be open to the more rigorous and critical versions of Marxism that were being advanced by the anti-Stalinist splinter groups and the free-lance literary radicals. The difficulty thus presented to the Communist cultural orbit was aggravated by the fact that the leading intellectuals of the anti-Stalinist left—men like Max Eastman, Sidney Hook and a bit later, Philip Rahv—were gifted as writers and political polemicists. At any given moment during the thirties the majority of left-wing intellectuals were likely to be sympathetic to Stalinism, yet the more independent minds among them were constantly drifting into heresy.

There was Max Eastman writing in *Artists in Uniform* a powerful attack on the suppression of writers in Stalinist Russia; even those who remained loyal to the Communist movement often felt this book as a splinter beneath their skin: it could be denied but not ignored. There was Sidney Hook writing his learned essays on Marxism, which clearly showed the absurdities, and worse, of the Stalinist ideology. There was James T. Farrell in his *A Note on Literary Criticism* pleading for the autonomy of literature, not in the name of some "pure estheticism," but on solid Marxist grounds.

This independent left tendency reached a climax in 1937, when the anti-Stalinist *Partisan Review* began to appear. Its immediate success and the considerable prestige it gained during the late thirties made the magazine a rallying point for left-wing intellectuals and writers who had turned away from Stalinism but, for a time at least, wanted to remain Marxists. Devoted to modernist values in literature and a quasi-Trotskyist position in politics, *Partisan Review* in its first several years provided a home of sorts for writers who could not be at ease with any of the established institutions that either accepted or rejected society. The magazine came to signify the fact that the Communist movement had failed in its effort to appropriate the political energies of a good many of the more gifted left-wing writers in America. That *Partisan Review* soon began a torturous intellectual journey of its own is another story. What matters here is a fact crucial for an understanding of our literary life in the thirties: anti-Stalinism, often of a brilliant left-wing variety, emerged sooner and more powerfully than in any other Western nation. In a dark time, this was a bright spot.

My readers will have noticed that until now I have been speaking mostly about the intellectual and literary culture of the thirties, rather than the literature actually composed at that time. This, for two reasons: the relationship between cultural context and literary work is especially important, indeed, problematic for that period, and the other contributors to this volume will get down to individual cases in a way I cannot attempt.

But I would nevertheless emphasize that it's a mistake to suppose the literary work of a given historical moment is solely to be regarded as a reflection of the intellectual and literary culture of that moment. If the writer is always tied to his moment, if he is implicated in its values and assumptions to an extent he can hardly measure, there is another sense in which, if he is at all serious, he writes apart from his moment, apart even from history. He writes in the blessed company of the writers of the past: that is what we mean by tradition.

A good many writers of the thirties, their names now forgotten, were burned out and left dry by their involvement with the Communist cultural apparatus. But there were others who survived, perhaps through some instinct for self-protection that kept them as writers somewhat apart from their experience as persons. Henry Roth was a Communist in the early thirties, but he was also a young man who had become infatuated with Joyce's lordship of language and thereby inclined to transplant some of that mastery to a New York locale. He was, in addition, a young man with a burden, *the* young man's burden: which is always the story of his immediate past as defined and exacerbated by the immigrant milieu. In struggling with this burden Roth had available to him the conventions of nineteenth-century fiction, with their stress on the growth of consciousness through the purgation of memory. If he had called his story *Great Expectations*, or *Ulysses' Son*, that would not have been inappropriate. All of the possibilities of tradition evidently played a stronger role in his creative work than the political commitment that at the moment undoubtedly seemed to him dominant.*

There was no inherent reason why good novels could not be written on the themes prescribed by "proletarian literature." Had the proletarian

---

*Roth's literary influences were wide-ranging and included Eliot's *The Waste Land* and Joyce's *Ulysses*. See Bonnie Lyons, *Henry Roth: The Man and His Work* (New York: Cooper Square, 1976). It is also interesting to note an important parallel if not direct influence, as Irving Howe did in his essay on Roth's *Call It Sleep* ("Life Never Let Up," *New York Times Book Review*, 25 October 1964, p. 1). There Howe quotes British critic Walter Allen, who says that the youthful hero of *Call It Sleep* "recreates, transmutes, the world he lives in not into any simple fantasy of make-believe—we're a long way here either from Tom Sawyer or the young Studs Lonigan—but with the desperate, compulsive imagination of a poet. He is, indeed, for all the grotesque difference in milieu, much closer to the boy Wordsworth of 'The Prelude.' " (See Walter Allen, *Tradition and Dream: The English and American Novel from the Twenties to Our Time* [London: Phoenix House, 1964], pp. 173–74.)—EDS.

novelists of the thirties been left to themselves, free to work out their own needs and work through their own errors, it is quite possible that something valuable might have resulted; some of them, like Robert Cantwell and William Rollins, were talented men. But the demands of party dogma, especially a dogma that kept shifting in the most erratic ways, forced them into a wrenching of the observed truth and a contempt for those aspects of experience that could not be contained by a narrow political utilitarianism.

Still, one wants to resist the facile readiness of literary historians to dismiss wholesale the radical fiction and verse of the thirties. There were writers influenced, to one or another degree, by the radical politics of the thirties whose work has survived; in fact, there are signs of a new interest, what we in America lamely call "revivals." Those works that were written out of a personal feeling of indignation or rebellion and kept at some distance from the explicit domination of politics have stood up best—one thinks of such major naturalistic fictions as Farrell's *Studs Lonigan* and Dos Passos's *U.S.A.* But there are other works of distinction also colored by, yet escaping the dogmatism of, thirties radicalism: Henry Roth's *Call It Sleep*, Daniel Fuchs's *Homage to Blenholt*, Nathanael West's *Day of the Locust*, William Carlos Williams's *White Mule*, John Steinbeck's *Grapes of Wrath*. What all these works reveal is that serious writers can surmount their influences, even the influences they embrace. Perhaps that's what influences are for. They need not be benign. They may constitute blocks of necessary resistance, barriers to mere preconception and ego, all that the creative energy must overcome. And in their various ways these writers did overcome, leaving signals of integrity, works of truth about their time. A "low, dishonest decade," said Auden about the thirties. No doubt; but about which decade of our time might that not be said?

The situation is less happy in literary criticism. Fragments of distinction remain, the early work of Edmund Wilson and Philip Rahv, the study of Whitman by Newton Arvin, a few other things. But most of these were composed in rebellion against the crude Marxism of the thirties, not in conformity with it. The truth is that the bulk of left-wing literary criticism was marked by an inquisitorial narrowness of spirit, by that form of presumption which consists in taking upon oneself "the conceit of history." All literary criticism suffers from rapid obsolescence; if no one reads the work of the *New Masses* critics, that is quite as it should be, and pretty much as it will be for others too. Who now reads the work of the New Critics? How many, a dozen years from now, will pay attention to the Yale Deconstruction Company?

Still, in fairness it ought to be said that the trouble with the criticism written in the thirties is not that it was Marxist in character. Marxism can be a powerful analytic instrument; indeed, it is often too powerful a tool for the critic to control. In regard to the thirties, however, discussion of the relation between Marxism and literary criticism is often beside the point; what really matters is the relation between an authoritarian party, its suffocating ideology, and a group of obedient critics. Criticism as the art of describing and evaluating works of literature could not be practiced by anyone deeply entangled in the cultural subworld of Stalinism, for such a critic could not allow himself the luxury of disinterestedness the enterprise demands. His mind lacked—or rather, he refused—the patience, delicacy, and passionate concern for problems of craft that are indispensable to criticism. Men with a persuasion that they are about to change the world, or at least take power within it, must find it hard to resist impatience with such questions as, What does this poem signify? How good is that novel? Yet it is a fundamental premise of criticism that somehow these questions do matter.

I have tried a little to resist the tendency to brush aside the thirties as a corrupt decade and have made some qualified claims for achievement. But concern for the truth must force us also to admit that it was a time in which talent betrayed itself to the wardens of authoritarianism. We end, therefore, with a question central to all reflection on twentieth-century politics and intellectual life: What is it that makes so many people, the sophisticated and the simple, yield their independence to one or another orthodoxy, one or another life-destroying apparatus? We end with a recognition of how enormous was the waste of that time and how four decades later we still suffer its consequences. Or in Empson's words: "The waste remains, the waste remains and kills."

CHAPTER 2

JOSEPHINE HERBST

Yesterday's Road

In 1943, when I was in Washington on the German desk of our war propaganda agency, I was interrogated by two investigators who asked, among other questions, why I had gone to the Soviet Union in 1930. The common-sense answer would have been, "Why not?" but common sense always looks treasonable in wartime.

The interrogators were an Irish Catholic and a Jew: middle-aged, nice, family men who were only doing a job. They had nothing to do with the procedure that required each charge to be introduced with a curious wording, such as, "It is Reported that in 1930 you went to the Soviet Union." There were a good many of these charges, linked to the events of the thirties and the role I had played in connection with each, and, put to me in bulk, I was impressed by the record.

In that big, impersonal room with its clean tables, shiny chairs, and vacant windows opening on a wispy sky, the voices of the men, in ritualistic devotion to the recurring phrase, *It is Reported*, began to sound like an incantation and to cast a spell. The scenes that flashed to my mind's eye were more vivid than the factual line of the wording, which meant less than the subtitles on a Charlie Chaplin silent movie, where that anarchic and immortal lily of the field, the tramp, gives a backward kick at the impassive form of a slow-witted policeman before he flatfoots it around the corner and wings his way beyond. I might say that in the whirlwind of events, doors had slammed. The vagabond road to the twenties was blocked. The inquir-

Written sometime during the 1950s, this memoir focuses upon Josephine Herbst's trip to Russia to attend the Second International Congress of Proletarian Writers. It first appeared in *New American Review* 3 (1968) and is reprinted here through the kind permission of Hilton Kramer, Herbst's literary executor, and Georges Borchardt, her agent. Except for minor corrections in the text, the memoir is reprinted as it originally appeared.—EDS.

ing journeys of the thirties, made for evidence, not for "kicks," had ended in this office.

In a pinch you may remember the wildest scenes, blown up like dust from a distant explosion. As I remembered *Nach Paris* scrawled in chalk on the German boxcars, which I had seen only in photographs in Berlin, the jubilant *Soldaten* of the First World War Wehrmacht jammed the doorways on their way toward Paris. But their *Nach Paris* had metamorphosed into our Versailles, and our Versailles into their Berchtesgaden, and Berchtesgaden into a new world war. And thus, I was in Washington.

Should I call up, from the debris of the twenties, Rilke's impassioned line, "Choose to be changed. With the flame be enraptured!"? Too literary for the present customers. But it had ignited the flambeau of the thirties, "Change the world," and no doubt about it, the world had changed. So had I. Should I try to go back to the crossroads where my own history intersected the history of our time? But every crossroad is a split diamond. And what would it get me? The real events that influence our lives don't announce themselves with brass trumpets but come in softly, on the feet of doves. We don't think in headlines; it's the irrelevant detail that dreams out the plot. You may have to go back to the blue bowl that held your infant bread and milk, or watch the sun shoot a dazzling arrow along the white tablecloth. Or listen for the squawk of the alarmed goose which once rode in a basket on the hard seat of a German third-class train. Or replay the scene where the doughboys gleefully sang, "How ya gonna keep 'em down on the farm, after they've seen Paree," before they went back to the farm to burn wheat in the thirties, to sell corn for a nickel a bushel, and to defy, with a dangling rope, the sheriff who came to foreclose the old homestead.

I had been fired, abruptly, without being told the reasons why and at a moment when I was due to be promoted to the New York office or overseas. Though this particular inquiry was to end with the approval of my qualifications by the investigators, they now began to look more like auditors who tally up the assets and liabilities of the alleged bankrupt before writing him off. I had the right of appeal, but I no longer wanted the post that now seemed to designate me more as a spook in a war poster than as an actor in a spectacular and moving pageant. What's more, I had no money to linger on in Washington to petition, to hang around in corridors and "present my case." Nor was I convinced that the paper bullets our outfit was firing over the airways could have any effect.

In those early days we were, of course, only tuning up, with a lot of raw recruits from the sticks as well as slick adepts from New York. My colleague on the German desk was a splendid young history specialist, trained at Princeton, and we both kept asking: Whom are we aiming at? The Nazis? The old Social Democrats? The Communists? The Junkers? Or that inchoate putty mass that can be pushed around and exists everywhere and nowhere? For if you hope to bend minds to a purpose, you must know to whom and to what you speak. We prodded, until one day we were summoned to an office and given a chunk of thick, typed "directives" to read, with the solemn proviso that we were to make no notes and must keep every comma incommunicado. A secretary was present as we sat sedately, and it was my mistake to laugh. Not that it mattered; I would have been fired anyhow. But who could help it? Even my more discreet colleague smothered a twitching mouth to mutter, "Quiet. There's a war on."

The directives, presumed to be of deep psychological import, were mostly for *hausfrauen* into whose unwilling ears we were to pour demoralizing suspicions concerning their absentee husbands. For wives with men on the western front: remember—not the French *poilu*, who had already officially capitulated—but the artful French sirens. Could a German housewife expect her man, on his return, ever to be quite the same again? Toward the east, the danger was equally insidious. Their women, too, might transform a potent warrior into a sex malingerer. But there were also paper bullets for the fighting men, who were to be twitched by their sexual roots and reminded that their home fire pullulated. Beware the horde of war prisoners and displaced persons—foreign types leaking in through crevices, who might be useful on the home front to spade the wife's garden, to plow, to feed the pigs, but many of whom were strong physical specimens. Could a woman's honor prevail over stark loneliness, dark winters, frost, the cries of the flesh? Did they want to come back from the gory front to find a stranger's chick hatched in their nest?

As propaganda, the directives struck me as about as effective as a loaf of our cottony bread. I knew a good deal about Germany, though not enough: I had lived there for two years in the twenties, had returned in 1930 and again in 1935 for the New York *Post*. I had learned something about actual war, that guns and bombs crushed more than a dozen eggs, when I was in Madrid in 1937 while the city was daily bombarded. As a woman, I felt a certain conceit in my awareness of the violent potentials simmering within situations and human beings. This stuff was silly. Hunger would have made more sense: older Germans remembered its pangs from the First World War; younger ones from the rickety legs of kids during the inflation. But *sex*—if I knew what I was talking about, damaged goods would have more appeal than empty arms, and the women knew it, the men knew it, and would be more likely to laugh than to weep at our piety. *Sex*—to *Germans*—who were pulverizing Jews and politicals, by the million!

I could remember some quoted lines from an old notebook where it was said that each man, according to his racial and social milieu and to the specific point in his individual evolution, is a kind of keyboard on which the external world plays in a certain way. All keyboards have an equal right to exist. All are equally justified. Something of the kind had even been built into our own Bill of Rights. But now these words sounded hollow, echoes from a departed summer twilight when the wooden croquet balls had jovially knocked against one another on the green lawn. In the convulsed knock of world upon world, could an individual keyboard hope to sound a single, clear, personal, or harplike note? In war, a mechanical master keyboard takes over, like some monster player piano, to drown out the piping of solitary and singular instruments.

The two investigators and I might add up a column of facts and *It is Reported*s without agreeing on the final sum. Nor did childhood memories count; they might hopelessly entangle. The two of them had doubtless saluted our flag in local grade schools, as I had in Iowa when a militant principal tapped her little bell like a drum major; on Washington's birthday she marshaled the troupe of pupils in a body to the main hall, where the drum rolled, a trumpet bugled, and the beautiful flag was unfurled. We stood, rows of impressionable infants, to chant in unison, "I pledge my heart (hand on heart, ready to be broken) and my hand (outstretched hand, ready to be blown off) to my country." One Country, One Nation, Indivisible, and One Flag. Drums. Star-Spangled Banner. Shivery, exalted, my voice rang out. Did we also promise our heads? Not as I recollect it. I had my own fable, and fables speak.

But if the headpiece was inviolable, could it be granted immunity from the flesh? No head versus heart, mind versus flesh, here. Words, too, are carnal. My own *doppelgänger* might split an apple with me, take the core and give me the fruit, but more often it spoke in riddles. Or hinted that immersion in the vital present, an immersion, alas, achieved by an uncritical acceptance of the drift of things, could defeat the aims of any goal. Ready and intoxicating spontaneity had its price. I could feel the pinch of it in that office, and if I seem to be putting on bland airs now, from an experienced distance, I was becoming sick at heart at the time. As often as I had rehearsed risky situations, dramatizing myself in major important roles, I had neglected this smaller domestic opening for a minor part. I wasn't in a maniac Gestapo cellar, nor confronted by a merciless judge in a Moscow trial. The sadism of the parlor and gallery that the surrealists had deliberately cultivated as a proof of their power to shock, and to delight, had passed over and beyond any of Max Ernst's bestiaries of animals with human heads, which now looked like benign beings compared with the factual evidence of the "real" world. But we were no police state, though it seemed we had engaged its footboys. The very politeness of my interlocutors unhinged me, made me regard trivialities with concern. I noted with alarm one ink-stained finger of my gloves; another finger was ripped. A bit more of this and I would begin to simper, "Shall I pour the tea?"

Moments like this can relegate you to a dungeon with nothing to contem-

plate except your own abyss. I had no intention of retreating to the
thirteenth century or to the fascinating eighteenth. Nor to call on Pascal,
Plato, or Thucydides to the extinction, for instance, of Rosa Luxemburg,
Madame Rolland, or Danton. Nor to apologize or stutter away my birthright or cede to strangers the ground rights to my own experience, my own
mistakes. Or even to my own ignorance. To do so would close the debate.
What I understood very well was that the dry rattle of all these *It is
Reporteds* might be calculated to reduce some of my best yesterdays to
outworn slogans, telephone numbers of people who were no longer there
or were dead, and foxed files.

They could take *It is Reported that in Madrid, in 1937, you broadcast in
behalf of the Spanish Loyalists*, turn it inside out, and find me involved in a
conspiracy, where I saw only evidence of my own well-grounded reasons of
the heart. Or what was I to make of the Report that I had signed a petition
in 1932 protesting the violating of civil liberties in Detroit? No details were
given and I couldn't remember what it had been all about. Or the one on
the piece for the *New Masses* in 1935, when Batista was shooting students
on the university steps, while in the mountains near Santiago peasants
stood with machetes, behind virgin trees, to guard their land and what they
took to be their rights from soldiers who were mounting the slopes in
obedience to commands from the sugar planters in the valley below. I no
longer wrote for the *New Masses*, nor would, nor *could*. But it had served
my keyboard once, as my piece had doubtless served theirs. And I stood by
the substance of it, which had its own life and veracity apart from either
author or publication. I had only to remember the frail wishbone from a
skinny chicken the mountain folk had shared with me and which a child,
who had never gone to school, had pressed into my hand at parting.

So I said, "Why do you keep saying, *It is Reported*, when it is a fact?"
But what is a *fact*? Who is to interpret it? What ideas ride on its back? And
a Protean Me wanted to break the cords that bind, and to soar, if only back
to my attic, where there was some hope of getting to the source of things. If
the truth about Me was what was wanted, they might better scrabble in the
old Gladstone bag, near the window where the squirrel got in. Nothing
within except a bunch of love letters, some tied together with a ribbon,
others with string or a busted rubber band; some in ink, pencil, or typed;
addressed to Madam, Mme., Mlle., Fraulein, Senorita, Mrs., or Miss.
One clawed with a stern warning, *Destroy*.

Or they could fumble on the shelf where old newspapers were stacked,
and where they might lay hands on copies of old little magazines such as
the *Little Review*, which I had carried to classes at Berkeley in 1917 instead
of a ball of wool to knit a sock for a soldier boy; or the number that was
banned when the editors printed a section of *Ulysses*. Or find the *Masses*
before its editors were indicted for treasonable intent in opposing the

Great War, and the magazine suppressed. Whatever happened to the seventy-year-old scholar with a shock of beautiful white hair, in a house in Berkeley, who had explained with enthusiasm what he believed to be the meaning of the Bolshevik takeover? Did he change his mind, or, like Victor Serge, stick with the Old Guard? They might stumble over a box of photographs to find a glum Hemingway in a stocking cap, with rod and reel. What could they make of Katherine Anne Porter, arms akimbo, posed with a rakish John Herrmann as a song-and-dance vaudeville team? I knew what they'd think of the jolly German soldiers in Madrid, lolling on the grass, who signed their first names on the back, but not their last. Or that one of Nathanael West and me as worthy old peasants on a wintry day, huddled in chilly coats: on his head, a sloppy hunter's hat; on mine, a shawl. While we brazenly held aloft a hammer and a sickle: he, the hammer; I, the sickle. Crossed, as duelists had once crossed swords. Or damning evidence: a photograph of me, taken in Moscow, 1930. Portrait of the Author, in a round cap, three-quarter view; eyelashes sloping downward over serious, downcast eyes; hand on table, open like an open book; expression watchful, listening, tender, and intense.

Were these courteous gents the hosts or were they my guests? It was nearing the cocktail hour. Why not take the deadweight out of facts and hand them a taste of mortal life? So I volunteered that they'd forgotten a thing or two, such as the day in Paris in 1935, when I had come out of Germany and had stood on the sidelines of the great funeral procession for Henri Barbusse. His body rode on a caisson, as it deserved to ride, for he had fought as a private in the First World War and had written his antiwar novel *Le feu* after he was demobilized. It had enlightened my green youth before our country came in as an ally. And that procession had been notable for me, not for its pomp, for it had none, but for the delegations from dozens of small towns, marching by the hundreds in formations of blue working-clothed ranks and bearing homemade wreathes; and for the huge glass hearses, of the old-fashioned, ornate type, that were loaded within and without with great bouquets of wilting field flowers: blue cornflowers, red poppies, clover, and sheaves of golden wheat, which had been brought to the funeral train as it passed through Poland, Germany, and France on its way out of Moscow, where Barbusse had died; and for the construction workers standing as silent witnesses on the scaffoldings at the tops of buildings; and the women and children, crowded in windows along the miles where the procession passed on its way to Père Lachaise.

And among this throng had marched a band of exiles from Germany: poor, dismantled, and conspicuous for the absurd precision of their disciplined marching among the more loosely jointed, more happily assembled French. Had their discipline been of use only to make martyrs? Or to divide themselves? For some of the marchers were to show up in Spain in the International Brigade in 1937, claiming that if you wanted to see

Berlin, go to Madrid. Nor had they foreseen in Madrid the fratricidal divisions to follow, or that concentration camps would await them in France after defeat, or death in the Moscow purges, or that they would flee to Mexico, Rio, or Buenos Aires, and some be denied America; or that some, brother against brother, might find themselves once more secretly at dagger's point with one another, but fighting together with the Resistance in Europe.

The two men listened—gentle, clerklike—and then let me go, toting up the figures to clear the bill of lading. Was their favorable verdict made out of pique against their rival investigators who had stolen their priority? I could not know or care: the job was gone. I did not fancy that without me the war might be lost. I was as certain we would win as I had been that Hitler would not last his thousand years, nor the Russians crumple in two weeks as the Nazi tanks moved eastward. Not that I prided myself on superior diagnostic powers: of such, I had none. Often I had miscalculated and misfired; often engaged in internal combat while in combat without. One Me, a jaundiced eye on Progress, was a gloomy prognostician; the other, a congenital cricket, ready to chirp, "While there's life, there's hope." No, what most struck me was that my interlocutors and I spoke the same tongue but lacked the elements of a common language. On my native soil, I was in a kind of no man's land, more strange than I had been when first I went to Germany and loved to drift anonymously with the crowd. And, just as I fancied then that because I could glibly read *Faust* in German I might hear and speak of Germany, so I had come to this outfit plumed with formal qualifications but unhanded by secret laws at cross-purposes with my own.

To blend our differences I would have had to sink myself in their total life, as once I had dissolved among Germans in the inflation days of 1923: when I had mingled with the rich in swank hotels and spas, or nibbled ersatz cakes with uneasy bourgeoisie in a pleasant pension on Kastanienallee while they regaled me with reports of outmoded delicacies, dishes now moribund: a dozen eggs, a pint of cream, split almonds, a fistful of orient spices, which took shape before their eyes, then exploded to their hysterical wonderment; or shared black bread and cabbage with students in their unheated *Studentenheim* in Marburg, where a youthful Pasternak had once climbed the steep, cobbled streets; or paid ten cents to take a train to Dresden to hear the opera, to look upon that Raphael Madonna that Dostoevski once complained had overenraptured Turgenev; or reveled at a different theater each night, where needy Germans strained to spend their paper marks before tomorrow made them trash and thronged for Ibsen, Strindberg, and Shakespeare, and for their own playwrights, who in fabulous stage settings set on fire the follies of their age, their bedevilment, their savaged predicament.

Or copied in my notebook, with a novitiate's pride, sage sayings: Georg

Kaiser, *Berliner Tageblatt*, 4 September 1923, on the poet as creator of the only history meaningful to man: "He orders the confusion. He draws the line through the hubbub. He constructs the law. He holds the filter. He justifies man." Or noted Werfel, hailing man as the name-giver, the one who expresses the unexpressed, lifts the world out of the unconscious and thus creates once more the cosmos. *Erkenntnis*, intellectual insight, was Heinrich Mann's motto; he claimed space for intellectual man to remake the social world according to the ideals of justice and reason. Shy and reticent, I circled around that circle about Herwarth Walden and his *Der Sturm*, where poets shucked off burdensome syntax, shed *Gemut*, elevated the noun and verb to do their work of reshaping and reseeing, and brought the arrow of their desire to its mark, shorn of all circumlocution, description, diffuseness. And I was drowned in awesome reverence for the new, and then drew back in fright; read Gottfried Benn's poem "Happy Youth," in which a drowned girl's body serves as a nest for a brood of rats—the Happy Youth are rats, not men. And saw its constructs reveal an icy vision of total indifference to human woe and universal death, where devouring rats could frolic—and nonmen.

And then? I don't know why I forsook this intoxicating realm, but there were echoes from the very paving stones, sounds in the air and black birds in the sky, and I dived down, and for months lived cheek by jowl with the poor in gloomy tenements of Moabit and Wedding. And you can say that the poor won, and that I came out of Germany, in 1924, pro-German, for whatever that implies for those days. Nor could the dazzle of Paris, the rich, heady air, or falling in love, or idling along the quay with a modest, happy Hemingway, or calling hello to a ruddy-bearded Pound: none of this could wipe away that vital decisive stain, which blended deep and harsh and took its toll in years to come. What could my interlocutors understand of this? The experience was my own; no outsider could subtract it from my totality. Who is to rob you except yourself? The heart must weigh the stone it earns.

By 1930 the road had lengthened out to reach to Moscow. Our government did not recognize the Soviet Union, no more than China now, but we could go to a writers' conference there provided the Russians approved our visas. John Herrmann and I sailed on the *Bremen*. We went third class, where there was no promenade deck, only a small space, about twelve feet by six, jutting out close to the water at the stern. This space was always packed with silent, intent men—looking back. "Third cabin" was a modern equivalent of the old-time steerage and now held many immigrants who were sad to return, pushed out by the crunch of rising joblessness and by the crackdown, too, on all those who held views contrary to the plan now engineered in the White House by the man who was to tell us, year by year, that prosperity was just around the corner and would soon appear.

We landed in Bremen and had to wait several days in Berlin, living cheap, hoarding the money we had raised, partly from selling books—a first edition of *Ulysses*, six of the early Paris copies of Hemingway's stories. Then, on a late October at 6 P.M., John and I stood, two posts, in a great train shed, while around about a crowd of Muscovites churned from up a flight of steps without, past us to their waiting trains. We tried to stop one, then another, but we had no speech they understood, until one man stopped in his tracks and moved back to tap on a pane of glass concealed by hurrying figures within the shabby waiting room.

Out popped a tall woman wearing a once-elegant suit of English tweed; her fair hair was knotted in a heavy bun, and she came up to us to ask in English with a Russian accent what she could do for us. We showed her the address of the magazine to which we had been told to go first; she took us to the street, called a droshky driver and gave him the address; told us how much to pay him and no more; and away we went, clattering over cobbled streets, up high on a teetering back seat, while lower down the driver hunched in a heavy patched coat, a foot thick; and shouted to his horse, whose fat sides were warmed by his native shaggy barklike covering.

And so we rode on our elevated raft along a street that surged with faces all lifted up to us as we rode, or parted to our vehicle without once breaking the current of their stride. How can I once more gather up the look they gave toward us? Of swift astonishment, deep curiosity, nor stopped a second, but hurried on to catch their trains in the station we had left. The faces are what I remember, bearing down upon us in a thick, pale flood, or upturned to us, as eye met eye. If you've only known an indifferent shopping crowd whose attention drifts toward a show of radios, female finery, or a shiny car, you hardly know how alive a crowd can be, stripped bare of all excrescences; how attentive to the human thing, or how antennae are thrust out, invisibly, from you to them, from them to you, so that like insects in the dark you are drawn toward the scent of the stranger and his curiosity. Their clothes made an odd array: all shabby, shoes broken down, and some legs wrapped in neat rags or paper; men wore caps, women had dark scarfs, the tails hanging down the back like the pigtails of girls. But as to clothes, the Russians all looked more or less alike; male or female: all dun-colored, except for army men, whose uniforms were spick and span and could stand up to our best-dressed man. The hollow murmur of many feet, and of our wheels on that street where no shop lights shone, was all the sound there was except for the crack of our driver's whip and a loud bray from his deep bass voice, shouting something as we passed. It was only later that I found out his bossy shout had been, "Make way for the delegation. Make way!"

We halted in a square where dead-eyed buildings stood and paid our man; got out with our two bags and typewriter; trudged inside the empty corridor. The elevator creaked, and we were the only moving bodies, it seemed; our footfalls echoed as we walked. The door had a name on it; should we knock? We took the American way and boldly flung it open and went in. The room was dim; a long cord dangled a feeble bulb above a group of desks where four men sat. But on our entrance, they all rose up, and, like those faces I had once seen on a faraway Montana ranch, where hospitality was a necessity of life not to the travelers alone but to the settlers who pined for outside news, the four showed their suspended eagerness. John had barely said our names, and that we were Americans, when they rushed to us, so it seemed to me, as the old-timers in Russia must have run when they heard the troika bells on the lonely road and welcomed the beginning of felicity. They threw their arms around us; we were kissed. We might have been a heavenly messenger who brings the *panis angelorum.*

Two were Russians: one, Dinamov, the editor of the *Gazette* and a professor at Moscow University; the other, a robust, dark youth, identified himself as a "specialist" in English and American literature. The other two were Hungarians: one ruddy, fierce, with stocky frame; the other, blond and frail, wore a curious rounded hole on his pale cheek, which puckered when he smiled or showed a glint of bone. He had been lined up against the wall when Hungarian Reds had been trapped in Budapest, and with a line of brother victims, shot down; they kicked him, but he lay still and waited and then after dark crawled off through the woods and thus escaped to Russia and to life, or so he thought.

But who could know what was to come? Not us, we knew so little. The room now buzzed with talk; yes, our names had been sent in but who could expect that we might really arrive? People were always promising things that never came to pass. And where to put us? Our new friends hardly knew; the hotels were packed. In a few days, a week, arrangements would be made for guests coming from afar for the conference; and at once, we were pressed to be their guests and to go to Kharkov to meet the writers of the revolutionary vanguard. Someone telephoned; the Critic, as we came to call the specialist on American goods, volunteered that John should stay with him; they had so much to talk about. As for me, they had just the spot, in the apartment of an agronomist who spoke German, came home late at night, and to whom I could talk German and tell my needs. So far, we had been talking mixtures of English, German, and French, and by touch and look, added to the sense.

John left first, and thereafter, for some days, we met only to exchange views or to wander, hand in hand, through the streets. He told how the Critic's "place," described in advance as "commodious," had turned out to be a narrow cell, furnished only with books stacked to the ceiling and a tight bed too short for John's long frame; his feet stuck out. The Critic insisted his guest must take the bed, and he himself lay grandly on the floor, covered by an overcoat. At night a rat pounced out and was squelched when our Critic nonchalantly threw a shoe. But night for sleep was short; the Critic was all aglow with talk and tea, a little vodka too. He was translating Proust, not for general consumption, but for the knowing few. He failed to pass the Kafka test but was impressed that we had been fishing with Hemingway in Key West a few months before. Dreiser and John Dos Passos should have come. He loved success. *Ulysses* was too deep, he felt, for present days; the translation problems too austere for him. He must learn the idiom, and, on that first night, had insisted we send him samples of *all* our magazines on our return. Especially the *Saturday Evening Post* and the detective-story publications.

As for me, the huge apartment building where the agronomist had a nook had once been a fancy club for dissolute rich young men and had been gouged out in wedges to accommodate some of the more modest bureaucracy. An elevator landed us on the sixth floor; the door was opened by a little girl with a round, chubby face. She wore a kerchief on her fair hair, and a tough sprong covered her from top to toe. My escort handed in a parcel that contained a hunk of precious butter and a jar of caviar for me. I stepped inside, but what to say? Our speech jangled odd sounds, we laughed, and from another room a plump woman sailed out, smiling, accompanied by an older, taller girl, slim and lovely, who asked me if I knew French; she was learning it. She would teach me Russian right away; she was dying to learn English; we could exchange. Right now, I must have something to eat. But first, a bath!

They took away my hat, my coat, my bag. There was a big open zinc tub in the room, near the fat kitchen stove on which pots steamed. The chubby one motioned me to undress, and the mother and her daughter withdrew. I undressed slowly and waited for privacy, but none came. The chubby one stood adamant; I was to get into the tub. I did, and knelt while she poured from a big tin pitcher a stream of warm water upon my head and me. I hadn't wanted my long hair washed, but washed it had to be. There was a tiny sliver of soap I feared would melt away, but it did not. I got out; there was a hot towel waiting, and I dressed, mounted a few steps from the kitchen to the dining room, where a beaded hanging lamp shone bright above a darned white tablecloth. My butter was set out, black bread and quantities of jeweled caviar. There was a fried egg, crisp and hot, a pot of tea, and so I began to eat, with a Russian lesson for dessert. A little boy with a thin, eager face joined us, leaning his chin upon the table. The mother worked away unraveling an old sweater to wind up its wool. My teacher would lift up a knife, say its Russian name; I would repeat, then give the English name; she echoed it and her little brother pantomimed. Before we parted for the night I knew the words for all the dishes on the table, how to say I would like some tea, thank you and good-bye, and how are you, and learned the name for where and what, for hot and cold, how to ask what time is it and what do you call this street.

The room where I was to sleep was choked with an enormous rubber plant resting against a tubercular window of a sickly hue, and two narrow beds. I was to sleep in one; the chubby girl in the other. But the little boy had given up his bed for me; he was to sleep on two chairs pushed together, on which a fat pillow served as mattress, with a thick blanket flung over all. I protested it wasn't right to put him out of his bed; but his mien was proud, he smiled, and in Russian said what may have been, "Please, it's nothing." The room went dark, the children fell asleep; the moonlight filtered through the rubbery leaves to make a greeny pool, in which we all three floated, the night through, in our aquarium.

I only saw and talked to the agronomist once, when late at night he sat in the room beyond the kitchen at the top of the flight of steps and looked then like some tired man on a stool who has been made to sit too long and may fall asleep before he has finished his bowl of soup. But the second I mounted the steps between, he woke up with a smile to shake my hand and to ask, how did I fare, was there anything he could do? By this time I had nosed around and could have asked a dozen questions but refrained. Would he have told me of the vast collectivization plan then afoot, which would uproot flocks of human beings from their ground, to starve or die? I doubt it. Perhaps he himself was not in on the plan, or what it foreboded. I knew far less, so told him of my youth in Iowa, where they raised corn and pigs and wheat. That was bait for him, he leaped at it, asked me a dozen questions about crops and machines; he had heard our farmers were not doing well.

The hour was late, but in low voices we talked on and on. What was said? I don't remember his words, only that he unwound a drama of a vast and suffering land, with the unnamed protagonist an absent Machine that could do the work of many hands. I was not making judgments but sopping up and taking in; or tutoring my backward keyboard to new tunes. How to reconcile Rimbaud's *la vraie vie* with the commune?

I only know those days were best before the delegations swept in; we could poke around, stare at pictographs in front of empty stores showing a fish, a loaf, a shoe to illustrate for the illiterate what was sold there once, but not now. Or at evening see the empty rooms light up with a lamp, a candle or two, while around a long table heads with caps or hooded with a shawl pored laboriously over a copybook, intent on the key that would release the clue. Or with an Englishman who spoke Russian and had lived there for months, visit a steel plant, the first I'd ever seen, doubtless the last: factories aren't my style. We moved around, electrified to see a great black bowl tip its scalding contents down, while a giant sheathed in leather wrestled with a huge red-hot snake that writhed until it was subdued to a long, dark shank for a train to glide upon. Or wondered when a little group of men, working at this and that, dropped their tools to follow us about, to press close. I'd ask, "What's he saying?" and they'd ask, was it true that in America every working man owned his own car? And, what did we think of Walt Whitman? Or, how did their steel plant compare with ours? Was Victor Hugo a revolutionary poet—what did we think?

Or once, wandering on the dim night streets with the Critic, we stopped to chat with a Russian night owl who stood with hands in pockets of a jaunty leather jacket and opined that he'd never had it so good, or thought to earn so much, except—alas—there was nowhere much to go and nothing much to spend it on. Or went with one of the Hungarians, as on a spree, to a factory meeting that turned out to be a poetry reading, and saw the intent faces, still as a clear flame, lighted up until the poem ended. One night we dropped into a basement den where the Critic promised other writers were sure to be. Rousing voices rumbled, tea was poured. We were introduced to a saturnine man, hunched in a black leather jacket. He was Leonid Leonov, a good writer, the Critic said, but like others of the older school, he found it difficult to make "the transition." The writer turned, bowed formally, and with an odd, faint, hostile smile, turned his back.

Where *were* the Russian writers? Did they hide? Mayakovski was already dead. Some years ago he had visited New York, had come arrogantly proud, bellicose, youthful, and intent. I had never met him, only felt the contagion of his presence: in an East Side dump he had enthralled a group of ardent youths and then departed, unheralded by the great, known by few:

> There's not a single grey hair in my soul;
> with nice old men I have nothing to do;
> the world shakes with my voice's roll,
> and I walk handsome,
> and twenty-two.

It was Mayakovski I had most hoped to meet; now he was dead, six months before: a suicide. But what of Babel or Pasternak? Gorki, too, was present only by his absence. Or what of the jolly pair who had written *The Golden Calf*? Or the ubiquitous Ilya Ehrenburg? Where was Pilnyak? Why was it that when the conference at Kharkov began, the general of the Red cavalry, Budenny, strode in like a hero, to great acclaim, but not Babel, who had ridden and fought with him? What was the cavalry without its bard, or Pushkin's statue in the square without Onegin?

Then the Germans streamed in, and, as you might know, order ruled. Our nonchalant strolling days were gone. Ludwig Renn, who had dropped his aristocratic *von* to take a name he coined, proved to be an inflexible as well as indefatigable lecturer on the pros and cons. John and I were now together again, in an old hotel, with delegates from twenty-two countries, so they said. But they said so much. The eight-hour day, the five-day week, the full employment as the rule: no beggars, no prostitutes. Museums, schools, nurseries. Under Renn's command the joy of riding on a streetcar strung with people swarming like bees was lost; he had to relate the history of the streetcar, its present degenerate state, its bright future as a going concern when more workers could be spared to build new cars again. Churches had become nurseries; here, too, we got a lecture on the bad air, which did not signify. A finger pointed at the rosy children who, in spite of clammy walls, thrived; they did. It almost seemed as if the robust kids should be carrying on their backs the tired mothers who fetched them away. Or we were taken to a big communal kitchen where hundreds of workers were fed; tasted the food and found it excellent; but got a lecture on the future plan that was to rescue housewives from kitchen slavery to work in factories of shiny glass, and would restore to communal brotherhood the eating habits of individual man.

The Germans boasted more delegates than anyone else. All were said to have written books which were declared to be "important" or "brilliant." Anna Seghers was there; she might have posed for Dürer, with her brow and hands. She'd written a sensitive novel about some anarchists, called *The Revolt of the Fishermen*. But where was Brecht?

Ernst Glaeser, a guest like us, not a delegate, was described as a "kind of Hemingway." His novel *The Class of 1902* was antiwar; and so was Ludwig Renn's novel *War*, which he proposed to follow up with one called "Peace." But where was the dramatist Ernst Toller, who had been outlawed from his homeland for years? He'd been a leader in the Bavarian Red Revolution, and his plays had drawn great crowds—some to riot, others to applaud.

You would think if pens were mightier than the sword, then war would have ceased. The twenties had been dominated by the theme that heroes were certain to back out, or to be blacked out by the catastrophe. By 1930 a last tide had swept in Hemingway's *A Farewell to Arms* and Robert Graves's *Goodbye to All That*.

But when the thirties came, Good-bye was turning to Hello, I'm here again. You realized in Moscow, and even more in Kharkov, that war was to be back on the track. It was as plain to see in Berlin or Rome as the sword that Ludwig Renn buckled on the night he made a speech, the sword he had won as a high-ranking officer in the Kaiser's Wehrmacht. Some held to a private view out of pride or indecision; some of the rich, loathing the wall-to-wall carpeted minds of their kind, moved sharply to the left; a few, who had the savor of the infinite in their mouths, wanted to see the worst of things and hoped for the apocalypse. Violence had so detonated since the Great War that no one could be quiet anymore. Some took it all in stride;

volunteered, so they said, for the duration, in the ranks of the social revolution.

We all bounced off to Kharkov in a train, with Ludwig Renn as a sort of paterfamilias to our car. The official delegation from the States had come: three ultraserious young men whom we had never met before and who looked us up and down as if to say, How did *you* get in the door? But neither did they think much of Mike Gold, the leader of their group, when he blew in solo at Kharkov. The fact was that the Russians loved Mike for his warm, breezy personality, and showed it. They also liked us. But it seemed to me the faithful three got little credit for their fidelity. Outside of official recognition and the satisfaction of chores done, they seemed to have little fun. Parties that went on late at night with champagne, vodka, and caviar did not note their presence. Nor did they approve of the sophisticated French, who brought a worldly gaiety, and Louis Aragon and his Russian-born wife, Elsa Triolet.

Now don't expect me to relate all the pros and cons of the debates that went on. It's all been done before. Nor was I one who, having sat on a park bench reading Marx, was to be rewarded by a sudden illumination. I had never read *Das Kapital* but came to explore other works, both Engels and Rosa Luxemburg, and to deplore that time was short and I had a great background to fill in. But platform speaking never gave me much; I need books and quietude. And the platform talk was barbarous as it trickled in translations. There were some sentences that rang out, bright and sharp, as when a handsome woman—from the Comintern, it was said—got on the platform and looking down, seemed to direct her talk to me and John and Aragon, and to reprove some of the talk that had brayed for workers' correspondence as the substitute for literature.

There was no time in this era of great depressions or threatened war to write long novels, poetry, or plays, the others had said. What was needed was patient explanation and reports from workers about their toiling lives; what was required were stories of their struggles and their aim, thus building the literature of the new class with the new man. When one of the gloomy three from the United States got on the platform to orate, he added his bit to the harangue, scolding that there was no time, no time; that what was needed was plain talk—works like one already printed in the States showing the life and death of a heroic worker.

I was trying to pay attention, to be serious, but at his words, and quite spontaneously, I got up and pushed past knees to leave the auditorium. In a drafty hall, I smoked a cigarette. Aragon came after me, took my arm, and said, "We all know what your position is. You mustn't mind that kind of talk. It's a kind of infantile disease and will wear out." I said, "But it's so funny. Don't you see, the speaker is the author of the very work he extols anonymously."

But when the handsome woman from the Comintern looked down at us, she seemed to understand the more that was at stake. She reminded the stubborn group, who sat stiff-faced, that the great revolutionaries who had brought October to triumph had come from bourgeois strains. That when the proletariat won its goal there would be no bourgeois class, only a classless world, but that in Russia the workers had as yet barely had time to learn to read and write. That the favorite author of Marx had been Balzac. By the time the workers had mastered the world they were to make, what would the term proletariat mean?

The words struck. They might have come from the outlaw Trotsky, whose brilliant book on literature and revolution I had read, as I was to read his *History* after Max Eastman had translated it. But why was it, in reports written by the faithful and printed back home, I never once heard mention of that speech or her name? Nor, for that matter, was Aragon's name ever brought to the fore or given the aplomb that would have added to the cause. I'll never know; there's too much I'll never know. But I knew enough then not to try to write about what I had seen, except for one small piece for the *New Republic*, reporting the conference in capsule.

What the faithful wrote you can't call lies; they thought it truth. That's the way ideas take root. Their keyboards were struck by winds I could not feel or respond to; dogma to them was the needed arm, not anathema. But one thing sure is that the whole affair told me to beware, beware! Don't get me wrong. In those early years I went as far left as you can go. But I was wary of the chatter, no matter by whom. (I steered clear of our New York political elite, as much as I could, because they knew it all.) I thought, something overwhelming is at stake, but what? I can't find out here.

We had never before met Aragon. We had some mutual friends who had described his "white-toothed" smile, his "Roman nose." But what are mutual friends compared with a mutual climate of the mind, a rebel's idealism? Still our keyboards hardly chimed, at least not his and mine. You might say he was of the Paris school and I of Berlin. The dadaists of the Café Voltaire had split into two camps, one to Paris, one to Berlin; one to become, in Berlin's terms, aesthetes; the other, in Paris's terms, political. So I, too, had been bent more toward the Berlin position, like the dadaist who had said he needed only to take a single look at the starved and maimed hordes of Berlin to discard his Byronic cravat. The ironic thing was that the Berliners had shed their earlier coats before the Paris dadaists, now turned surrealists, took up the political role as 1930 rolled in.

Perhaps the Paris crowd had had their fill, had tired of wandering Paris streets, courting chance: the vertigo of the unknown. Only vaguely aware of the great industrial strikes that paralyzed their country's economic life, they had wanted freedom; but the free man, as they conceived him, was not so much a man among the living as a dark angel—experimenting, destroying, and from whose ideal point of view all human ends pale into pure gratuity. The role of the terrorist, the spy, the saboteur, the traitor had become transformed. They had named Saint Just the Divine Executioner.

But who of our literary generation was not a crime snob of a sort? Who did not lean toward the underdogs, peddlers, thieves, prostitutes, beyond the call of duty: all the underbelly of the world, which looked so fat and smug on top? Perhaps we had gone to Russia because it had been so almost universally despised by the cautious and the respectable. But no surrender to either nirvana or compulsive obedience.

Who of us had not dreamed of freedom, limpid affections, intensity above all, passionate friendships; and had not become as well, demanding, possessive? We wanted the universe; we wanted *all*. And leaning out from our traveling trains to wave farewell, good-bye, we rounded that long curve, back to war again.

CHAPTER 3

TOWNSEND LUDINGTON

Friendship Won't Stand That:

JOHN HOWARD LAWSON AND JOHN DOS PASSOS'S
STRUGGLE FOR AN IDEOLOGICAL GROUND TO
STAND ON

Late in August 1937 the dramatist and screenwriter John Howard Lawson
wrote from Hollywood to his friend John Dos Passos. Lawson was attempting to convince him that there was merit in trying to make a film of Dos
Passos's novel *The Big Money*, the third volume of which would be published the next year as the trilogy *U.S.A.* Lawson admitted he would like to
work on the film: he needed the job; and, as he told Dos Passos, who was
skeptical of the project, he thought "certain vital things could come out of
it," by which he meant that he hoped a film with a social message might be
produced. Lawson by this time in his career was deeply committed to the
Communist party yet was writing film scripts that had little if any social
import, so his comments to Dos Passos were in part a justification of the
clash between his radical politics and Hollywood commercialism. "I have
no control over what's done with [*The Big Money*] any more than you
have," he declared in his letter, "and I think it's perfectly proper to work
under those conditions."

"So you see I don't agree with you about the movies," he continued,
adding, "nor about religion or politics—for that matter." By 1937 he had
been arguing politics with Dos Passos for several years. The strain was
showing; earlier Dos Passos, attempting to continue their relationship
despite growing ideological differences, had written that friendship was a
matter of "gratuitous illogical and purposeless bonds." No, responded
Lawson, it was not just that, but "a rather serious business, and is based on
a good deal of understanding—not only understanding of where people
agree, but of all the vast and complicated and psychoneurotic and intellectual and emotional factors which may and do cause people to disagree. . . .
As long as friends have a decent respect for themselves and their
friendship, they say anything they damn well think, and I don't see why
either should get angry about it." But Lawson, in fact, was simmering.

Their friendship had strained to the breaking point, and two years later, after the publication of *The Adventures of a Young Man*, Dos Passos's novel of protest against the Communists, it would end.[1]

What irritated Lawson in August 1937 was Dos Passos's article "A Farewell to Europe," which had been published in the journal *Common Sense* the month before. In it Dos Passos decried European ideologies, which, left or right, now seemed to him futile and, fascist or communist, totalitarian. He had journeyed to Spain the previous spring along with Ernest Hemingway to investigate conditions in the civil war and to make a film supporting the Loyalists' struggle against the rebel Franco. But once in Spain, Dos Passos had been shocked to learn of the execution of his close friend José Robles Pantoja, an educated man whom he had known since 1916 and who had returned from a post at Johns Hopkins University to fight for the Loyalists. The more Dos Passos learned about the circumstances surrounding Robles's death, the more certain he became that it had been at the hands of the Communists, whom Robles had apparently observed covertly organizing to assume power in Spain, were Franco to be defeated. "Behind the lines," Dos Passos asserted about the situation among the Loyalists, "a struggle as violent almost as the war had been going on between the Marxist concept of the totalitarian state, and the Anarchist concept of individual liberty."[2] Disillusioned and bitter, Dos Passos had returned to the United States in June 1937, any allegiance with the Communists entirely vanished, and his farewell appeared a month later.

When he wrote Lawson after the "Farewell" was published, he said in effect that he had washed his hands of foreign ideologies and had "settled down to getting [his] own private menagerie into [his] own private ark," to which Lawson responded in the August letter, "That's a perfectly dignified thing to do. I don't think much of ivory towers, but I can certainly respect a friend who wants to sit in one and says, 'Come in and have a drink, but be courteous enough to respect my feelings and let's lay off politics'—but when you say that, and at the same time issue extremely political statements in the public prints, I say you're either kidding yourself or kidding me, and I don't respect your alleged 'privacy.' "

Dos Passos in his letter to Lawson had referred to "the intricate and bloody machinery of the Kremlin," a reference to Stalin's purge trials as much as to the party's power plays in Spain. Though distressed at the reference, Lawson responded that he did not see why disagreement about Soviet policies should destroy their friendship. After all, the core of both their thinking processes had been "the passionate belief in human rights and liberty and dignity which we both share." But Dos Passos seemed to Lawson to be guilty of "plain ornery red-baiting," because he appeared unwilling to differentiate his hatred of Moscow's policies from "the implication that everybody who disagrees with you and approves this intricate and bloody machinery is *also, a priori* and whether they like it or not, pretty damn intricate and bloody." In other words, Lawson accused Dos Passos of blaming all Communists for the violence and terror he had found in Spain.

"What I'm concerned about," Lawson wrote, "is you and myself and America." Dos Passos, he asserted, must draw a line between committed Americans and Kremlin policy. Lawson, unwilling to believe his friend would not make the distinction, was concerned to point out that not to do so was "a very real danger, and the farthest thing in the world from the free-thinking and free exchange of opinion" which Dos Passos insisted on. "It happens," Lawson noted, "that a large number of progressive and serious people *do* get together to wage what they feel is a clear-cut fight *against* something, against reaction and fascism. Communists play a large part in organizing this movement." He conceded that Dos Passos might be correct in believing that the situation was more complex than merely a struggle of good (that is, the left) against evil (that is, reactionaries and fascists) and that creating "an instrument of power" (the Communist machinery of government) created "a continual contradiction between the aims of the fighters for liberty and the result. Alright," Lawson continued, "but in finding your way through this complexity don't cut yourself off from the whole complex of people and ideas which is the very thing you're trying to analyze." He thought that the two of them could argue constructively about how to achieve individual liberties, unless Dos Passos now believed that "the fight against Communism, as an 'alien' philosophy," was more important than the beliefs that he and Lawson held in common. If that were the case, then Dos Passos was guilty of "witch-hunting and red-hating and prejudice."

Finally Lawson ended his impassioned August 24 letter to the man whom he had respected perhaps more than anyone else. After criticizing Trotskyites, for whom Dos Passos had some sympathy, Lawson concluded, "Lots of us are dumb enough to think that [loyalty and cooperation, and faith in the honor and courage and decency of people] are the qualities that brought the anti-fascists from all over the world and especially from Russia to fight in Spain and we're pretty sick and hurt when it's described as an 'intricate and bloody machinery.' Think it about Russia if you want to. Say it if it makes you feel any better. But don't twist it into an unforgivable prejudice against your own sort of people, and the work they're trying to do. I assure you, friendship won't stand that."

Unlike Lawson, who had committed himself to communism in 1934, Dos Passos was only in 1937 becoming sure of the political ground he stood on. He responded to Lawson quickly, trying to elucidate his stance as precisely as possible while attempting as well to keep the strained friendship alive. "You must have patience with unbelievers," he urged Lawson, and he declared that the real difference between their two political attitudes was that Lawson thought that ends justified means, while Dos Passos was positive that "all you have in politics is the means; ends are always illusory." And, making what was for him a significant declaration, he continued: "I think that Anglo-Saxon democracy is the best political method of which we have any and I'm for or against movements in so far as they seem to me to be consistent with its survival. To survive its got to keep on evolving. I have come to believe that the CP is fundamentally opposed to our democracy as I see it." Lawson had been correct in his previous letter: Dos Passos now saw Russian communism if not Marxism—exactly—as "an 'alien' philosophy"; and he would no longer give the American Communist party the benefit of his doubts. Communists were wrong, he believed, and those who did not take orders overtly from the Kremlin were nevertheless its dupes. His response was typical of the man; emotional at least as much as intellectual, it was one which tried to define issues too starkly. He found it difficult to accept a middle ground and had thrown out the baby with the bath water, which was what so irritated Lawson. "You cannot tell me what *my* intentions are," was Lawson's point. "You don't *know* what your intentions are," was Dos Passos's response, "because they are what the Kremlin dictate [*sic*], and the Kremlin reveals no secrets."

Although Dos Passos in his own mind might make some distinction between the communism of Stalin and the theories of Marxism, he admitted little. "Marxism," he declared to Lawson, "though an important basis for the unborn sociological sciences, if held as a dogma, is a reactionary force and an impediment to progress. Fascism is nothing but marxism inside out and is of course a worse impediment." To the argument that not supporting the Communists was aiding the Fascists, Dos Passos answered, "Rubbish: free thought can't possibly give aid and comfort to fascism." He defended himself against Lawson's accusation that he had not seen enough of what was going on to reach the conclusions he did. "Naturally [my] position was reached after considerable travel," Dos Passos continued, asserting:

> I now think that foreign liberals and radicals were very wrong not to protest against the Russian terror all down the line. There's just a chance that continual criticism from their friends might have influenced the bolsheviks and made them realize the extreme danger to their cause of the terror machine, which has now, in my opinion, eaten up everything good in the revolution. What we have in the U.S.S.R. is a new form of society—but I don't think it shows any sign of being a superior frame for the individual human than the poor old U.S.A. And waving the fascist spook at me isn't going to make me think any different.

Sensing that he was venturing out into unpopular territory, he added, "the fact that my particular slant in thought has few adherents at present, doesn't make it any less valid in my opinion."[3]

Lawson immediately responded, and while he agreed that they must have patience with each other, the breach widened. "You see," he admonished Dos Passos:

> where my goat is gotten, and starts not only to bleat but to neigh like a horse, is that, starting from a disagreement about certain facts (what is happening in the Soviet Union, the actual functioning of the Soviets, the Russian foreign policy, etc.) you jump . . . to the *realm of theory*: that is, in order to justify your version of the facts . . . instead of proceeding to at least attempt this verification, you assume that Communists and their friends *must* have a lot of theories which fit your version of the facts; the next step: since these theories are obviously contrary to what Communists say *they* believe, they must be a bunch of the most unprincipled liars.

Lawson told Dos Passos he was "nuts" to think that Communists believed that ends justified means. Instead, not believing such was exactly what distinguished Communists from Fascists. The former, in fact, believed that "only honorable and democratic means can be used to achieve democratic ends." To Lawson it seemed clear that the war in Spain demonstrated conclusively the difference between the ends-justifying-means Fascists—who slaughtered people and destroyed property indiscriminately—and the Communist-supported Loyalists, who Lawson was convinced "*strictly*, and with no exception, employ honest, democratic means . . . for honest, democratic ends." These means Lawson enumerated as being "a People's Army, a people's education and culture, an extension of the rights of the workers and farmers and shopkeepers and professionals, observance of the most humane principles possible in war-time, open and completely frank diplomacy."[4]

Dos Passos had to have been incensed by Lawson's rhetoric, particularly when Lawson went on to say that his impression of the situation was that "there is no case, in the Soviet Union or in Spain, of people being imprisoned or executed for their beliefs." Dos Passos was thoroughly convinced of the Communists' duplicity behind the scenes, was positive of their murderous methods as in the case of his friend Robles, and was aware of their terrorism in 1937 against the POUM (*Partida Obrero de Unificacion Marxista*) and anarchist elements among the Loyalists, whom the Communists accused of subversive Trotskyism. He knew, further, of their execution of Andres Nin, the POUM leader, and of their forcing Largo Caballero to resign as premier of the Loyalist government in favor of Juan Negrin.

Lawson was sure of *his* intentions as a Communist; and he could not tolerate—for that matter, could hardly comprehend—Dos Passos's conviction that being such, he, Lawson, was an unwitting victim of the Soviets. He accused Dos Passos of a "tragic isolation from activity," while Lawson and others working for the movement had learned a "deeper and richer democracy," which they were committed to protect, as were Communists in the Soviet Union and in Spain. "You don't know what you're missing," he concluded his letter, "and what you're missing is a first-rate education in actually working democratically, by democratic means, for democratic ends."[5]

The friendship was not entirely sundered in 1937. Dos Passos in November wrote Lawson to praise a revival of the dramatist's play *Processional* while noticeably avoiding any reference to their political quarrels.[6] Then in December Dos Passos published in *Common Sense* a piece entitled "The Communist Party and the War Spirit: A Letter to a Friend Who Is Probably a Party Member," an essay which was as much directed toward Lawson as toward any of Dos Passos's other critics. "As I take it," he wrote to his hypothetical friend, "your argument is, in its simplest terms, that the world situation consists of war between Fascism, demagogic military dictatorship for the purposes of reaction on one side, and the principle of progressive popular rule on the other side, of which you feel the Communist Party is the spear head." Dos Passos went on to spell out the Popular Front line, but he disagreed with it, stating that he did not think his friend's assessment was a true picture of international politics. Dos Passos could agree that "the declared aims of the Bolsheviks were admirable," but he noted, "The question is whether the dictatorship method didn't make these aims impossible to attain." He recalled that only after twenty years of totalitarian rule did the Communist party reintroduce "at least a facade of what Marxists used sneeringly to call bourgeois democracy" to coincide with the Popular Front. Americans wondered if the price had not been too high. Wouldn't it have been better to retain the democratic processes all along, and hadn't the result of the "human misery and repression" been "to warp the whole great enterprise in the direction of personal and bureaucratic despotism?" Clearly he thought so; American democracy had become his ideal; in fact, he now believed that "the one hope for the future of the type of western civilization which furnishes the frame of our lives is that the system of popular government based on individual liberty be not allowed to break down." Fascism, he had decided, "is a disease of sick capitalism, not a disease of democracy," and its cure was "intelligent popular government." As for Spain, liberal and Communist support of the Loyalists had been their life blood; but, he wrote, "the terrible thing for Spain's confused and vigorous movement for social renovation was that the Communists entered Spain at a moment when their party was infected by the internal feud of the Trotsky heresy hunt, at the moment in its history when it was least flexible. . . . The Communists took to Spain their organizing skill, their will to rule, and their blind intolerance," and the result had been that, instead of rallying progressives to it, the party had, "as it gained in power, set itself to eliminating physically or otherwise all the men with possibilities of leadership who were not willing to put themselves under its orders."[7]

There, apparently, the matter stood between Lawson and Dos Passos for the next year and a half. Lawson went his way in Hollywood, while Dos Passos went his, studying the origins of the American republic and emphasizing his stance to whoever would listen. From the Warm Springs Inn in Virginia, for example, he wrote Upton Sinclair in March 1938, expressing precisely the ideas he had the previous December in *Common Sense*, while adding that as for the United States, he believed increasingly that the Communists were "introducing the fascist mentality [he first wrote "methods"] that [had] made Europe a nightmare." "After all," he noted in an aside, "its the Bolsheviks that invented all of Hitler's and Mussolini's tricks." As a result he had come to think American Communists were "a pestiferous nuisance—Stalinist and Trotskyite alike."[8]

In the summer of 1938 Dos Passos and his wife Katy traveled to Europe, where during July and early August they sailed in the Mediterranean with Gerald and Sara Murphy. During the cruise they landed at Paestum, Italy, the site of an ancient Greek colony along the shore south of Salerno. Twenty years earlier, Dos Passos and Lawson with two other friends had visited Paestum while on leave from their Red Cross ambulance unit. From the site in 1938 Dos Passos wrote Lawson a postcard, reminding him that "just a little more than twenty years ago . . . you suddenly appeared here in a horse cab under the most extraordinary auspices—the temples [are] still doing well."[9] Significantly, shortly before his death Lawson recollected that Dos Passos's postcard had read in part, "I wonder if anything has changed since that time?" Lawson saw this as Dos Passos's attempt to reconcile their differences. He further recalled that he had never responded to the card, nor had he ever written Dos Passos again until he thanked him for a copy of *The Best Times*, Dos Passos's memoir, which he sent Lawson after it was published in 1966.[10]

Lawson's memory in 1974 tricked him. The postcard did not say what he would have had it say, and he did write Dos Passos again. While in his old age Lawson wanted to believe that he and his erstwhile friend had merely drifted apart, the final break came from more than that. Dos Passos, although firm in his convictions, was willing to overlook political differences to preserve friendship. Lawson, on the other hand, could not stay away from ideological differences, so in what was almost assuredly his last letter to Dos Passos, written the end of August in 1939, he berated Dos Passos for *The Adventures of a Young Man*, his statement in fiction of his break with the left wing. The novel, Lawson declared, had so shocked him that he had not recovered. He accused Dos Passos of violating "known and available truth." "The book made me angry—but anger isn't very helpful," he concluded, "and I'd really like to be helpful—although I doubt if it's possible. In fact, I doubt if there's any common ground on which we can talk about these things. I think that's tragic. . . . I also think . . . that you're to blame—for turning so far away from the sort of agreed fun-

damentals of feeling and purpose, the groundwork for common thought—
which is also common action—that we started with. That's not a nice thing
to say—and it probably won't have any effect—but there it is. Jack"[11] Of
their relationship—except for the brief interchange around *The Best
Times*—the rest was silence, and a sad, if revealing, conclusion to the
friendship of two politicized American writers in the 1930s.

No two figures could be exact prototypes for the many intellectuals who
struggled with politics during the decade; yet Lawson's and Dos Passos's
ideological struggles had striking similarities to others, while their diver-
gent paths represent two of the several routes writers chose as they found
their ways through ideological thickets. Lawson ended farther to the left
than most American writers. Some like Granville Hicks moved that far but
drew back after the close of the "red decade" and the signing of the
Soviet-Nazi pact in 1939, leaving only a few like Lawson and Mike Gold to
carry the red banner. Dos Passos ended farther to the right, in a region
located in Goldwater's Arizona and Dos Passos's version of Jefferson's
Virginia, where few American intellectuals had strayed. Among his companions, people who like him had also tried the left, were Max Eastman,
Will Herberg, James Burnham, John Chamberlain, and Russell Kirk. Their
spokesman became William Buckley; their journal, the *National Review*.

Lawson and Dos Passos had come to their early political positions
through similar experiences. They had first met aboard the S.S. *Chicago*
steaming toward Europe in June 1917. During that summer they had
observed World War I along the western front as ambulance drivers, then
had served together in Italy again as ambulance drivers through May 1918,
before being released. Dos Passos was threatened with a dishonorable
discharge for writing harsh comments about the war and the Italians. He
had to return to the United States to clear up his case with Red Cross
authorities in Washington before he could enlist in the army medical corps
as he did, sailing for Europe the day after the armistice. It was not long
before he joined Lawson, who had remained in Europe by taking another
post with the Red Cross in Rome after his release in May 1918. During the
spring of 1919, the two of them, radicalized by their contempt for govern-
ments and the military, talked protest in the charged atmosphere of a
politically volatile Paris with other Americans like the journalist Griffin
Barry, Robert Minor—a cartoonist for the defunct *Masses*—and the novelist Mary Heaton Vorse. Dos Passos's and Lawson's feelings might be
summed up by a letter Dos Passos wrote in April 1919. "A false idea, a false
system, and a set of tyrants, conscious or unconscious," he lectured his
young friend Rumsey Marvin, "is sitting on the world's neck at present and
has so far succeeded in destroying a good half of the worthwhile things in
the world."[12]

Dos Passos and Lawson during the first half of the twenties were against the Establishment, be it in government, business, or art; yet they were hardly political activists. They wished to protest conventionality through their art, and a good part of their protest was against art itself, although, of course, they opposed what they saw contemporary society to be. Dos Passos during the spring and early summer of 1919 labored at three manuscripts: a never-to-be-published novel entitled *Seven Times round the Walls of Jericho*; his first published novel, an essayistic protest against war entitled *One Man's Initiation: 1917*; and a larger novel he first called *The Sack of Corinth*, which became *Three Soldiers*, his statement against the war, but more, against organizations and mass society.

Lawson, meanwhile, worked at an expressionistic drama that he hoped would revolutionize the theater while striking a blow against contemporary society. By 1921 he had completed *Roger Bloomer*, a play which, as Dos Passos noted in his foreword to it when it was published in 1923, examined "the continuously increasing pressure in the grinding machine of industrial life." Lawson, Dos Passos asserted, was attempting to convey a sense of "the unprecedented fever and inhumaneness and mechanical complexity of American life."[13]

During the first part of the twenties their revolt was a generalized one that opposed the "normalcy" of Warren Harding and strived to celebrate The New in art. Dos Passos's next important novel after *Three Soldiers* was *Manhattan Transfer*, published in 1925, a work, he wrote a friend as he was about to begin it, that would be "a long dull and arduous novel about New York and go-getters and god knows what besides."[14] *Manhattan Transfer* would become his monument to New York and another record of "the unprecedented fever and inhumaneness and mechanical complexity of American life." He was a social, not political, critic then, a satiric observer rather than a committed radical.

So, too, was Lawson, whose next play, *Processional: A Jazz Symphony of American Life in Four Acts*, was produced in 1925. The piece, according to his own account, "caused a sensation, and established my reputation as a playwright rebelling against the form and content of the contemporary theatre." He wrote in an introduction to *Processional* that he hoped to express something of "the reality of America spiritually and materially." Hidden beneath the country's "hokum of advertisements, headlines, radio speeches" was "some inner necessity, a sense of direction," but he admitted he did not have the key to find it. Through *Processional* ran themes about the rhythm of contemporary life, about labor conflicts, capitalist exploitation, and urban problems. While it was "America well spanked," as Stark Young noted in his review, it was not a precisely political drama.[15]

Nevertheless, the two writers were edging toward political commitment, although it would fall short of what the activist Mike Gold desired from them. Lawson was instrumental in the production of Dos Passos's expressionistic play, *The Moon Is a Gong*, early in 1926, as a result of which Lawson invited Dos Passos to become a director, along with himself, Gold, Francis Faragoh, and Em Jo Basshe, of an avant-garde group to be called the New Playwrights Theatre, which Lawson later described as a "workers' " theater, an experimental organization whose aim was to present "mass plays, done for workers at prices that workers can afford."[16] *Moon*, in theme and technique somewhat similar to *Processional*, was distinctly unsuccessful; yet that did not discourage Dos Passos, and he joined the New Playwrights, thus putting himself in close touch with people like Gold, for whom politics was a way of life.

In addition, Dos Passos became in 1926 a member of the executive board of the *New Masses*, the reincarnation of the *Masses*, which had died at the hands of Woodrow Wilson's administration in World War I. In the June 1926 issue of the *New Masses*, Dos Passos wrote a piece describing the sort of journal he would like to see. His essay was in part a response to Gold, who, Dos Passos asserted, had earlier referred to him as a "bourgeois intellectual." The most interesting aspect of his piece is his independent, questioning stance, one that, to the annoyance of committed Communists like Gold, he would maintain during the next six years when many people considered him a convinced fellow-traveler, and some, a Communist in fact as well as in spirit.

"As mechanical power grows in America," Dos Passos wrote in 1926, "general ideals tend to restrict themselves more and more to Karl Marx, the first chapter of Genesis and the hazy scientific mysticism of the Sunday supplements." The present, he was sure, was no time for "spellbinders" to lay down hard and fast laws about anything. "Particularly," he emphasized, "I don't think there should be any more phrases, badges, opinions, banners, imported from Russia or anywhere else." From the days of Columbus, in fact, the American continent had been cursed by "imported systems"; what was needed now was not another import, but a native brand. The best thing for the *New Masses* to be was "a highly flexible receiving station that will find out what's in the air in the country." "Being clear-sighted" at a time "when the pressure is rising and rising in the boiler of the great imperial steamroller of American finance" that was always trying to grind down contemporary civilization was a matter of life and death. Introspection and doubt were what the *New Masses* needed, not any set of instructions, be they from Moscow or the steel mills of the United States.[17]

Understandably, Mike Gold, who made a habit of trying to goad bourgeois intellectuals leftward, was peeved. In the same issue as the one where Dos Passos's statement appeared, he responded, crying out "Let It Be Really New!," which was an attack on what he termed the "vague esthetic creed" of writers such as Dos Passos and Lawson. Gold's thrust at

Dos Passos came early in the era of ideological struggle; it is remarkable how consistent it is with the complaints lodged against him by the radical left all during the period when he was their literary almost-darling. The trouble with Dos Passos, Lawson, and their ilk, asserted Gold, was that they "hug chaos to their bosoms, and all the heroes of their fiction wind up in chaos and failure." This mood of "pessimism, defeatism, and despair," however, was not the only possible route for writers who opposed the status quo. Gold had seen younger writers discover a new path, that of "the world of revolutionary labor."[18]

As if to reaffirm what he had written, Gold's review of *Manhattan Transfer* appeared in the *New Masses* two months later. Calling the novel "a barbaric poem of New York," he observed that Dos Passos's work reflected "bewilderment." The central protagonist, Jimmy Herf, "is tortured by American commercialism and always seeks some escape." Dos Passos, however, did not understand how to help Herf, who at the conclusion of the book can only try to escape the chaos of Manhattan by plodding along a highway out of the city looking for a lift. "How fur ye goin?" asks the driver of a truck. "I dunno," answers Jimmy, "pretty far"—a response that, Gold was correct, is an affirmation of nothing except the negative effects of urban life.[19]

The answer to Dos Passos's problem, Gold wrote soon afterward, was to "read history, psychology, and economics" and to become active in the labor movement. Dos Passos, instead of standing aloof, needed to "ally himself definitely with the radical army, for in this struggle is the only true escape from middleclass bewilderment today." More acutely than perhaps he was aware, Gold observed, "Dos Passos suffers with nostalgia for a clean, fair, joyous and socialized America," by which Gold meant the egalitarian, individualistic democracy that had been the ideal before the young nation a century earlier.[20]

Dos Passos and Lawson thought they *were* allied, as artists, with the labor movement. Such an alliance was the intention of the New Playwrights. But still they created works in which artistic experimentalism was as important as protest. Lawson stood with Dos Passos in 1926, his concern at the time reflected in a response he made to Stuart Chase in the same issue of the *New Masses* as the one in which the exchange between Gold and Dos Passos appeared. Chase, in what he termed "A Yell from the Gallery," had decried three avant-garde dramas: Lawson's *Nirvana*, Dos Passos's *The Moon Is a Gong*, and Eugene O'Neill's *The Great God Brown*. Lawson defended them and lectured Chase that "it is a mistake to think of the New Art of the theatre in terms which are either new or artistic. It is an attempt to apply a very ancient form of showmanship to the needs of current and vital entertainment." Lawson meant to be socially aware, but his primary interest was in "the New Art of the theatre," a point that he would reiterate many years later. During the life of the New Playwrights Theatre, he stated, only Mike Gold represented the orthodox left, and only Gold wanted the group's productions consistently to take a well-defined left-wing stance. Contrary to what people who knew of the New Playwrights believed, their short history was not one of constant political bickering. Their arguments were more often about staging, sets, and other theatrical matters.[21]

In essence, the stances of Lawson and Dos Passos as the New Playwrights were forming in 1926 remained their stances into the 1930s, despite a degree of increased activism on Dos Passos's part when he made a symbolic but ineffectual visit in the spring of 1926 along with other intellectuals to observe a strike against textile mills in Passaic, New Jersey; despite Dos Passos's and Lawson's involvement in the protests against the convictions of Sacco and Vanzetti, culminating in both Dos Passos's and Lawson's arrests for picketing in Boston prior to the Italians' executions on 23 August 1927; and despite Dos Passos's subsequent lengthy trip in 1928 to Russia.

In the wake of Dos Passos's disgust with American justice after Sacco's and Vanzetti's deaths—"The black automatons have won," he declared in October in a prose poem; and later, to describe his emotion at the time, he wrote, "We are two nations . . . we stand defeated America"—and in the wake of earlier encomiums such as Lincoln Steffens's about Russia, which he asserted was the future, and it worked, one would have expected Dos Passos to embrace the Soviet system. As he visited Leningrad and Moscow, traveled through the provinces, and voyaged down the Volga River, he talked with many Russians and came quickly to admire their enthusiasms and social fervor. The poverty and desolation he saw, however, caused him to wonder if the ground was "being cleared for future building, or was [the situation] just the results of oldfashioned ignorant centralized oppression?" He was no closer to an answer about the rightness and wrongness of political systems than he had been in the United States, while his doubts about the Soviet order in particular increased, if anything, after an evening he spent in Moscow with an Englishman and his Russian wife. The husband had come to Russia to work for the Communists; his wife favored them as well, but she was one of the pre-Communist intelligentsia, and nothing she could do could ingratiate her with the new wave. Purge after purge had occurred; now the couple feared for their lives. First it had been the nobility and the "middleclass social revolutionaries" who had been purged; at the moment it was the Trotskyites, the very people who had worked alongside the bolsheviks. The Englishman was most disturbed by the Communists' brutal suppression of the Kronstadt rebellion in 1921, where members of the Cheka had sadistically punished the rebels. "It was terror I'd seen in the man's eyes," Dos Passos recalled; nothing he could say could lessen the Britisher's fear, which would only end when he and his wife either died or escaped. "We are doomed," he concluded, and his pathetic plight left Dos Passos unable to decide where he stood politically.[22]

Lawson admitted to the same doubts before becoming a confirmed Communist. He said that his two plays which had been produced by the New Playwrights, *Loudspeaker* and *The International,* "reflected the confusion, the romantic groping and petty handling of great themes, which afflicted me in the later twenties." The theater's policy, in fact, seemed to him to suffer from these difficulties; but its importance was that, "in spite of its weaknesses, its aesthetic manifestoes and vacillating policies, it was an important forerunner of the more mature social theatre of the nineteen-thirties."[23]

As the twenties ended, Dos Passos and Lawson went separate ways, although remaining on the same ideological ground. Lawson departed New York for Hollywood and MGM, where his first assignment was to supply titles for a silent movie, *The Pagan.*[24] Dos Passos, back in New York after Russia, oversaw the production of the last New Playwrights production, his drama *Airways, Inc.,* in early 1929. The show was a disappointment, and in the wake of it, he resigned angrily from the theater group, which soon thereafter collapsed entirely.

Despite the demise of the group, Lawson and Dos Passos remained close friends. Yet Lawson later believed the whole New Playwrights Theatre episode had put a strain on their relationship that he never sensed at the time. He came to think that he had been naive about pushing Dos Passos into drama by producing *The Moon Is a Gong.* At the time it did not occur to Lawson that his close friend did not savor being forced to work with a group like the directors, or that he did not really appreciate being committed to left-wing theater. Partly the idea titillated him; as another director, Francis Faragoh, commented, Dos Passos saw the experience as "a sort of slumming." He willed his commitment, and the same part of him that enjoyed talking tough with his friend Hemingway enjoyed Mike Gold's political brashness or late-night set painting in cramped, proletarian quarters. But the experience chafed also against his penchant for solitude and his basic distrust then of doctrines and systems. Nevertheless he worked for left-wing causes, protesting—as in a letter to the editor of the *New Republic* in 1930—the jailing of labor organizers throughout the country and asking for funds for the Communist-dominated International Labor Defense organization. While he continued during the first half of the decade to work for such causes, however, he kept asserting his uncertainties privately. "I guess the trouble with me is I can't make up my mind to swallow political methods," he wrote Edmund Wilson in January 1931. Intellectually Dos Passos was probably closer to Wilson than to anyone else at the time—the two of them had an even more probing, because more dispassionate, political dialogue during the thirties than had Dos Passos and Lawson—so to Wilson he poured out his concerns. "Most of the time I think the IWW theory was right—Build a new society in the shell of the old—but practically all they did was go to jail," Dos Passos went on. "Anyway the extraordinary thing about Americans . . . is that while they strain at a gnat of doctrine, they'll swallow an elephant of experiment—the first problem is to find a new phraseology that we'll be at home with to organize mentally what is really happening now—This is all very confused," he fretted; but his basic point was clear enough: he distrusted political doctrines and their concomitant terminology. He would not embrace the left wing entirely; in the summer of 1930 he described himself in the *New Republic* as "a middle-class liberal, whether I like it or not," and he located himself politically as neither a member of the Communist party nor a procapitalist. Two years later, despite the fact that he would vote for Foster and Ford, the Communist candidates for president and vice-president, he considered himself a "middleclass intellectual," a " 'camp follower' of radical parties." So when Wilson sent him a copy to endorse of a manifesto that Wilson, Waldo Frank, and Lewis Mumford had written, Dos Passos objected to some of the rhetoric which smacked too much of the Communist party for his tastes. "I think the only useful function people like us can perform," he told Wilson, "is introduce a more native lingo into the business—and Goddamn it, I haven't enough confidence in the C.P. to give it a blanket endorsement." A year later, in the spring of 1933, he was praising the new president, Franklin Roosevelt, writing Wilson that Roosevelt was a "fascinating performer" and "a sleek wire artist," someone, Dos Passos implied, who might pull the country out of the depression by revising and reinvigorating American democracy. Then early in 1934, Dos Passos signed "An Open Letter to the Communist Party," which appeared in the *New Masses*, protesting "the disruptive action of the Communist Party which led to the breaking up of the meeting called by the Socialist Party in Madison Square Garden of February 16th." The *New Masses* was pained, and in an editorial entitled "To John Dos Passos" its editors deplored his joining the company of Lionel Trilling, John Chamberlain, Robert Morss Lovett, and Edmund Wilson, among others. "To us," declared the *New Masses*, "you have been, and, we hope, still are, Dos Passos the revolutionary writer, the comrade."[25]

When Wilson wrote his friend about the exchange in the *New Masses*, Dos Passos responded that he had not intended to imply by anything he said that the Socialists were any better than the Communists. "What is happening," he was convinced, was that "the whole Marxian radical movement is in a moment of intense disintegration—all people like us, who have no taste for political leadership or chewing the rag, can do, is to sit on the sidelines and try to put a word in now and then for the underdog or for the cooperative commonwealth or whatever." Dos Passos remained convinced for the moment that the Marxists were correct in their analysis of the situation, but it seemed to him that everything they did helped their opposition. "The only alternative," he wrote, "is passionate unmarxian revival of Anglo Saxon democracy on an industrial basis helped by a collapse in the directors' offices. That would be different from Nazi social- ism only in this way: that it would be a reaction towards old time Fourth of July democracy instead of towards feudalism. . . . How you can coordinate Fourth of July democracy with the present industrial-financial set up I don't see. Maybe Roosevelt is already as far as we can go in that direction."[26]

During these years when Dos Passos was backing away from the Com- munists, Lawson appeared to be in a kind of political limbo, caught between the demands of his work in Hollywood, the "progressive" stance he had taken in the twenties, and the politics of Mike Gold. In retrospect Lawson could believe that his first years in Hollywood had contributed to his political education. "I was deeply interested in the art of the film," he wrote, "and troubled by the ruthless and irresponsible methods of produc- tion which prevented writers from dealing honestly and creatively with their work." Perhaps so, one might agree; however, until 1934 he appeared not unduly dissatisfied. But that may be unfair to Lawson. He worked to organize the Screen Writers Guild and was elected its first president in 1933. His politics, nevertheless, remained non-Communist. Harold Clur- man, who knew Lawson well, later wrote that early in the depression, although "of progressive, even radical opinion, he was violently opposed to official communist doctrine," a position Lawson apparently espoused in his play *Success Story*, which opened in September 1932. It departed from the experimentalism of his earlier work and evinced Lawson's criticism of materialistic society, even implying that a person should make a political commitment; yet the main figure, Sol Ginsburg, does not, announcing that he is "sick to death of radical meetings an' sour-faced people an' cheap gab." Little matter if he repented; the left-wing critics disapproved of the play, Mike Gold declaring that Lawson's intended criticism of his protago- nist was nothing more than "the mask for an overwhelming craving for money and bourgeois success."[27]

Clearly Lawson faced a moral dilemma. He recognized that Hollywood films conveyed little or nothing of the social messages he favored. And clearly as a result he was struggling while the thirties wore on to clarify his own political ideology. He could have been speaking of his own work when he wrote Dos Passos early in 1934, criticizing Dos Passos's third play, *Fortune Heights*, a copy of which Lawson had just received. Its themes were murky, he protested; the play "introduces all sorts of social ideas and has a very strong unresolved social content which isn't worked out ideologically." He assured Dos Passos that he did not take "a stiff Marxian Stalinistic attitude" but then exploded, "Christ Almighty, it seems to me obvious that if you undertake certain revolutionary problems—evictions, the hunger march, things that are part and parcel of the whole life around us—you've got to have some revolutionary ground on which to stand." Lawson resented Dos Passos's "inconclusiveness," reflected in "the fact that, although the play contains a revolutionary hypothesis, three quarters of it are concerned with a semi-satirical picture of middleclass break-down, that it ends up with an ironical defeatist twist, and that the Proletarian angle is ignored!" Dos Passos had shortly before criticized Lawson for his most recent plays, *The Pure in Heart* and *Gentlewoman*, which Dos Passos—rightly, Lawson conceded—thought were "removed from life." Lawson was groping toward a firmer ideological ground. "I'm not at all sure I know *how* to write the Proletarian plays which I am thinking about," he confessed, "but I feel there's got to be *something said* beside the pathos of middle-class breakdown." The pathos lent power on occasion to *Fortune Heights*, he admitted; yet it was not enough, "the sense of groping is not enough", and "phrases (which might be interesting if developed) about 'finding the United States' are not enough." To which, Lawson acknowledged, Dos Passos might reply, "This is exactly the stage at which people find themselves." But Lawson did not believe that; he believed that there was "a great deal more stirring."[28]

More accurately than Lawson knew, he was defining exactly the stage where Dos Passos found himself. Lawson, unlike his friend, was on the verge in early 1934 of making a deep commitment to communism. He was stung once by the failures of *The Pure in Heart* and *Gentlewoman*, both of which flopped on Broadway during March, and stung again by the attack of Mike Gold, who upon the appearance of the two plays immediately branded Lawson "a bourgeois Hamlet of our time." The 1925 play *Processional*, Gold wrote in the *New Masses*, had been futilitarian. Now, almost ten years later, Lawson was "still lost like Hamlet, in his inner conflict. Through all his plays wander a troop of ghosts disguised in the costumes of living men and women and repeating the same monotonous question: 'Where do I belong in this warring world of two classes?' " To the question, "What have you learned in these ten years?," Lawson, according to Gold, had to respond, "Nothing. I am still a bewildered wanderer lost between two worlds indulging myself in the same adolescent self-pity as in my first plays." Gold hammered away at his target: "To be a 'great' artist," he declared, "one must greatly believe in something," but Lawson had "no real base of emotion or philosophy," nor had he "purified his mind and heart."[29]

One might expect Lawson to have come back fighting, but he did not. While acknowledging privately to Dos Passos that he resented "the idea of my friends that either Hollywood or 'Gentlewoman' were making inroads on my fundamental plan to use the theatre as a medium for revolutionary expression," he began issuing what amounted to *mea culpas*. Gold's attack had been "bitter and exceedingly dirty," he told Dos Passos, adding that his answer was "what I think is a reasonable statement of my position." But instead of struggling against Gold's accusations, Lawson concluded his letter to Dos Passos by acknowledging that he felt "very strongly the necessity of a much closer contact with Communism, and much more activity in connection with it."[30]

In the issue of the *New Masses* following that in which Gold's attack appeared, Lawson responded. He admitted the truth of 70 percent of the criticism, remarking in his defense that for persons like himself, "a genuine acceptance of the proletarian revolution is a difficult task." "The majority of American fellow-travellers are struggling with the problem of their own orientation," he continued, noting that it was "strikingly evident in the work of John Dos Passos, which combines great revolutionary fervor with all sorts of liberal and individualistic tendencies." Lawson also offered in his defense that, regardless of the inadequacy of his works' political orientation, he was demonstrating an "ideological advance." *Gentlewoman*, he claimed, despite its faults, was "a play along Marxian lines about a dying bourgeois class."[31]

He did not end his confessions here, however. He moved with the fervor of a religious convert, reevaluating his work, joining the party, and accepting blame for his past ideological failure. Harold Clurman recounted the tale of going in 1934 to a meeting of a John Reed Club, a radical literary group to whom Lawson was to speak about his plays. But before he spoke his audience pounced on him for his ideological confusion. Lawson, Clurman recounted, was "not only humble but apologetic" when he rose to speak: "He talked like a man with a troubled conscience, a man confessing his sin, and in some way seeking absolution. He wanted his present critics to like him; he wanted to live up to their expectations, fulfill their requirements. He knew his plays were faulty; he was seeking in his heart and mind for the cause and remedy."[32]

Lawson had taken sides and now strove to match words with deeds. Twice—in May and July of 1934—he traveled into the South as part of a delegation sponsored by the National Committee for the Defense of Political Prisoners, the American Civil Liberties Union, International Labor Defense, and a committee to defend Angelo Herndon, a labor organizer jailed in Fulton County, Georgia. The delegation's purpose was to investigate the situation of Herndon and others in Georgia and that of the Scottsboro boys, the eight young blacks imprisoned in Alabama for the supposed rape of two white prostitutes. On both visits Lawson was arrested; he was profoundly affected by the experiences, not only of being arrested, but of discovering some things about southern justice. "I learned for the first time of the oppression of the Negro people," he wrote later, "of the greatness and nobility of these people, and of the significance of their struggle in the whole nation's life and history."[33] He returned to the North, more committed than ever to activism. "I do not hesitate to say that it is my aim to present the communist position, and to do so in the most specific manner," he declared in November 1934 in *New Theatre*, the drama journal of the Stalinists. He had become, in Gerald Rabkin's terms, the "dean of the revolutionary theatre."[34]

Lawson's stance was now firm, and from this point on the rift between him and Dos Passos would grow as the latter refrained more and more from any fellow-traveling. The seeds of the rift, as we have seen, were already planted by early 1934 when Lawson had criticized *Fortune Heights*. Then during that spring or early summer, around the time Lawson was making his southern journeys, they exchanged more correspondence. Dos Passos, in a letter that offended Lawson, blamed the failure of Lawson's plays, as well as the intolerance of the left wing, partly on what he termed "New York neo-ghetto ignorance." "The whole New York jewish theatre guild, Damrosch, Otto Kahn, Mike Gold culture (I mean jewish in the best sense)," Dos Passos asserted, "is an echo of the liberal mitteleuropa culture that has just bitten the dust with such a fearful crash in Europe." This left people only their "feudal reflexes," he believed, which took the forms of Mussolini and Hitler. The United States, on the other hand, lacked "feudal reflexes"; rather, it would fall back on "desire under the cemetery elms, lynching bees, General Motors and the Ford car" when a political reaction such as had hit Europe set in. He felt that what was now happening in America was a retreat away from socialism, and he preferred the retreat to occur within the framework of politics native to the United States rather than within a communist structure or under the aegis of the Communist party, whose "New York jewish leadership" was indulging in a foolish delirium of martyrdom. He told Lawson he had not seen Mike Gold's remarks but could imagine them. What he referred to as "the whole Marxist-German socialist and Russian Jewish communist" seemed to be "frittering away into vicious and childish nonsense." Recently he had been reading the Industrial Workers of the World (IWW) weekly, and he confessed that he still felt more in common with its line than with any other.[35]

Lawson's response was an impassioned, thirteen-page typed letter which began, "I am extremely disturbed by what you say about the Communists and the general situation. . . . I think you're terrifically wrong in this approach." The situation was not as Dos Passos saw it. "For Christ's sake, Dos," Lawson burst forth, "we're seeing the death-throes of Capitalism, and we're seeing it take the most brutal and bloody fascist forms in order to preserve itself a little longer." Lawson went on at length to refute Dos

Passos's views about the American scene, the Communist party, its leadership, and its mentality. Dos Passos's views about the Jewish mind pained him; moreover, they were narrow and simplistic. To Lawson, only the Communist party with its grounding in Marxist theory stood truly for the working class. Liberals, socialists, and men like Edmund Wilson were nothing but "propagandists for the bloodiest reaction."[36]

As Lawson wrote on, his passion mounted. In the full heat of his new commitment he lectured Dos Passos: "You and myself and all the people we know, people like ourselves, are individualists, and we're soft, and we're not particularly given to accepting any kind of discipline. I feel that the Communists have the fullest justification for their distrust of the intellectuals—and the first thing for someone like myself to learn is to choose a line and then be damned humble and damned disciplined about it." Lawson told Dos Passos that at a John Reed Club meeting he had attended, presumably the same one that Harold Clurman had observed, members of the audience had accused Dos Passos of "consorting with their enemies" by writing for the magazine *Common Sense*, which they said was "directly aiming toward fascism." They were right, asserted Lawson, for whom "the day of *general* revolutionary tendencies is past." And, separating himself from the majority of leftist American writers, he declared: "The Dreisers and Sherwood Andersons and Bunny Wilsons and Archibald MacLeishes and Hemingways and Menkens [*sic*] and Nathans and Heywood Brouns and Calvertons and Eugene O'Neills and Roger Baldwins and Sidney Howards—The whole caboodle of 'em are lining up exactly where they belong—in the name of their aesthetic integrity, they're serving fascism and war and Jew-baiting and negro-baiting. A few of 'em will find out they made a mistake and start to scream like stuck pigs—when it's too late." Finally he closed his letter, first reiterating his own plans to work closely with the Communists, become involved in strike activity, and accept party discipline. Then he ended with a sort of plea to his friend: "You've always (far more than myself) followed a revolutionary idea—it seems to me that now you (and all of us) are faced with a clear-cut revolutionary choice. I maintain that there is only one revolutionary line and one revolutionary party (Be as sentimental as you like about the Wobblies, but they do not represent the working class, or any portion of it, in a modern sense). And what's needed now is not sentimental adherence, but the will to fight a disciplined difficult fight."[37]

There the matter stood. Dos Passos had a brief stay in Hollywood later in 1934, the chief results of which were his increased scorn for the big money and for the left-wing involvement he thought the screenwriters played at. He and Lawson contributed papers to the first American Writers' Congress in 1935—Dos Passos's paper called for "bold and original thought" to be supplied by writers who should not "make of themselves figureheads in political conflicts." Lawson's essay was a Marxist analysis of the techniques of drama.[38] But Dos Passos did not attend the congress; and he and Lawson had little contact, apparently, until 1937, when they discussed a filmscript of *The Big Money* and picked up their arguments that ended with silence in 1939.

After 1935 Lawson published only one more play, *Marching Song*, intended as a model revolutionary drama. He continued as a screenwriter and polemicist for communism but cannot be said to have attracted national attention until 1947, when he was indicted by the House Un-American Activities Committee for contempt of Congress. As one of the Hollywood Ten he refused to say whether he was a member of the Communist party. It was a brave stand; his reward was imprisonment from 1950 to 1951 in a federal penitentiary in Kentucky. He remained unrepentant, to the end of his life asserting that the communist ideal was desirable, even if the Soviets had botched their experiment.

Dos Passos, on his way to Goldwater country, gave himself a course in the roots of the republic. He found them in an Anglo-Saxon self-governing tradition, his first celebration of which was a long essay introducing a selection of Thomas Paine's work. Dos Passos saw something of himself in Paine, whose "reckless dedication to the truth" and the "extraordinary courage and steadfastness with which he held to his basic conceptions" made him of interest to the present.[39] A more significant statement was Dos Passos's next book, *The Ground We Stand on: Some Examples from the History of a Political Creed*, published in 1941. Here he praised Paine again, but more, Roger Williams, Daniel Defoe, Benjamin Franklin, Samuel and John Adams, Thomas Jefferson, Joel Barlow, Alexander Hamilton, and H. H. Brackenridge. "In times of change and danger when there is a quicksand of fear under men's reasoning, a sense of continuity with generations gone before can stretch like a lifeline across the scary present," Dos Passos wrote in his introductory chapter, entitled "The Use of the Past." Observing that "Americans as a people notably lack a sense of history," he asserted that during the twenties "the social revolutionists [had] swallowed the millenial gospel of Marx in one great gulp." But their fervor had blinded them to the realities, and despite the "agony of Europe," Americans remained unsure of the values of "our poor old provincial American order," which was framed from "the largest heritage of the habits and traditions and skills of selfgovernment there has ever been in the world."[40] The United States and its republican government had become his. Repeatedly thereafter, he celebrated the early republic, marveling especially at Thomas Jefferson, while relentlessly attacking Marxism, socialism, or, as time went by, any politics to the left of Senator Robert Taft's. He jabbed painfully at Lawson in 1954, harshly satirizing him and the Hollywood left in the novel *Most Likely to Succeed*. Lawson was aware of it and was hurt, but that had been Dos Passos's intention, because he felt betrayed and forced into isolation by the left, of which Lawson was an extreme example, for his refusal to condemn the excesses of HUAC, Joseph McCarthy, and his kind.

What is to be taken finally from this story of a friendship? For one thing, Lawson's and Dos Passos's struggles before and during the 1930s were like those of numerous other American writers. The two debated Marxist doctrine, severely questioned the fundamentals of capitalism and democracy, searched for roots and a usable past, and attempted to deal with sometimes contradictory elements of American character and culture such as individualism, egalitarianism, racial and ethnic bigotries, a love-hate relationship with industrialization, and a profound commitment to liberty. For another thing, like other American writers Lawson and Dos Passos reacted to the shifting political winds of 1920s capitalism, the New Deal, and the Popular Front. Further, in the cases of these two writers, as with others, the thirties marked the end of their best work. It was as if their efforts, emotional as much as intellectual, had exhausted them. Nevertheless, their struggles, their processes of defining a ground to stand on, were important for their self-definition; one might add, for their world, because these writers were defining issues and ideologies that remain with us even until the present.

Part II

THE TRIUMPH OF LITERATURE: WRITING IS NOT OPERATING A BOMBING-PLANE

There is no sense in pursuing a literary career under the impression that one is operating a bombing-plane. On the one hand, imaginary bombs kill no actual enemies; and on the other, the development of a war psychology prevents one's real work from having value. When you "relax the aesthetic and ethical standards," you abandon the discipline itself of your craft.

> Edmund Wilson,
> "American
> Critics, Left
> and Right," 1937

CHAPTER 4

DONALD PIZER

James T. Farrell and the 1930s

There is much precedent and considerable usefulness in discussing a writer and his work in relation to a specific moment in time. Artists of course differ in the degree to which they respond to the issues and events of their day, but few have successfully created works that are completely "out of space, out of time." And if the nature and quality of an art work can be clarified by reference to its moment, then we should by all means not neglect this avenue of approach. One difficulty with this platitudinous defense of historical scholarship is that it is often based on the assumption that the "past" is a recoverable entity. There is a distinctive period—the American 1890s, say—and there is a writer who flourished during the period. Compare one's notion of the 1890s with the work of the writer and, presto, important and commanding "insights." What we frequently do not recall in undertaking this form of criticism is that much of what we conceive of as the 1890s is a construct of ideas which derives both from seventy years of speculative thinking about the period and from the needs and values of our own time. We think we are writing history, as R. G. Collingwood has noted, but in fact we are creating a kind of myth.[1]

Which is not to invalidate the myth-making process. As we all know, myth has a truth of its own—the truth of felt beliefs expressed in symbolic form—and literary criticism, like most speculative activities, needs all the truth of human experience it can muster. But we are required, I think, to be aware of what we are about as "historians" if we are not to construe our enterprise falsely. When we discuss a writer in the context of the 1890s, in other words, we do so by creating a symbolic device that we agree to call the 1890s. We then use this device to cast light on the writer's work, but the light we cast may reveal as much about our own preoccupations as about those of the writer and his period.

I make these not very original remarks about historiography because of their special relevance to any discussion of the work of James T. Farrell. Few major American writers have been so neatly and permanently pigeonholed in time as Farrell has been. Farrell is a writer of the 1930s and that's that. The fiction of the 1930s is characteristically proletarian, naturalistic, Marxist, sociological, and documentary. Farrell writes proletarian, naturalistic, Marxist, sociological, and documentary novels.[2] Ergo: the writer and his time are one and the job of criticism is completed.

Much of the impulse behind this quick dismissal of Farrell derives from the belief that both he and other characteristic writers of the thirties sought to describe the surface of experience without regard for either profound meaning or artistic form. We know, of course, that the self-conscious call for a literature that is moral and artistic—for a literature of high culture, in other words—has often disguised a powerful social fear or need. In the 1870s and '80s, for example, the attack on realism as superficial, inartistic, and morally thin reflected a deep distrust of the new urban society from which the ideals of realism were assumed to have sprung. The pejorative cast of the phrase "a thirties writer" (what is usually meant is "a thirties writer *and nothing else*") has a somewhat similar origin. During the 1940s and '50s, an entire generation of critics found themselves questioning many of the ideals and values they had held in the 1930s. Men of the caliber of Lionel Trilling, Edmund Wilson, Philip Rahv, and Malcolm Cowley discovered that ideologically speaking the thirties were now suspect. Marxism in its various political manifestations was not a pure road toward revolutionary progress and human brotherhood but a tool of political oppression and literary conformity abroad and a potential threat at home. But they, and others, had believed, and there is no bitterness like that of the apostate. And who better to represent the limitations of the age and its now discarded faith than Farrell, a writer who had been in the forefront of Marxist theorizing and whose major work appeared to be a massive example of the indictment of capitalism through a sociological depiction of the emptiness of lower middle class life. I do not intend to imply by these comments that some of the major critics of recent American literature have engaged in a conspiratorial attack on Farrell's work or that they have all shared a simplistic view of it. Rather, they contributed in the 1940s and '50s to a literary climate that tended to find most naturalistic fiction of the thirties deficient and that tended to identify Farrell as a leading figure in that movement. Some of the critics (such as Rahv and Cowley) wrote specifically about Farrell in condemning the literary tradition of which he was a part; others (such as Trilling and Wilson) condemned the tradition without naming him but nevertheless contributed implicitly to the attack on his work.[3]

There is much irony in this use of Farrell as a symbol of the thirties. Most obviously, he himself in the 1930s had frequently been the butt of vicious attacks by more orthodox radicals because of his early anti-Stalinism. Now he was often viewed as part of a monolithic left-wing orthodoxy during the decade. Also, and in a more literary context, Farrell in the 1930s had been a vigorous opponent of a reductive Marxist literary creed. His *A Note on Literary Criticism* (1936) had angered such writers as Granville Hicks and Mike Gold because of his attack on formula notions of the collectivist and proletarian novel and because of his defense of fiction as "a branch of the fine arts." And finally, in a far more useful and significant way, there is irony in designating Farrell "a thirties writer," given his roots in the literary ideals and techniques of the 1920s. Farrell himself in 1965 commented ruefully on the conventional "decimalization" (as he put it) of his work: "I have been rubber-stamped as a novelist of the thirties. In some instances, I have been treated as though I were born a writer, full-blown, after the stockmarket crash of 1929. It is as though I had no infancy, childhood or youth which affected and influenced the formation of my consciousness as a writer."[4]

Farrell in this comment opens up a potentially rich vein of inquiry into the nature of his best work. How, we might ask, does a consciousness formed largely in the 1920s (Farrell was twenty-six in 1930) respond to conditions of life in the 1930s when writing both about the twenties and the thirties in his major fiction? An account of Farrell's work along these lines need not imply the existence of an integral body of values, beliefs, and techniques that flourished during the 1920s and another such body that flourished during the thirties. Rather, the terms *1920s* and *1930s* can serve as convenient critical symbols to represent various ideas about literature and life, some of which can be called 1920s ideas and some 1930s. This designation will probably have some historical justification, but the aim of the designation is not to characterize an age but to make certain historical reference points symbolic of certain tendencies in fiction.

The work by Farrell that I wish to discuss in this way is *Studs Lonigan*. One reason for choosing *Studs* is that it has been and will probably continue to be the foundation of Farrell's permanent reputation; any valid critical approach to Farrell should therefore aid in the understanding and appreciation of this novel. Another reason is that the work bridges the twenties and thirties in a number of obvious ways that suggest a deeper and more significant link between the decades and the origin and nature of the novel. The trilogy was begun in 1929 before the crash and its first two novels—*Young Lonigan* and *The Young Manhood of Studs Lonigan*—were largely completed by mid-1931.[5] *The Young Manhood of Studs Lonigan* ends on New Year's Day 1929. The third volume of the trilogy, *Judgment Day*, is set during the depression. It is against a background of a collapsed market, failing banks and businesses, strikes, mass unemployment, and growing left-wing agitation that Studs moves toward his death. This novel is also far more documentary in technique than the first two, with Farrell drawing heavily on the use of headlines, songs, and slogans in the manner of Dos Passos. But it is less on the grounds of depression subject matter and a documentary method that the trilogy as a whole is identified with the 1930s. It is rather the dreariness and failure of Studs's life that have been felt to be symptomatic of the tragic waste and misdirection of American society as a whole during the decade.

This is, I think, a valid symbolic use of the novel. *Studs Lonigan* is here made to represent an idea that we have about the decade. But the novel itself, when understood in relation to its sources in the 1920s and to its close texture, is not something contrary to this symbolic use but rather something that is also much finer and richer than is subsumed by the symbol. It is along these lines that I would like to take up *Studs Lonigan*.

Much of the discussion of the major influences on Farrell's thought and writing has centered on the problem of his naturalism. On the one hand, the concern with the origin of Farrell's naturalism has contributed to the longstanding and widespread belief that he can best be understood as a disciple of Dreiser. On the other, several recent critics—notably Edgar Branch and Lewis Fried—have argued that Farrell's basic ideas can more properly be located in the social philosophy of John Dewey and George Herbert Mead, figures whom he read and admired during his years at the University of Chicago in the late 1920s. Farrell himself, no doubt in part because of his resentment at being labeled a lesser and simpler Dreiser, has also tended to find the roots of his ideas in the Chicago school of philosophical pragmatists.[6]

There is profit in viewing Farrell's work from the perspective of both Dreiser and the Chicago pragmatists, but there is also some hazard if these serve as the only avenues of approach. Like Dreiser, Farrell was deeply moved by the American dilemma of the warping of potentially admirable yet weak minds by the overwhelming attraction of socially corrupt goals and values. One of Farrell's epigraphs to *Young Lonigan*—a quotation from Plato's *Republic*—could, for example, apply equally to *Studs Lonigan* and to *An American Tragedy*. The passage reads: "Except in the case of some rarely gifted nature there never will be a good man who has not from his childhood been used to play amid things of beauty and make them a joy and a study."

Our full understanding of the implications of this passage for the character of Studs, however, requires as well a recognition of the impact upon Farrell of the beliefs of Dewey and Mead that the relationship between an individual and his culture is one of functional interaction rather than dominance by either the individual or his world, and that a beneficial interaction requires above all that an individual be aware of as full a range of options for belief and choice as possible.

This approach to Farrell through ideas, however, does not render either the pull or the feel of his fiction at its best. The method is somewhat akin to discussing Zola largely in relation to the influence of Claude Bernard and to Zola's programmatic philosophizing about literature in *The Experimental Novel*. One knows what Zola believed, but one does not really know his fiction. For Zola's fiction itself, one might more profitably begin by his obvious indebtedness to some of the giants of the nineteenth-century novel, and particularly to the work of Dickens and Balzac. It is in their novels that Zola found much of his own fictional style—how character is portrayed and how action is unfolded—to which he gave his own characteristic emphasis and shape. For Farrell, an understanding of his relationship to the work of two of the major writers of the 1920s, James Joyce and Sherwood Anderson, can serve a similar purpose.

Farrell wrote in his 1938 introduction to *Studs Lonigan* that Studs was "a normal American boy" who was bred in a milieu of "spiritual poverty" and that in the course of his life "his values become the values of his world."[7] This account of Studs by Farrell locates the center of the novel in the 1920s belief that it was the novelist's function to commit himself above all to the dramatization of the inarticulate felt life (what Farrell calls the "spiritual") as that life interacts with a social reality that informs and often collides with it. Of course, all fiction is, in one way or another, devoted to the depiction of the relationship between distinctive individuals and a particularized outer world. But the fictional shape given this relationship changes from age to age, and in the 1920s the shapes that were both most characteristic among major writers and most influential on Farrell were those of Joyce and Anderson.

Farrell himself has noted the powerful effect these writers had upon him during the period when he was forming his literary sensibility and fictional method in the late 1920s. As an author concerned with the inhospitality of Irish-American lower middle class culture to the life of the mind and spirit, Farrell could not help but be drawn to similar themes in Joyce. But, more significantly, he was especially attracted—as were so many others of his generation—by Joyce's striking portrayal of the interplay between the minutia of everyday life and the free-ranging consciousness. It is this aspect of Joyce that Farrell stressed in his *A Note on Literary Criticism* when he sought to defend Joyce's work against its simple-minded dismissal by Marxist critics and to place it affirmatively within the development of naturalism. Naturalism, Farrell noted, had begun as a fiction of "extensiveness"—that is, as fiction devoted to the depiction of a panoramic social milieu. In the work of Joyce, however, it had progressed to a fiction of "intensity," in which the novelist represented both a narrower and more minutely portrayed social world and "the individual consciousness."[8] Indeed, if Farrell had wished, he could have offered as additional evidence of this progress his own work of Joycean naturalism, the novel *Gas-House McGinty*.

Gas-House McGinty was written in mid-1931, in Paris, after Farrell had completed drafts of the first two volumes of *Studs Lonigan* but before he had begun *Judgment Day*. *Gas-House McGinty* is in part a 1930s slice-of-life novel. Set principally in the dispatcher's office of a large express company, it renders in mind-numbing repetitive detail the noise, horseplay, bickering, small-mindedness, and prejudices of men at work. McGinty is a leading figure in this setting, and our sense of him in this context is of his grossness and inflated self-importance. But McGinty also has an active though usually repressed aesthetic sensibility and a great need to be loved, qualities of his inner life that express themselves in his enthusiasm for the elegance and beauty of applied mathematics—what McGinty calls "figures worked out"[9]—and in the wild fantasizing of his dream life.

Farrell later noted that the impulse behind the long chapter in *Gas-House McGinty* in which he presented a dramatic account of one of McGinty's dreams was his desire to experiment with this form of stream-of-consciousness material before exploiting it at even greater length and complexity in the portion of *Judgment Day* he intended to devote to Studs's deathbed delirium.[10] The Joycean model for fiction of this kind—the Nighttown episode in *Ulysses*—is clear enough. What is perhaps less clear is that in both *Gas-House McGinty* and *Studs Lonigan* the desire to work closely with the paradoxes offered by a mundane and restrictive outer world and an emotionally vital inner life also had its origin in Anderson.

Farrell has often commented on his debt to Anderson, perhaps most explicitly in 1954, when he noted that Anderson "influenced and inspired me perhaps more profoundly than any other American writer." It was not only Anderson's sympathy in *Winesburg* "for the grotesque, the queer, the socially abnormal" that moved Farrell, but more significantly—as Farrell realized in 1927 when reading Anderson's autobiography *Tar*—his concern for "the inner life of a boy in an Ohio country town." Farrell intuitively felt, he recalled, that in Anderson's work he was discovering the potential source of his own art. "Perhaps my own feelings and emotions," he wrote, "and the feelings and emotions of those with whom I had grown up were important. . . . I thought of writing a novel about my own boyhood, about the neighborhood in which I had grown up. Here was one of the seeds that led to *Studs Lonigan*."[11]

Joyce and Anderson had, of course, a number of distinctive meanings for Farrell. Joyce confirmed Farrell's awareness of the potential for satire and burlesque in the pompous self-certainties of middle-class Irish life. And

Anderson helped shape Farrell's understanding of the deformities in character that occur when the human need for love is frustrated. But together the two represent as well a powerful single impulse toward the depiction of the felt inner life as this quality exists in conjunction with a social world that provided few "things of beauty" for the cultivation and satisfaction of man's "spiritual" nature. Joyce in particular, through his massive demonstration of the fictional possibilities present in the blending of a particularized scene and a specific consciousness, provided a powerful encouragement for Farrell's own experiments in stream-of-consciousness fiction.

It is now conventional wisdom, because of the seminal studies by Robert Humphrey and Melvin Friedman, that stream-of-consciousness fiction is not a technique but rather a subject matter which can be presented through various techniques, and that this subject matter appeared in fiction long before its vogue in experimental fiction of the 1920s. We also now know, because of the recent suggestive study by Roy Pascal called *The Dual Voice,* that one of the important early modes for depicting internal states of mind and feeling is the device that Pascal names "free indirect speech."* In brief, the device of indirect discourse is that of depicting in a third-person narrative voice the thoughts and feelings of a character, yet doing so, as Pascal notes, with "the vivacity of direct speech, evoking the personal tone, the gesture, and often the idiom of the . . . thinker reported."[12] The "dual voice" of the device derives from the circumstance that the narrator is present as reporter, structurer, and summarizer of the character's frame of mind but that he presents this material in the language and grammatical form habitually used by the character.

Obviously, indirect discourse is a device capable of much variation, and Pascal notes the range in its use from its occasional appearances in eighteenth-century fiction to its centrality and increasing sophistication in the nineteenth-century novel. In particular, he notes the importance of the technique in the fiction of Flaubert and Zola. Flaubert made it the means by which he depicted the inner life of his characters with a seeming authorial detachment, and Zola exploited it to lend a texture of working-class raciness and crudity to the narrative language of specific novels. In the twentieth century, in the work of Virginia Woolf, for example, the device intensifies both in the depth of psychic experience depicted and in the exclusiveness of its presence as a narrative technique.

---

*Pascal's "free indirect speech" is an attempt to translate into English the well-known French phrase for the device, *"style indirect libre."* The German term for the technique is *"erlebte rede."* I prefer and will use the alternative term in English for the device, "indirect discourse," since "free indirect speech" as a term does not contribute to an understanding of the technique while "indirect discourse," because it at least refers to the syntactic form of the device, is more descriptive.

Perhaps a few examples from *Studs Lonigan* would be helpful at this point, both to suggest the nature of indirect discourse in general and to illustrate some of the distinctive uses Farrell makes of the device. Here, for example, is Studs's father early in the trilogy ruminating on the future of his family: "When he'd bought this building, Wabash Avenue had been a nice, decent, respectable street for a self-respecting man to live with his family. But now, well, the niggers and kikes were getting in, and they were dirty, and you didn't know but what, even in broad daylight, some nigger moron might be attacking his girls."[13] It is clear in this passage that it is the narrator who is reporting Lonigan's thoughts, but the thoughts themselves appear in the verbal and syntactical form Lonigan himself might use if he were articulating them.

And here, in a somewhat more complex and rich example, is Studs, late in the trilogy, walking with his girl Catherine on a Sunday morning:

> Jesus, if only he could walk along with her on a sunny spring morning like this one and not have a worry in his head, no worry about his dough sunk in Imbray stock, about his health and weak heart, and the possibility of not living a long life, and not be wondering would he, by afternoon, feel pooped and shot. And then it was so gloomy at home that it could be cut with a knife, and it was bound to affect him, the old man's business going to pot, his dough lost and going fast, his expenses, unrented apartments, the mortgage. Just to have none of these things on his mind, and to be able to stroll along Easy Street with Catherine at his side, perfectly happy all day, and not having to feel that when he woke up tomorrow all these thoughts would pop back and keep going off like fire-crackers in his mind all day. And he had to decide about holding or selling his stock. Which?[14]

The language and grammar of this passage are, as before, principally those of the mind being depicted. But the passage also now contains a free association movement backward and forward in time, a movement shaped and controlled by Studs's emotion of the moment—his anxiety. There is as well more rhetorical emphasis through structural parallelism and colloquial imagery ("cut with a knife," "Easy Street," "going off like fire-crackers") than would be characteristic of Studs's speech. In short, the passage seeks not only to report the details of Studs's state of mind but also, by means of authorial shaping, the emotional reality of that state. It is not Studs's mind that is speaking directly to us but rather his mind filtered through the controlling rhetorical skill of the narrator.

One might ask, If indirect discourse of this kind is the principal narrative device of Studs Lonigan—as indeed it is—why hasn't Farrell's participation in modern stream-of-consciousness fiction been more widely noted and discussed, particularly when Farrell himself has often commented on his efforts at a "free association" depiction of Studs's internal state and indeed once even used the term "stream of consciousness" to describe his method in the novel?[15] One reason, of course, is that Farrell's indirect discourse presents few problems in immediate apprehension and is therefore less noticeable than the free association devices of Joyce or Faulkner or even Virginia Woolf. Another reason—and one more pertinent for our purposes—is that whereas Stephen Dedalus, Quentin Compson, or Mrs. Dalloway are capable of imaginatively questioning and exploring themselves and their worlds with much verbal virtuosity, Studs for the most part resists disturbing new ideas or experiences and reflects principally the values, goals, and language of his immediate culture.

Another question one might ask about Farrell's reliance on indirect discourse is its appropriateness as a narrative strategy when it is to be used as a means of disclosing the inner state of a figure as shallow in intellect and experience as Studs. One obvious response is that the dramatic depiction of Studs's shallowness is Farrell's subject. Farrell himself has remarked that his intent in the novel was not to depict Studs's world but rather the effect of this world upon Studs.[16] His intent, in short, was less to render objective experience than to render objectively (that is, dramatically and vividly) the impact of experience on a consciousness. Indirect discourse also had the advantage of permitting Farrell a necessary authorial detachment from the highly evocative material of *Studs Lonigan*, a need that is suggested by a comparison of Farrell's early short story "Studs" (written in the spring of 1929) and the trilogy.[17] In "Studs," an autobiographical first-person narrator attends the wake of an old neighborhood chum—Studs—who has died of dissoluteness at the age of twenty-six. The story is marred by the overt contempt of the narrator for Studs and his world, a contempt that transfers our interest from the tragedy of Studs's life to the emotions of the narrator. In *Studs Lonigan*, however, the technique of indirect discourse commits the narrator to the dramatic depiction of his characters' inner life and thus assures authorial detachment. True, Farrell's own sentiments are occasionally boldly evident, as in the indirect-discourse account of the beliefs of the autobiographical figure Danny O'Neill. But for the most part *Studs Lonigan* resembles *Madame Bovary* in that our awareness of authorial attitudes arises out of the ironic contrast between what is reported of the characters' sentiments and beliefs and what we assume—because of the evident limitations of these sentiments and beliefs—to be the author's values.

Nowhere in *Studs Lonigan* is Farrell's attempt to involve us in Studs's inner life through indirect discourse more central and powerful than in Studs's feelings about sex and love. It is in Studs's thoughts and emotions about this range of experience that we come to know fully the meaning and tragedy of his life. We come to know, that is, of Studs's need for emotional communion, of his lifelong repression of this need, and of his substitution of street-culture roles for his essential nature.

It is almost a given in Studs's world that all expression of deep personal feeling is either repressed or severely channeled, since to express one's emotions openly is both to expose potential weaknesses and to suggest a lack of aggressive manliness. Our first encounter with Studs, on the evening of his grammar-school graduation, reveals this habit of mind. He has become fond of one of his teachers, Battleaxe Bertha, and after the ceremony thinks of speaking to her: "He wanted to go up to her and say goodbye, and say that he felt her to be a pretty good sport at that, but he couldn't, because there was some goofy part of himself telling himself that he couldn't. He couldn't let himself get soft about anything, because, well, just because he wasn't the kind of bird that got soft. He never let anyone know how he felt" (*Young Lonigan*, p. 36).

Studs's terms of rejection—goofiness, softness—are those he will use throughout his life to identify what he believes are self-threatening needs and feelings. At fourteen, however, Studs is still not fully confirmed in his role of toughness; he still wavers during this phase of early adolescence between the desire to share his feelings and his fear of deserting a group-sanctioned role. The incident that helps shape the direction he will take occurs that summer. He and his former classmate Lucy Scanlan spend an afternoon in Washington Park, sitting in a tree. Studs responds to the peace and beauty of the park and to Lucy at his side and has what he himself realizes are a series of poetic insights into the wonder and pleasure of natural beauty and of love. He has what we might call an epiphany, and he wishes to share it with Lucy: "He wanted to let her know about all the dissolving, tingling feelings he was having, and how he felt like he might be the lagoon, and the feelings she made inside of him were like the dancing feelings and the little waves the sun and wind made on it; but those were things he didn't know how to tell her, and he was afraid to, because maybe he would spoil them if he did. He couldn't even say a damn thing about how it all made him want to do things and be big and brave for her" (*Young Lonigan*, p. 114).

Studs is not given another opportunity to overcome his fear, since his street world discovers and ridicules this adolescent romance and Studs resolves to be more careful: "He liked Lucy. He liked her. He loved her, but after what had happened he was even ashamed to admit it to himself. He was a hard-boiled guy, and he had learned his lesson. He'd keep himself roped in tight after this when it came to girls. He wasn't going to show his cards to nobody again" (*Young Lonigan*, p. 124). Studs's acceptance of the role of "hard-boiled guy" is also an acceptance of a street ethic toward sex, in which girls are to be used sexually if possible but otherwise avoided as marriage traps. Studs, as he matures, has little difficulty in conceiving of most girls he has known in this way, but Lucy evades him: "He tried to tell himself that he didn't really love Lucy, and that loving a girl the way he loved Lucy was goofy, because a big tough guy should only want to jump a girl, and think that all the rest and the love was crap."[18]

Studs dismisses Lucy but he cannot rid himself of thinking about her, and he does so, for the remainder of his life, at moments of free-association reverie. We come to know that Lucy and the afternoon in the park recur again and again in Studs's consciousness not merely because they represent nostalgia for an idyllic moment in the past but because they symbolize a life of feeling that though rejected and repressed is still intensely needed and longed for.

Studs seemingly has a chance to recover Lucy—and thus recover part of himself—when, in his early twenties, he and Lucy have a date. Again a kind of epiphany combining nature, love, and the moment occurs, and again Studs is incapable of expressing himself:

> It was like a picture that Studs wanted never to forget. The warm spring evening, the promise it offered to him, a mist in the lush air, Sheridan Road ahead, with traffic lights, people crossing the street, automobiles going by, the Victrola, Lucy singing, so pretty that he wanted to look at her, touch her, kiss her, love her, take her arm, say something to her of what it all meant, and of how all along he had really wanted nothing like he had wanted her. And he couldn't say anything, because it all stopped him. He guessed that when you felt like he did, you just had too many feelings to tell them to anybody. [*Young Manhood*, pp. 277–78]

Unable to express what he feels, Studs slips unthinkingly into the form of expression with girls that is now habitually his—that of himself as sexual aggressor, with the girl merely a figure to be aroused and then used. He attacks Lucy in the cab; she repulses him; and their relationship is now permanently ended. But there is still the need. In the long New Year's Eve section that closes *The Young Manhood of Studs Lonigan*, Studs gets drunk and longs for Lucy. The incident represents the history of the relationship between Studs's inner and outer life, a history in which that which Studs refuses to accept within himself is transformed in outward expression into the squalid and filthy.

> Studs staggered, and draped his arms tightly around a lamppost. He vomited.
> "I'm sick. I want Lucy. I love Lucy. I want Lucy. I want Lucy," he cried aloud, a large tear splattered on his cheek. The vomiting caused a violent contraction and pressure, as if a hammer were in his head.
> "I'm sick! Lucy, please love Studs!" he cried.
> A light flurry of snow commenced. Studs tenderly kissed the cold post, which lamp suddenly seemed to be Lucy.
> "I've always loved you, Lucy!"
> Tears rolled down his drunken, dirty face. [*Young Manhood*, p. 395]

Judgment Day brings the judgment of a life spent in the acceptance of a group ethic of emotional repression. Studs still occasionally has periods of "goofiness," usually in conjunction with moments of peace in nature. But for the most part he feels alone and deserted, particularly because of his need to share the worries brought on by his illness and the depression. He tentatively thinks of opening himself to his sister Frances or to his father, the members of his family he has been closest to, but does not because—in a key word now in Studs's life—he discovers that he is a stranger to them, as they are strangers to him. He makes the same discovery about Catherine, the girl he plans to marry: "After all, he was really a stranger to her. He was really a stranger to everyone else in the world also, and they really did not know what went on inside of him, and how he felt about many, many things. He wasn't sure that he would want to live so intimately with anyone as he would have to do with Catherine if he married her" (*Judgment Day*, p. 26).

Toward the end of *Judgment Day*, Studs's life draws to a close not merely in the sense of his imminent death but also in the sense of his bleak recognition of the emptiness and falseness of his life and thus of its lack of a future. He is at the beach with Catherine, who is now pregnant by him:

> He . . . asked himself how . . . did it come about that he was marrying Catherine when she seemed to him suddenly like a stranger he could never know. And that a child of his was, at this very minute, growing inside of her. He scratched his puzzled head. He felt alone, so completely alone that it seemed as if there were no one near him. All these people, too, strangers. He closed his eyes and held in his mind the naked image of Catherine, and he imagined her with him in that act that was supposed to make a guy and a girl so close, and still she seemed a stranger, and he still felt all alone. His thoughts and feelings were padlocked, completely padlocked in his mind, and when he talked, most of the time, instead of expressing them he was using words to prevent himself from letting them out, fooling people by putting into their minds a picture of himself that was not at all Studs Lonigan. [*Judgment Day*, pp. 334–35]

A locked mind and feeling, projecting out to the world in sex and speech false images of self that make all strangers—such is Studs's final realization of himself and of the road he has come, rendered in an almost poetic moment of indirect discourse. In the image of E. M. Forster that sums up the central theme of much of the major fiction of the 1920s, Studs has failed to connect.

I would like to return briefly at this point to the general problem I raised earlier about Farrell as a writer of the 1930s. *Studs Lonigan* is indeed a novel of the thirties in that we have grown accustomed to identifying in the work qualities that we associate with the decade. We find particularly in *Judgment Day* that the juxtaposition of Studs's personal collapse and the failure of his social world is a powerful expression of what we believe to be characteristic strains of both thirties life and the fictional portrayal of that life. But *Studs Lonigan* is also a novel of the 1920s in Farrell's exploration of the inarticulate felt life of a character by means of indirect discourse. Perhaps I can clarify the presence in the trilogy of the two decades—still thinking of them, of course, as symbolic critical constructs—by again referring to the work of Joyce and Anderson. One of the significant similarities among *Winesburg, Ohio, Ulysses,* and *Studs Lonigan* is the importance of a moment of epiphany in the three works. In each of the novels, a character has a semimystical insight into his relation to the nature of things, and in each he seeks to share this vision with someone else. In this sense, all three works are novels of the twenties. However, there is a major difference between *Studs Lonigan* on the one hand and *Winesburg, Ohio* and *Ulysses* on the other, both in the placing of the major moment of epiphany in the novel and in the success of the character in expressing and sharing his vision. In *Winesburg* and *Ulysses,* the moment occurs toward the end of the novel—George Willard and Helen White holding hands in the stands of the Fair Grounds in the story "Sophistication," Bloom and Stephen together in Bloom's garden on a warm June night after their long separate wanderings during the day—and in both instances there is connection. In *Studs Lonigan,* however, Studs and Lucy sit in the tree in Washington Park at the opening of the novel, and Studs is incapable of reaching out to express and share with Lucy his emotional exaltation and understanding. *Ulysses* and *Winesburg* thus suggest the possibility of struggling through to at least a temporary connection as understanding and need grow in experience; *Studs Lonigan* suggests that experience only increases the isolation of the spirit. *Studs* is therefore a work of the 1930s as well as of the 1920s, since the theme that life fails to provide answers to the seeking heart is one we associate most of all with a period when life provided few answers of any kind to human needs. *Studs Lonigan,* in short, incorporates both in theme and form attitudes toward character and experience that we have come to identify with both decades. Like most major works of art, it can usefully be placed in its moment of time, but its "moment in time" is a complex construct which is an index of the complexity of the work itself. Indeed, one way of describing the permanence of *Studs Lonigan*—though not of course the only way—is to view it as a work whose strength derives from the distinctive strengths of the two impulses that I have called the 1920s and the 1930s.

CHAPTER 5

SYLVIA JENKINS COOK

Steinbeck, the People, and the Party

In 1930 Michael Gold, the left wing's literary hit man, provided a vitriolic foretaste of the controversies of the coming decade in his review for the *New Republic* of the works of Thornton Wilder. Gold attacked Wilder for turning his back on the ravages of capitalism in America and for retreating into remote historical settings and decadent religiosity. The *New Republic* was immediately flooded with letters exhibiting such extremities of partisanship on both sides that Edmund Wilson later recognized in the exchange the advent of "the literary class war." In this intellectual milieu—New York in the early 1930s—few young writers could remain unaware of the ardent political debates of the day, the urgent prescriptions for a revolutionary proletarian literature or the immediacy of the social crisis. However, it was at exactly this point in his career that John Steinbeck was farthest removed, geographically, intellectually, and politically from the left-wing ferment in New York. When the literary class war was declared there in 1932, Steinbeck was in California working on *To a God Unknown,* a novel examining the mystical, pagan instincts that inform the relationships of people to the land they tend. Of his two previously published books, one dealt with the adventures of a seventeenth-century Welsh pirate and the other with the propagation of a curse in a utopian western valley. His favorite reading was neither the *New Republic* nor the *New Masses* but Xenophon, Herodotus, Plutarch, and Sir Thomas Malory, and at this time he was beginning to find the greatest stimulus to his intellectual life not in the Marxist dialectic but in the tide pools of the Pacific, where he became something of an expert in marine biology. To borrow some of the terminology with which Michael Gold scourged Wilder, it all seems rather "erudite and esoteric." Yet in 1941, when Michael Gold summarized the literary 1930s at the fourth and final Congress of American Writers, he chose Wilder and Steinbeck to measure the two poles of achievement in that decade, arguing that "what had happened . . . between Wilder and Steinbeck was a revolution of taste, morals, aspirations and social consciousness. American literature and the audience that read it had reached a certain maturity. A people's culture and hundreds of fine novels, plays and poems impregnated with proletarian spirit had battered down the barricades set up by the bourgeois monopolists of literature."[1]

One might well assume that nothing less than a revolution could have caused the author of *Cup of Gold* and *The Pastures of Heaven* to create a novel of such remarkable timeliness and ideological appropriateness for the 1930s as *The Grapes of Wrath*; yet there is no evidence in Steinbeck's fiction, his letters, or the outward course of his life that he underwent any dramatic conversion away from the remote, heroic, and mystical concerns of his early work to the more topical, naturalistic, and political orientation of *The Grapes of Wrath*. What there is ample evidence for is a gradual and logical evolution of the social metaphors in which Steinbeck embodied his biological interests, which caused him to shift his focus from the marine life of the tide pools to the Communist party and thence to the Joad family. This shift was aided not by literary ideologues in New York but by his empirical observations in California, where he spent almost the entire decade. In this environment Steinbeck had the advantage of detachment from the endless wrangling over revolutionary art and posturing over proletarian causes; however, he was also isolated from the significant reaction that was forming, in a writer, for example, like James Agee, against artistic portrayals of squalor and poverty that seemed to pander to a fashionable taste for exposés of suffering. He was more innocent of both ideology and its exploitation than a writer in Agee's world could ever be. Thus the tumultuous reception of *The Grapes of Wrath* bewildered Steinbeck; he had neither anticipated becoming, as he did, an immediate public institution, nor being characterized, as he was, as a liar, a Communist, and a Jew. He had set out to search for fictional vehicles for rather arcane biological theories and had arrived, in the context of a decade of social upheaval, at the heart of the depression's last literary class war.

The artistic stimulus that Steinbeck found in his biological studies is first articulated in a letter to his friend Carlton Sheffield, dated 21 June 1933. The fact that Steinbeck bothered to date a letter with precision indicates that it had an unusual significance for him, and indeed the text is often incoherently excited. Three years of random scientific observations had suddenly taken a clear philosophical direction so that he now felt the urge to seek what he called "the symbolism of fiction"[2] to act as a vehicle for them. These observations and experiments are derived largely from his study of the coral insect, but in the context of the United States in the depression they all have obvious human and political dimensions. There are three main issues of importance, the first of which he called the group or phalanx idea. This concerns the properties of a group organism and their difference from the properties of the individual units that compose the group. The ideological extension of this interest in the society of the 1930s is the clash of totalitarianism and individualism, communal and selfish behavior. The second concern is with the advantages and disadvantages of nonteleological thinking; in this area Steinbeck's friend and mentor, Ed Ricketts, urged on him the value of constantly seeking to understand and accept what is, rather than a "preoccupation with 'changes and cures' "[3]— that is, the role of the detached scientific questioner rather than the advocate of a cause. This issue manifests itself not only in the technique of Steinbeck's fiction, where he experiments with the idea of having what he calls "no author's moral point of view," of being "merely a recording consciousness,"[4] but also in his version of naturalism, wherein the best-laid schemes of mice and men are inevitably destined to defeat. Steinbeck was not optimistic about dreams of a more perfect future, yet in the 1930s, the alternative pattern of American pragmatism, of limited and nonidealistic thinking, seemed increasingly inadequate to deal with the magnitude of the social crisis. The last of Steinbeck's biological themes is a sense of the unity and interdependency of all life forms and their environment. It appears early in Steinbeck's fiction as an instinctive veneration of the natural world by man; however, when this kind of pantheism is placed in the contemporary context of the decay of agrarian life, the mechanization, industrialization, and despoilage of land, it clearly may provoke political as well as religious responses. None of these biological concerns ever became systematized for Steinbeck into rigid theories; they are constantly reex-amined in his fiction in changing circumstances. However, the fact that these circumstances include Communist efforts to organize a strike among fruit-pickers and the exploitation of migrants who are forced off their land lures the reader of Steinbeck to measure him against the orthodoxies of his time, even if his progress there was oblique and unorthodox.

Steinbeck's interest in the phenomenon of group behavior was certainly not new to American fiction, as Mark Twain's description of the mob in *The Adventures of Huckleberry Finn* will testify: "The pitifulest thing out is a mob . . . they don't fight with courage that's born in them, but with courage that's borrowed from their mass." In the 1930s a more positive characterization of group behavior emerged in the many proletarian novels that dealt with the solidarity of the union, where workers could acquire dignity, strength, and power, all inaccessible to the exploited and impotent individual. What distinguishes Steinbeck's interest in group man from either of these examples is his reluctance to attach any moral judgment to the group phenomenon. In his original letter describing his fascination with the possible manifestations of the group, he writes that "Russia is giving us a nice example of human units who are trying with a curious nostalgia to get away from their individuality and re-establish the group unit the race remembers and wishes. I am not drawing conclusions." By the following year he had begun work on what he called "the Communist idea" which was to become *In Dubious Battle*. That Steinbeck's stated intentions for this novel are not wholly congruent with the effect it achieves is a measure of the gap in Steinbeck between the behavioral theories of the amateur biologist and the broader perspective of the artist, a gap that was to increase throughout the 1930s. He denied that the novel was anything other than a harsh scientific investigation of "man's eternal warfare with himself," saying, "I'm not interested in strike as means of raising men's wages, and I'm not interested in ranting about justice and oppression. . . . I wanted to be merely a recording consciousness, judging nothing, simply putting down the thing." Steinbeck felt that he had found in this study of the manipulations of a group of migrant workers by Communist party organizers an ideal crucible for testing the development of his group-man notions; but as soon as the material took form in a specific historical setting, Steinbeck's more complicated sympathies and prejudices altered the novel's supposed impartiality: it is not propaganda, but it clearly illustrates the problems of nonpartisanship.[5]

Group man in *In Dubious Battle* is illustrated by a crowd of striking apple-pickers in the Torgas Valley in California. Individually, they are as far as is imaginable from the conventional image of the deserving poor: they are lazy, careless, cruel, cowardly, envious, and selfish. They refuse to cooperate voluntarily to secure even minimal sanitary arrangements for their camp. The men exploit the women sexually, and the women provoke the men to blood lust. It could never be said of these strikers, as it was of the Okies in *The Grapes of Wrath*, that they bear only the physical but not the spiritual stigmas of poverty and injustice.[6] Yet Steinbeck refuses to indulge in such rationalizations here for the repulsive qualities of his protagonists. When these same men are unified into a group animal by the skill of Mac, the Communist organizer, the new creature is powerful, reckless of danger, savagely ferocious. It is neither more nor less decent than the individuals who compose it, but it is vitally different in many of its attributes. There is no alternative view in the novel of American working men en masse. The two characters who conduct the intellectual debate of the novel over Communist tactics are in complete agreement with this vision of group man though they differ in their responses to it. Mac, the doctrinaire field organizer, sees the group animal as something to be fed and goaded in the service of Communist political ideals; his images for the group are inevitably contemptuous animal analogies. Doc Burton, the "dreamer, mystic, metaphysician" who gives free medical attention to the strikers, but is himself "too God damn far left to be a Communist,"[7] sees group man as something to be studied and analyzed in the service of knowledge; he rejects Mac's animal images but substitutes for them images of germs and cells that are certainly no less dehumanizing. The only denial in the novel of the totalitarian implications of this vision of human nature comes from the hypocritical president of the Fruit Growers' Association, who has most to gain by it. Yet the brutal detachment Steinbeck professed and aimed at in *In Dubious Battle* is not absolute; while the group animal and its analysts Mac and Doc Burton clearly engaged his intellectual interests, it was not apparently a sufficient vehicle for his less impersonal artistic sensibility. Thus the novel contains two characters, a father and son, who remain completely outside the theoretical scheme of the novel but who clearly have Steinbeck's sympathy. These are the Andersons, who operate a small, independent farm and a low-profit lunch wagon; they are genial, self-reliant, and efficient men who have their livelihoods destroyed because they side with the aims of the strikers. Since they are so much closer than the fruit-pickers to a benevolent image of the people, they suggest a possible evolution for Steinbeck away from the mechanical and faceless mob—the product of his emotional detachment—to the more heroic and dignified people with roots in history, culture, and region who will form the group animal in *The Grapes of Wrath*.

This is not a simple transition from scientific detachment to emotional involvement on Steinbeck's part—it is also a recognition that the context in which the group phenomenon is studied alters its significance. Thus one Marxist critic of *In Dubious Battle* called it the most lifelike and satisfying proletarian novel of the 1930s.[8] The label is false if used in the conventional sense of the term since the novel does not seek to promote the cause of revolution, but it indicates the partisan nature of Steinbeck's chosen set-ting—any fiction that dealt with labor activities in the depression and stopped short of opposing it might incur such a label.

Between the publication of *In Dubious Battle* in 1936 and *The Grapes of Wrath* in 1939, Steinbeck wrote a short story, "The Leader of the People," that may serve to emphasize further how the "fictional symbols" in which he embodies the group theory can alter its ideological effect. The story is about an old man who, at one time in his life, had found himself a special kind of cell in a group organism, much as the Communist Mac had in *In Dubious Battle*. He had been the leader of a group of westward-trekking pioneers who had survived a grueling journey across the continent. When they finally reached the Pacific the leader's function had disappeared and to his family he has now become a boring and garrulous figure, endlessly recalling his adventures. The old man is eventually trapped into admitting the authentic nature of the experience: it was a group phenomenon rather than a heroic act. "It wasn't Indians that were important, nor adventures, nor even getting out here. It was a whole bunch of people made into one big crawling beast. And I was the head. It was westering and

westering. . . . I was the leader, but if I hadn't been there, someone else
would have been the head. The thing had to have a head."[9] However, his
grandson Jody, like the reader of *The Grapes of Wrath*, cannot shake off
the heroic associations of westering. In that novel they are revived forcefully, together with all the resolution and hope of the earlier pioneers.

Steinbeck presents the movement of the Okies to California as mysterious and biologically determined, but the context of the people and the
evocative associations of their journey recall other, more human standards
by which to judge it. The historical context of pioneering is only one of the
differences in setting between the filthy, cowardly, and brutish workers of
In Dubious Battle and the noble and enduring Okies of *The Grapes of
Wrath*—two groups of people who might otherwise seem so contradictory
in their conception as to suggest that Steinbeck radically altered his whole
view of human nature between the two books. The Okies, unlike the
striking fruit-pickers, are presented as victims of a natural disaster as well
as an economic crisis: since the earth has failed them, they must begin
anew. Thus there is an impelling logical reason for their migration that
makes it both sensible and sympathetic. The Okies are also placed in a
cultural tradition that gives dignity and stature to their predicament; they
are the descendants of the people who helped clear and settle the continent, who fought in the Revolution and the Civil War. They carry suggestions of the chosen people as they seek for the Promised Land in California.
None of these dignifying factors negates the essential biological nature of
the mass movement of the group in *The Grapes of Wrath*, but they add an
epic and legendary quality to the adventure that suggests that Steinbeck's
evolving concern for the migrants has led him to a new and less dispassionate metaphor for his scientific interests.

The group unit itself is given a more varied portrayal in *The Grapes of
Wrath*; it is no longer limited to the single feral body of strikers but may be
seen in the Joad family moving into unified action to slaughter pigs; it may
be a camp of migrants that comes into existence for one night only; it may
be a field of cotton-pickers or a chorus of fanatical Jehovites; it may be the
massive migratory group, crawling like insects along the highways; or it
may be the ultimate macrocosmic group, Manself. These groups, true to
their original biological conception, have properties different from those of
their individual members: "The bank is something else than men. It
happens that every man in a bank hates what the bank does, and yet the
bank does it. The bank is something more than men, I tell you. It's the
monster."[10] However, with the illustration of such a variety of group
formations, Steinbeck also reveals group properties that are clearly differ-
entiated from each other and on which he now appears to make moral and
political judgments. The howling, whining, and thumping of the religious
enthusiasts does not make an admirable contribution to the life of the

people, while the instinctive communal behavior in the roadside camps does; there, "in the evening a strange thing happened: the twenty families became one family, the children were the children of all. The loss of home became one loss, and the golden time in the West was one dream" (p. 264)—this is clearly beneficial to the mutual welfare as laws are established and property shared. The groups continue as in *In Dubious Battle* to respond to emotional goading, but unlike the arbitrary scenes of bloodletting created by the callous and opportunist Communists to stimulate the strikers' lust, in *The Grapes of Wrath* the provocation is completely integral to the situation, and the reader responds to it even before the Okies themselves:

> The people come with nets to fish for potatoes in the river, and the guards hold them back; they come in rattling cars to get the dumped oranges, but the kerosene is sprayed. And they stand still and watch the potatoes float by, listen to the screaming pigs being killed in a ditch and covered with quicklime, watch the mountains of oranges slop down to a putrefying ooze; and in the eyes of the hungry there is a growing wrath. In the souls of the people the grapes of wrath are filling and growing heavy, growing heavy for the vintage. [p. 477]

Anger changes in this novel from a carefully fostered biological urge to a moral obligation; and the mob man is now labeled Manself, willing to "suffer and die for a concept, for this one quality is the foundation of Manself, and this one quality is man, distinctive in the universe" (p. 205).

Had Steinbeck rested *The Grapes of Wrath* on this ideological refinement of group man, it might well have been a more satisfactory proletarian novel; instead he chose to extend the context of the group not just beyond the biological to the political and moral level, but beyond that to the mystical and transcendental: the final apotheosis of group man in *The Grapes of Wrath* is not to socialist unity but to the Oversoul. In *In Dubious Battle*, the subversive Doc Burton had posed the question, "Can't a group of men be God?" (p. 261) only to be rebuffed by the practical Communists; in *The Grapes of Wrath*, when Casy says, "Maybe all men got one big soul ever'body's a part of" (p. 33), there is no spokesman for an opposing point of view. Set in a highly topical situation, *The Grapes of Wrath* shows a keen awareness of man as a political animal, existing somewhere between the tidepool and the stars, but, true to his personal and empirical attitude, Steinbeck refuses to be limited exclusively to that consciousness.

Steinbeck's interest in nonteleology as a way of approaching life and literature was first stimulated by his association with Ed Ricketts at the Pacific Biological Laboratories, and like the group-man theory, it rapidly moves in the fiction far beyond its scientific sources. Ricketts felt that people in a complex universe tended to search for its purpose before they had any comprehension of what it was—they asked the question, Why? before they tried to answer the question, How? Ricketts advocated instead what he called "is" thinking, which sought understanding without judgment and was therefore "capable of great tenderness, of an all-embracingness" that is rare otherwise.[11] Steinbeck's fascination with this theory is indicated by the frequency with which he creates fictional characters who voice Ricketts's opinions: Doc Burton in *In Dubious Battle*; Casy and, to some extent, Ma Joad in *The Grapes of Wrath*; and Doc in *Cannery Row*. But, especially in the novels written in the 1930s, Steinbeck consistently questions the social consequences and dangers of this rather passive view.

Doc Burton is one of the more appealing characters in *In Dubious Battle*; in a world of cruel and self-assured fanatics, he is gentle and tentative in his opinions; in a world of violence and destruction he aids and cures. He serves humanity without judging it; in a partisan setting, he has avoided taking sides. In his many debates with Mac, the Communist, he emphasizes his quest for pure knowledge, uncontaminated either by moral or historical labels: "I don't want to put on the blinders of 'good' and 'bad', and limit my vision. . . . I want to be able to look at the whole thing" (p. 169). Burton denies beginnings and ends, seeing only constant flux that prevents any practical, goal-oriented action. He is an enigma to Mac, who responds to his arguments with a mixture of revulsion and admiration, "In one way it seems cold-blooded, standing aside and looking down on men like that, and never getting yourself mixed up with them; but another way, Doc, it seems fine as the devil, and clean" (p. 201). Doc's mysterious disappearance from the novel indicates that in this particular dubious battle, when the ranks are drawn, there is simply no place for the man who tries to remain unsullied by partial commitment. To be "fine as the devil, and clean" is also to be intolerably isolated from human endeavor, as his departing remarks in the novel assert: "I'm awfully alone. I'm working all alone, towards nothing" (p. 262).

The Grapes of Wrath traces in more detail the wholesale transformation of two of its heroes, Casy and Tom, and the imminent conversion of the third, Ma Joad, away from "is" thinking to the search for both causes and ends. At the beginning of the novel, the former preacher, Jim Casy, is very much in the nonteleological mold of Doc Burton; he has given up his ministry to study his fellow mortals, of whom he says, nonjudgmentally, "There ain't no sin and there ain't no virtue. There's just stuff people do. . . . And some of the things folks do is nice, and some ain't nice, but that's as far as any man got a right to say" (p. 32). Casy, too, has a sense of living in a directionless flux, but unlike Doc Burton he gradually comes through his experiences to see a meaning and purpose in it—on the road west he observes of the migrants, "They's gonna come somepin outa all these folks goin' wes'—outa all their farms lef' lonely. They's gonna come a thing that's gonna change the whole country" (p. 237). Despite his initial rejection of sin, Casy is soon brought to the assertion that "they's somepin worse'n the devil got hold a the country, an' it ain't gonna let go till it's chopped loose" (p. 175). By the time of his death, Casy appears to have identified what is worse than the devil as California's rampant capitalism, and he gives his life to the ideal of defeating it.

Tom Joad is at first stolidly unimpressed by Casy's vaguely apocalyptic vision of the future; to Casy's admission that he mentally climbs barriers that have not yet been built, Tom replies, "I'm still layin' my dogs down one at a time" (p. 237). However, he is gradually led to realize, much as Steinbeck himself appeared to be doing, the dangers of such aimlessness. When his conversion to social activism comes, it is the result of personal experience rather than the preacher's rhetoric. This is a crucial difference between the radicalism of *In Dubious Battle* and that of *The Grapes of Wrath*: in the earlier novel, a rigid ideology is furthered by the emotional manipulation of the group; in the latter, the people themselves are educated empirically into their new activism. Tom's first advice to Ma Joad when she worries about the future is to "jus' take ever' day" (p. 124), an attitude that is qualified for the reader by the knowledge that it is the product of Tom's prison experiences in a powerless and dependent role. When Ma attempts to live by this ideal, it becomes a struggle to preserve the family unit against its assimilation into any wider group. As the futility of that struggle gradually becomes apparent, Ma, too, finally comes to recognize the need for a new vision of the future. She never relinquishes altogether her concern for the immediate future to the extent that Tom and Casy do, but she knows by the end that if people are ever to exist in more peace and security, it will be because of those who dedicated themselves to a final purpose instead of just "taking every day." Steinbeck's original attraction to the nonteleological view of the scientist is reversed when the fictional symbols in which he embodies it are the peculiar disasters of the depression for people who have formerly dedicated themselves to "is" thinking.

The last of Steinbeck's biological interests that found fictional symbols in his work during the 1930s is his sense of the mystery of ecology and especially of the mutual and sacred dependence of people and land. Like other American writers in the thirties, notably Faulkner and Caldwell, Steinbeck was interested in the special nature of the agricultural bond, since agribusiness and natural disasters seemed about to end it forever. It is explored early in his fiction in the pagan religious context of *To a God Unknown* in 1933; only later in the decade does the topic come to have a political dimension. *To a God Unknown* deals with the mystical union between the farmer, Joseph Wayne, and the homestead he acquires in

California. Joseph's cult begins in a simple lust for the land, symbolized in a ritualized mating with it. He glories in its fertility, identifies a tree as the spirit of his dead father, makes sacrificial offerings to the land, and ultimately comes to identify with it so completely that he kills himself in a dry season in the certainty that his blood will water and renew the earth. Although this novel was seen by most critics as a kind of anthropological curiosity, the same identification with the land, both physically and spiritually, is apparent in the more contemporary and realistic Okies in *The Grapes of Wrath*, who affirm that the "place where folks live is them folks" (p. 71).

In *The Grapes of Wrath*, Steinbeck depicts what happens to the land as well as the people when the agrarian bond is broken. The tractors that come on to the land, driven by machinelike men who eat machine-made food, rape the land that had formerly been loved and cause its symbolic death. Thus the banks that drive the people off the land are shown to be committing not only a crime against humanity but also a sacrilege against the religion of agriculture. This attitude is identified by critic Chester Eisinger with Jeffersonian agrarianism, and he argues that, appealing as this philosophy may be, it is certainly an outmoded way of dealing with the problems of the Okies in the 1930s.[12] However, while Steinbeck clearly displays some nostalgia for such notions, he also identifies them as part of the past that is irretrievable; in addition to the banks that tractor the people off the land, there are the dust storms that would ruin their livelihood anyway; their legal or moral right to stay is undermined by nature itself turning against them. The pantheism of the novel is rooted in hunger for fertile, productive land; it is useless to continue to worship land that is already dead, as Muley Graves and Granpa Joad do. Steinbeck demands adaptability as well as resilience in his species of farmers so that even at the nadir of the Joads' suffering in California, when Pa wishes only to return to Oklahoma, Ma insists that California, which has treated them so badly, is nevertheless "better land."

The religious element in Steinbeck's agrarianism that made reviewers of *To a God Unknown* wish that he could find more stable and relevant principles on which to build future novels proves capable in *The Grapes of Wrath* of supporting a highly political and topical thesis: "when property accumulates in too few hands it is taken away. . . . when a majority of the people are hungry and cold they will take by force what they need. . . . repression works only to strengthen and knit the repressed" (p. 324). Land hunger in Steinbeck is from his earliest works both a physical instinct and a religious need; in *The Grapes of Wrath*, when the days of homesteading are past, it becomes also a political principle.

The fact that Steinbeck's biological interests took the direction they did in his fiction in the 1930s is, of course, a direct consequence of the times in which he lived. Although Steinbeck was largely estranged from the cliques of radical literary activists, he was throughout the depression coming into more and more intimate contact with the human suffering it spawned. In 1934 he had written sardonically to a friend in New York, "I am pegged as a pessimistic writer because I do not see the millennium coming." By 1936, after he had done a series of reports for the *Nation* on migrant labor in California, he was writing to the same friend, "There are riots in Salinas and killings in the streets of that dear little town where I was born. I shouldn't wonder if the thing had begun. I don't mean any general revolt but an active beginning aimed toward it, the smouldering." This is a considerable progress in millennialist rhetoric in the space of two years, and what was largely responsible for Steinbeck's rather late awakening was the peculiar experience of California. Since much of the suffering and exploitation there arose as a consequence of the Dust Bowl migration, the exposure and consciousness of it came much later in the decade than the circumstances that gave rise to the main flowering of proletarian literature. By 1938 Steinbeck's letters show a repeated anguished emphasis on the explosive situation in California, the starvation and disease among migrant families, and the sabotaging of all efforts to help them by what he calls the "fascist" utilities and banks. Steinbeck was torn between his desire to write his fury into a work of fiction and a more pressing need to take direct action, "to help knock these murderers on the heads." One of his letters ends, "funny how mean and little books become in the face of such tragedies"; a few days later, he arranged for the proceeds of his articles to buy serum and codliver oil for the migrant children and then concluded in despair, "Of course no individual effort will help." A week or two later, he apparently decided that reporting might be the best medium: "I want to put a tag of shame on the greedy bastards who are responsible for this but I can best do it through newspapers." *The Grapes of Wrath* is thus very firmly grounded in the immediate turmoil of the California scene although it is necessary to add that it was not an immediate product. The first book Steinbeck wrote out of his anger was a bitter satire called *L'Affaire Lettuceberg*; he later rejected it because it was "mean" and "nasty" and, by dealing in half-truths, more likely to cause hatred than understanding. When he began work on *The Grapes of Wrath*, the need to take immediate action had been satisfied by his journalism and personal generosity; the need to vent his rage had been poured into the abandoned propagandistic novel that he knew was bad. Thus into *The Grapes of Wrath* he could distill the more measured results of a whole decade of intellectual and literary apprenticeship with a topic that was almost exclusively apt to his worldly experience. [13]

There is one final factor in Steinbeck's intellectual background that plays an important role in his political novels and indeed, according to his friend

Toni Ricketts, was the "real clue to his writing": this was what she characterized as "his hatred of the middle class."[14] This appears to be not so much a class-conscious attitude in a political sense as a preference in cultural and moral values for lower-class people who lived with excess and abjured moderation. The excess might take the form of sexuality, drunkenness, gross appetite, or religious enthusiasm; Steinbeck was not so much interested in the specific manifestation of a zest for life as in abhorring the prudence, prurience, rigidity, and conformity that robbed people of the capacity for heroic conduct or the pursuit of dreams. His earlier, largely unpolitical fiction—*Cup of Gold, The Pastures of Heaven,* and *Tortilla Flat*—had all examined the stultifying effects of respectability, mediocrity, and stability on the human tendency to wildness and eccentricity. Although the Joads in *The Grapes of Wrath* are never so extravagant as the people in these early novels in their appetite and indulgences, they are certainly immoderate and nonconformist. Every member of the family is introduced by a tale of excess, from Tom's murder to Granma's religious ecstasies to Al's tomcatting, Uncle John's binges, and Ma's attack on a peddler with a live chicken. The Joads, however, are also generous, compassionate, and able to restrain their impulses when it is necessary for the common good. They are hardworking, not for acquisition but for survival and the pleasure of performing well. Only in *The Grapes of Wrath* do these qualities become politically class-conscious, since they are deliberately opposed to the "shit-heels"—the worried, insecure businessmen with their languid, discontented wives, rushing across the country to California to indulge in gossip and vicarious living because they no longer have any vitality in themselves. Steinbeck's comments on the decadence of these people, of their pursuit of the artificial and perversion of the natural, come very close to the standard conventions of proletarian fiction, but for him they are very far from being leftist clichés, or a sentimental indulgence in primitivism. They are rather the logical development, in the political atmosphere of the depression, of an early and instinctive prejudice.

When *The Grapes of Wrath* was published, it shocked, offended, and made enemies for Steinbeck, but it also brought him instant fame, offers from Hollywood, membership in the Press Club, and a Pulitzer prize; he was now an acknowledged member of the literary set. He was completely unprepared for such a response. While the novel was in the publication process, he wrote repeatedly warning Viking against a large first edition. His later letters express surprise but little elation at the reception of it; he seems to have been exhausted, both physically and mentally, skeptical of any political action, and wholly disillusioned with the genre in which he had been working: "I've worked the novel . . . as far as I can take it." He loathed the newfound intrusions on his privacy and feared for his future integrity the consequences of "this damnable popularity."[15] He determined to change directions, to abandon fiction altogether for scientific studies, to write a good book that few people would want to read. He foresaw himself becoming what he had so detested—respectable, consistent, satisfactorily assimilated. As with his late and largely empirical conversion to radical politics, Steinbeck needed to feel the actual destructive force of success on himself before he doubted the validity of his particular approach to art. It was a position to which one other notable radical writer had come by the end of the 1930s, but for James Agee the revulsion from the public's appetite for aesthetic images of human suffering preceded the writing of his great depression effusion, *Let Us Now Praise Famous Men*. With a topic and a political philosophy remarkably close to Steinbeck's, Agee's work helps to dramatize, by its almost nihilistic originality as well as by its ideological torment, both the advantages and disadvantages of the enduring value of *The Grapes of Wrath*, of Steinbeck's estrangement in California during the 1930s.

Let Us Now Praise Famous Men grew, like *The Grapes of Wrath*, from a specific experience of human suffering and from Agee's background in the depression, which was markedly different from Steinbeck's—at the center of the New York literary and radical world. From that he had acquired a distaste for the chic, left-wing affectation he observed, as well as for the fashionable new relevance of the artist. It was a distaste that led him to reject all the successful literary conventions of the 1930s for a work that he determined would be as unpalatable to the aesthetes of suffering as he could possibly contrive. He succeeded in creating a book that had in its own day no popular appeal and limited critical enthusiasm but has risen steadily in critical estimation ever since, so that it is not unusual now to see it hailed as the greatest literary achievement of the depression.[16] By contrast, the reputation of *The Grapes of Wrath* in America had declined so much that in 1962, when Steinbeck was awarded the Nobel Prize, the *New Republic* rather ungraciously editorialized that it could not in any sense acknowledge that he was a great artist, or even nationally esteemed.[17] Steinbeck's novel had succeeded in the 1930s not merely because of its topicality but also because of the skill with which he had documented the voices and lives of the migrants, the carefully fostered dialectical debate between the chapters and interchapters, the compassion with which the novel demanded a moral response from its readers. In contriving a technique, as well as an ideology, Steinbeck had come to discover the use of conventions such as documentary journalism, folk idiom, multiple protagonists, and ideological irony and symbolism that had become common in the thirties in the fiction of other left-wing writers, but in the eyes of a writer like James Agee, hackneyed and discredited. Steinbeck's isolation from Agee's world permitted his education in the field rather than the radical drawing-room; it enabled him to explore his biological interests free of ideological harassment and to evolve new vehicles for them in accordance with his emotional sympathies. Nevertheless, this freedom cost Steinbeck something in the loss of the kind of intellectual stimulus and debate that helped direct Agee towards the creation of a new literature of the left, rather than, as *The Grapes of Wrath* finally seems to be, the climax and culmination of the old. Perhaps, in this sense, Michael Gold's enthusiasm is its most fitting epitaph.

CHAPTER 6

LOUIS D. RUBIN, JR.

Trouble on the Land:

SOUTHERN LITERATURE AND THE GREAT DEPRESSION

It is a painful thing sometimes to read history books that are written for children, and to realize the view of the past that is being given them. Recently I happened upon volume 14 of the *American Heritage New Illustrated History of the United States*. It was subtitled *The Roosevelt Era*. The author of volume 14 provided his young readers with a year-by-year chronicle for the 1930s. I quote from the section for the year 1935:

> During the year, Technicolor came to the movie screen, and the WPA Federal Arts Project came to the aid of hungry artists, many of whom had a built-in predilection for the "Ash Can School" of painting—stark slum scenes being a favorite subject. Plays expressed the same preoccupation with social messages in this period. . . . In the world of fiction, William Faulkner was gaining world-wide praise for his naturalistic novels portraying for the most part sordid slices of low-class life in the South. Within this realm, Erskine Caldwell had recently contributed *Tobacco Road*. The third book of James Farrell's *Studs Lonigan* trilogy appeared in 1935, looking at squalor further north, in Chicago.

It saddens me to think that this is the picture that today's young readers will receive of William Faulkner, and of southern literature for the period. For the 1930s were the high point, the culmination, of the South's literary history, and relatively few of the books written by southern authors during the period had much to do with "sordid slices of low-class life."

From roughly the coming of the Great Depression up to the attack on Pearl Harbor, the southern literary renascence was at perihelion. A roll call is in order. Faulkner published *The Sound and the Fury, As I Lay Dying, Light in August, Absalom, Absalom!*, and *The Hamlet*. Thomas Wolfe published *Look Homeward, Angel, Of Time and the River*, and two post-humously edited novels. Robert Penn Warren published his first book of poems and his first novel. *Gone with the Wind* came, was read and then seen on film, and has endured. Caldwell published *Tobacco Road, God's Little Acre,* and other novels; until censorship standards were relaxed in the 1950s they were unsurpassed as popular pornography. Carson McCullers published *The Heart Is a Lonely Hunter.* Katherine Anne Porter published almost all of her best work. Allen Tate wrote most of his best poems and his novel, *The Fathers.* Eudora Welty's first book, *A Curtain of Green,* was published. James Agee published his first two books. Richard Wright wrote the stories in *Uncle Tom's Children.* In drama, Lillian Hellman did most of her best work. And so on.

From the standpoint of what is now almost a half-century's perspective, it does seem undeniable that a disproportionate share of the more impressive literature by Americans during the depression years was written by southern authors. Yet not only is there only a moderate amount of "sordid slices of low-class life" included in that literature, but the truth is that most of it does not importantly concern itself with what many of our historians and critics still seem to believe was the major and almost the sole literary theme of the period: social consciousness, as manifested in exposés of capitalistic society, greed, sympathetic delineation of the downtrodden, depictions of class struggle, and so on. There are, of course, exceptions, but mostly that sort of thing was not what seems to have kindled the literary imagination in the South of the 1930s.

Now I trust that nobody needs to be reminded that if this is so, it is certainly not because the southern states were in any way exempt from the consequences of the debacle of 1929 that in the Northeast sent most of the intellectuals off to the Finland Station. "It is my conviction," President Roosevelt declared in 1938, "that the South presents right now . . . the Nation's No. 1 economic problem." The depression brought widespread joblessness and deprivation. The region had for many decades lagged behind the remainder of the country in all the relevant economic indices as it was, and the depression hit with devastating effect. Banks failed, farm prices hit rock bottom, mortgages were foreclosed, tenants evicted, businesses folded, factories and mines shut down. Few if any of the social themes that the depression made available to the American writer were barred to southerners. There were strikes, agitation, violence. Communists showed up to exhort the strikers, and the police treated them with the expected enthusiasm. There were fascist movements here and there. Huey Long proposed to Share the Wealth. When President Roosevelt and the New Deal took hold to do something about the situation, the South voted for him overwhelmingly and continued to do so for as long as he lived. The Great Depression and the ensuing recovery were very much a part of the southern way of life.

Writing about the impact of the crash upon American writers, Malcolm Cowley has declared that "thousands were convinced and hundreds of thousands were half-persuaded that no simple operation would save us; there had to be the complete renovation of society that Karl Marx had prophesied in 1848. Unemployment would be ended, war and fascism would vanish from the earth, but only after the revolution. Russia had pointed out the path that the rest of the world must follow into the future." Clearly Cowley was not thinking about the southern writers when he summed up the literary scene in such terms. Neither was Alfred Kazin when he wrote that "more than the age of the ideologue, of the literary revolutionary and the proletarian novelist, roles usually created within the Communist movement, the Thirties in literature were the age of the plebes—of writers from the working class, the lower class, the immigrant class, from Western farms and hills—those whose struggle was to survive." None of the southern writers of the period was a plebe except for Richard Wright, who was a black plebe. With but one or two exceptions, all the better writers had university educations. Though they had problems, personal economic survival was not one of them.

In the South, therefore, we have a region hard hit by the catastrophic crash, with severe ramifications felt throughout rural and urban southern society. The decade in which the crash occurred was that in which the literature being written by southern authors was reaching the very height of its artistic achievement. Almost none of that literature was so-called escapist literature: it dealt with human beings in struggle and travail. Yet even though we know that what was happening economically, socially, and politically within the region, the nation, and the world was of great concern to the men and women who were writing the literature, relatively little that they wrote was *about* the depression and its impact. Moreover, what was written about it was for the most part only moderately successful at de-lineating that particular experience.

There would seem to be something of a conundrum involved here, and so what I want to do is to examine it. I want to deal with three southern authors of stature who did try to write about the depression, in order to get at what it may have been that prevented them from succeeding in what they set out to do. My hope is that in so doing, it may be possible to throw a little light, however wavering, on the nature of the southern literary imagination, through what it was *not* as well as what it was.

My concern is not with the avowedly proletarian novelists among the southerners, who sought to write fiction in accordance with the approved party formulas. There were in point of fact a few of them. Olive Tilford Dargan, until the crash a local-color poet of the Carolina and Tennessee mountains, assumed the pen name of Fielding Burke and wrote several protest novels. Also there were Mary Page and Grace Lumpkin, and doubtless others of whom I know not. The fullness of time, however, has not ratified their literary importance. As novelists they are forgotten. It may be that if ever the revolution does arrive, the work of these writers may be revived. For now we must turn elsewhere.

Erskine Caldwell asserted, in fiction and nonfiction both, his political and social militancy during the decade. He did write about an actual textile strike in *God's Little Acre,* and in *Tobacco Road* he produced a work of formidable reputation, though it may be that the Broadway play adaptation was equally responsible for its long vogue. The Caldwell novels, which sold in the millions in paperback editions, did not, however, enjoy their vogue on the merits of their political assertion. They made their popular mark because they were bawdy and suggestive, even though they avoid four-letter words of the wrong sort and the sex act is never described clinically. If in recent years they have lost their popularity on the drug-store paperback rack, it is because now that the standards for pruriency have been dispensed with, few would purchase *Tobacco Road* when *Emmanuelle* or *Fear of Flying* is available. I wouldn't even buy it myself.

Assuredly there is considerably more than pornographic suggestibility to *Tobacco Road.* For one thing, it is *funny.* So are *God's Little Acre* and *Journeyman.* Jeeter Lester, Dude Lester, Sister Bessie, Ellie May are sterling exemplars of a southern literary tradition that goes all the way back at least to William Byrd II's *Dividing Line* histories of 1728. The tradition is of low-life highjinks; as in all such buffoonery the art consists of depicting human beings as animals. It is a Georgia freak show that Caldwell offers us, and like all theatrical ventures it is successful in direct proportion to the extent that the strangeness can be dramatized.

Caldwell's contemporary William Faulkner was not above providing similar entertainment for us. I don't suppose there is anything in Caldwell's low comedy that offers more raunchy subject matter than Ike Snopes's romance with the cow in *The Hamlet.* As I. O. Snopes puts it, "A man cant have his good name drug in the alleys. The Snopes name has done held its head up too long in this country to have no such reproaches against it like stock-diddling." The difference is that Faulkner's lowborn rustics are complex human beings. However grotesque in form the expression of their humanity may seem, they are not often turned into beasts. Faulkner's lyric apostrophe to Ike Snopes's romance with the heifer, with its rhapsodic depiction of the idiot courting his inamorata, is amusing because Faulkner comically ennobles the liaison. He celebrates Ike's tryst in language that would be appropriate for the courtship of Romeo and Juliet, and though the contrast between what is happening and the language used to describe it is comically ridiculous, it works the other way around, too. The idiot and his cow are, in their own fashion, neither more nor less in their love than Shakespeare's star-crossed lovers.

Erskine Caldwell offers little such comic dignity to his *Tobacco Road* folk. When Sister Bessie asserts of her yen for the sixteen-year-old Dude

Lester, "The Lord was speaking to me . . . He was telling me I ought to marry a new husband," the comedy resides in her sorry effort to justify her biological compulsion by biblical reference. The language of Scripture is used to cloak sexual urge. The result is to make her less human, more animal; the laugh is at the expense of the humanity.

In *Tobacco Road* low-life comedy is made to exist side by side with political and social message. Caldwell ridicules Jeeter Lester and his companions as comic degenerates, and he proclaims their victimization by society. Jeeter wants to plant a crop, but he can't because the soil has been exhausted and the merchants won't sell seed and guano on credit. "You rich folks in Augusta is just bleeding us poor folk to death," he complains. "You don't work none, but you get all the money us farmers make." But he will not abandon the land: "We was put here on the land where cotton will grow, and it's my place to make it grow. I wouldn't fool with the mills if I could make as much as fifteen dollars a week in them. I'm staying on the land till my time comes to die."

The political message, the proletarian agricultural motif, is in no important way fused with the low comedy. On the contrary, they work against each other. It is next to impossible to maintain a serious concern for the plight of the Lesters when throughout the novel we are invited to laugh at them for their degeneracy. No doubt it was Caldwell's intention to have us view the degeneracy and squalor as the result of the economic victimization: privileged society has turned the Lesters into swine. But except when making his political pitch Caldwell gleefully expends his rhetoric in making us guffaw at his bestiary. Regard how comically lewd and depraved these Lesters are! he tells us. Watch them fornicate in full view of an audience! Note the way that the woman preacher with the hideous nose quotes Scripture to justify her venery! Ain't it diverting?

We are informed by Robert Cantwell that "as a social document, *Tobacco Road* was a highly effective instrument in the various projects of soil conservation and social welfare of the time. . . . Had the characters of *Tobacco Road* been drawn sympathetically, the tragedy they embody would have been at best an echo in prose of the elegy in a country graveyard; as comic characters, they make that poverty unforgettable." There may be some truth to that, but if the New Deal had been forced to make dependence upon the influence of the Caldwell novels in its efforts to marshal public opinion in favor of the Soil Conservation Act, my guess is that the late Henry A. Wallace would have abandoned Washington to return to chicken farming in his native Iowa a number of years earlier than he did.

An altogether more imposing depiction of southern low life is James Agee's *Let Us Now Praise Famous Men*. Agee spent his boyhood in Tennessee, studied at Philips Exeter and Harvard, then went to work for Henry

Luce's *Fortune* magazine. During the 1930s Agee found himself increasingly drawn to communism. Though hardly an adherent to the official party line, and at all times distrustful of the shallow leftist formulations of his day, Agee declared of the Marxist hypothesis that "an awful lot of things do seem somewhere near and right from that, or essentially that, point of view, as the same things don't from any other." In the summer of 1936 Agee was delighted to receive an assignment from *Fortune* to go south with the photographer Walker Evans and "do a story on: sharecropper family (daily and yearly life): and also a study of Farm Economics in the South (impossible for me): and also on the several efforts to help the situation: i.e. Govt. and state work; theories and wishes of Southern liberals; whole story of the 2 Southern unions." It was, he added, the "best break I ever had on *Fortune*."

It was indeed a break; it was pivotal to his literary career. Though the articles he was hired to write proved unacceptable to *Fortune*, they developed into a book that some critics feel is almost a classic. In Genevieve Moreau's summation, *Let Us Now Praise Famous Men* "is an intense spiritual adventure, a search for innocence, and along the way all literature, all culture, is brought into question. It is an experimental, polyphonic work in which all the arts—literature, music, film—fuse. And though Agee repeatedly disavows its artistic purposes, it is as a work of art that *Famous Men* is ultimately valued."

What the assignment to go down to Alabama and write about sharecroppers did for Agee was to get him into the rural South, and into a confrontation with his own origins. For the downtrodden tenant farmers and sharecroppers of Alabama were his father's people. Though the Agees of the Tennessee hill country had not themselves descended from the mountains and into the squalor, deprivation, and hard toil of the Gudgers, Ricketts, and Woods whom Agee encountered in Alabama, James Agee discovered in the houses, lives, and ways of these depressed agriculturalists of the rural South a concreteness and significance such as seemed otherwise missing from his adult life in the urban literary and journalistic world of the metropolis. Their lives seemed anchored in actuality. These people were *real*. As he prepared to spend a night in the rickety farmhouse with the Gudgers,

> the feeling increased itself upon me that at the end of a wandering and seeking, so long it had begun before I was born, I had apprehended and now sat at rest in my own home, between two who were my brother and sister, yet less that than something else; these, the wife my age exactly, the husband four years older, seemed not other than my own parents, in whose patience I was so different, so diverged, so strange as I was; and all that surrounded me, that silently strove in through my senses and stretched me full, was familiar and dear to me as nothing else on earth, and as if well known in a deep past and long years lost; so that I

could wish that all my chance life was in truth the betrayal, the curable delusion, that it seemed, and that this was my right home, right earth, right blood, to which I would never have true right. For half my blood is just this; and half my right of speech; and by bland chance alone is my life so softened and sophisticated in the years of my defenselessness, and I am robbed of a royalty I can not only never claim, but never properly much desire or regret. And so in this quiet introit, and in all the time we have stayed in this house, and in all we have sought, and in each detail of it, there is so keen, sad, and precious a nostalgia as I can scarcely otherwise know; a knowledge of brief truancy into the sources of life, whereto I have no rightful access, having paid no price beyond love and sorrow.

It is because of this experience, reported retrospectively like the *madeleine* episode in Proust, that the involvement with the Gudgers in *Let Us Now Praise Famous Men* is artistically important to the author. The "half my blood" and "half my right of speech" are his father's family heritage. Hugh James Agee was killed in an automobile wreck when his son was six years old. James Agee's subsequent life—the years with his mother and her well-educated family of northern antecedents, at Saint Andrews School in Sewanee, Tennessee, at Philips Exeter, Harvard, and in New York City—had constituted a distancing from the social and cultural legacy of his birth and his childhood in Knoxville. Now, in a sharecropper's shack in Alabama, he is made aware of the extent to which that portion of his identity and his heritage had become obscured. But the memory of the past—"so keen, sad, and precious a nostalgia"—can give him renewed access to the circumstance of his own identity in time. *Let Us Now Praise Famous Men*, therefore, comprises the monument and record of James Agee's rediscovery of his southern birthright. The writing of it would ultimately make possible for him the recreation of remembered experience that is *The Morning Watch* and, most important of all, *A Death in the Family*.

For that very reason, however, the sharecropper book is ineffective as a work of political and social reportage. For despite the extremely detailed portraiture of the sharecropping families, how they looked and talked, where they lived, what they ate, how they worked, how degraded their situation, Agee isn't really imaginatively concerned with them in their own right. It is *his experience there* that fascinates him. The tone painting, the evocations of scenery and circumstance, the continued questioning of his own motives, the expressions of outrage at those who dare to look down upon and pity the humanity of the sharecroppers, the apostrophes to human endurance constitute nothing more, and nothing less, than an exploration of his own sensibility.

Agee isn't interested in the Gudgers, but in how to think, feel and write about the Gudgers. Under the guise of declining to oversimplify and distort through imposition of any sort of formulaic, stereotyped presentation of sharecropping, Agee is recording his experience in Alabama. As one critic points out, the "lack of order is the order in the text: Agee's straining to communicate reality, and failing, and straining again to give the narrative its form. . . . The form imitates the process of consciousness wherein perception is sudden, inexplicable, quickly lost, and always beginning again. What one feels constantly behind the words on the page is a consciousness laboring toward the world, Nature, the truth." The inability to impose meaningful shape probably comes because the real meaning was not the Alabama experience as such, but his own alienation from what it represented, and how the alienation happened. The place to look for that was not in the details of sharecropper families in Alabama, but in his memories of Knoxville, his childhood, his parents, his divided heritage—"the sources of life, whereto I have no rightful access, having paid no price beyond love and sorrow." Rightful repossession could come only through the resources of memory and understanding: the writing of *The Morning Watch* and *A Death in the Family*, an artistic travail which, pursued intermittently, occupied the remainder of his life.

That Agee declares that the usual ways of writing a book about sharecroppers won't work is quite correct, for he was not writing a book about sharecropping. Agee possessed a deceptive—deceptive to him—ability to engage himself thoroughly and completely in whatever topic came to hand or was assigned to him by an editor or a film maker. As a writer he could get involved in almost anything, and force his energies upon it, without any immediate insight into the relationship of the project at hand to any other aspects of his career or his work. It is the aptitude of the good journalist, the journeyman writer. But Agee was also an artist—an artist who was in search of his true subject and who had not yet discovered it. In this instance his aptitude misled him, for what Agee was really drawn to wasn't sharecropping and sharecroppers but their symbolic relationship to his own imagination, something that he sensed was tied in with his memories and his origins, but without knowing quite why. So he tried to invest his portrayal of the sharecroppers with the imaginative dimensions of a significance that really belonged not to the sharecroppers but to the relationship with his past.

Even so, it was not finally wasted. The discovery had been made that led ultimately to *A Death in the Family*. So we can only be grateful for the Alabama book.

The other southern writer of consequence who sought to deal literarily with the depression of the 1930s, of course, was Thomas Wolfe. Most of what he wrote about the economic and social experience of the crash is contained in the work entitled *You Can't Go Home Again*, which was put into shape by Edward Aswell of Harper and Brothers and published in

1940, two years after Wolfe's death, as a "new novel by Thomas Wolfe." We now know that it wasn't any such thing. Aswell pieced it together from a vast heap of published and unpublished writings, some of it dating back to the period of *Look Homeward, Angel*, some of it published in magazines as short novels, some of it written shortly before Wolfe's death. Working from a rough outline left by Wolfe, Aswell cut, spliced, rearranged, rewrote descriptions for consistency, incorporated portions of letters, and wrote transitional passages himself when he thought they were needed. It is dangerous, therefore, to deal in more than very general terms with Wolfe's actual achievement in reference to *You Can't Go Home Again*. Of all the important American writers of the 1930s Wolfe was by far the worst edited, both at Scribner's and Harper's.

During the years from 1929 until his death in 1938 Wolfe lived for most of the time in New York City, with several extended stays in Europe. The publication of his first novel and the stock market crash both occurred in the fall of 1929. It was not until six years later that his second novel, *Of Time and the River*, was published. All of his work is intensely autobiographical, and since the second novel carried his autobiographical protagonist only up to the late 1920s, he could make no direct commentary there on the ravages of the Great Depression as such. We know that his editor at Scribner's, Maxwell Perkins, was at some pains to insist that Wolfe not allow his Marxist views of the 1930s to become part of Eugene Gant's consciousness during the period covered in *Of Time and the River*, when Thomas Wolfe had held no such views.

Perkins's attitude was that since Wolfe was writing avowedly autobiographical fiction, it was essential that he be faithful to the way his protagonist thought and felt during the time being chronicled. But the difficulty is that Wolfe's fiction is autobiographical not only in the sense that it is about his own life, but also in that he, the writer, is overtly present—*as writer*. Though he does not say "I" (in actuality he did just that in the manuscript entitled *Of Time and the River*, but his editors changed it to the third person for him), he makes his reader quite conscious of his presence as authorial commentator on the events being related, events that earlier had happened to *him*. Thus Perkins's insistence upon chronological authenticity had the result of working against any kind of growing maturity on Wolfe's part as to the meaning of his earlier experience as a writer, and Wolfe needed all the emotional maturity he could muster.

Most of what Wolfe had to say about the Great Depression can be found in two sequences in *You Can't Go Home Again*. One of these is set in New York City a week before the crash and describes a lavish party given by George Webber's mistress, Esther Jack, at her Park Avenue apartment. A fire breaks out in the apartment house, the building is evacuated, and the residents and their guests wait outside as the firemen go to work. To extinguish the fire it is necessary for firemen to flood the basement, which in turn floods out several levels of railroad trackage underneath. The episode is interpreted by Wolfe as emblematic of the approaching collapse of the wealthy, privileged society of the metropolis in the wake of the stock market debacle and the depression. When the fire has been put out and the tenants return to their apartments, George Webber vows silently to leave the world of Esther Jack and the immense wealth, social inequity, and artistic philistinism that it symbolizes. Wolfe published a shorter version of the sequence, entitled "The Party at Jack's," in novella form. Aswell combined it with additional material, wrote a new ending, and incorporated it in *You Can't Go Home Again*. It is not known whether the additional material was written before or after the version that was published in magazine form. Certainly the novella version is considerably more focused artistically than that in the book.

A second depression sequence describes the frenzied business activity of predepression Asheville, which is called Libya Hill, and the calamitous impact of the crash. Wolfe drew the inspiration for much of this material from his own family's experience. Several sections were originally published as short stories. Aswell combined, spliced, and rewrote to fit it into *You Can't Go Home Again*.

Let it be said at once that there is a great deal of very powerful writing in this later work of Thomas Wolfe's. While I am not convinced that Wolfe ever really found an artistic substitute for the intense lyric self-consciousness of Eugene Gant, his protagonist for the first two novels, he was writing well toward the end, and it may be that as C. Hugh Holman and other good critics have declared, Wolfe was indeed working toward a new and different mastery of his material in a dramatic and social rather than lyrical and personal mode.

It seems to me, even so, that an episode such as "The Party at Jack's" is not altogether convincing as the indictment of the overrefined wealthy that it sets out to be. For George Webber's decision to reject Esther Jack's world seems to come as the result of at least several impulses on the part of George. On the one hand, the society of Esther and her friends is depicted as materialistic, wasteful, callous, effete; ultimately it is based upon the exploitation of the lower levels of society, as personified by the two elevator attendants who die from smoke suffocation in the fire. A second reason for George's distaste for the world of Esther Jack, however, appears to be that it is composed primarily of highly cosmopolitan, successful, supercilious urban folk, many of whom bear such names as Mandell, Heilprinn, Hirsch, and Abramson, and who are extremely unappreciative of the merits of earnest young artists from the provinces. The host at the party, Frederick Jack, takes delight in "seeing some yokel, say, fresh from the rural districts, all hands and legs and awkwardness, hooked and wriggling on a cunning word—a woman's, preferably, because women were so swift and deft in matters of this nature." After the party is under way, precisely this is what is done to awkward, ill-at-ease young George Webber. Are all these New Yorkers false, vicious, amoral, predatory because they are wealthy and philistine, or because they are New Yorkers, many of them Jews? One isn't so sure. Still a third reason for George Webber's renunciation is his mistress's age; she is considerably older than he is, and as we see when she pretends that a youthful painting of her was done later than in fact it was painted, she tries to conceal her relative antiquity.

The dramatis personae of "The Party at Jack's" are for the most part a thoroughly unpleasant and unattractive assortment of human beings, and if an earthquake of a stock market crash should come to destroy or cleanse the society they inhabit—preferably a little of both—we might not feel entirely overcome with grief and loss. Still, if what is wrong with them is that they have the misfortune to be New Yorkers—that is, not Anglo-Americans in origin and ways of speech and appearance—and therefore not to have been born in the South or the Midwest, then isn't the author's attitude a trifle insular and undemocratic? And if what is wrong with George continuing to inhabit the world of Esther Jack is that Esther is considerably older than George and tends to be overly possessive, then is it quite honest to attribute the decision to leave that society principally to the wealth, philistinism, and social callousness?

In other words, mixed in with the social commentary of "The Party at Jack's" is a considerable amount of provincial insularity and personal self-justification.

Now we can understand young George Webber, fresh from the provinces and an unpublished author, feeling this way. Indeed, it would be somewhat surprising if he did not. The difficulty is that the older, much more mature author whose autobiographical surrogate young Webber manifestly is, seems also to entertain such emotions. Young George, for example, wasn't present earlier in the episode when Esther Jack's husband looked forward so eagerly to the possibility of a young man from the province being humiliated by one of the sophisticates at the party. The author-narrator was there, however, and told us about it with quite the same intensity of feeling that George displayed when later on it happened to him. The author-narrator is quite indignant about the kind of wicked metropolitan society and the kind of nasty urban sensibility that would not only tolerate but actually relish such cruelty to young provincials.

If Wolfe's excoriation of wealth and privilege in the metropolis is compromised by his provincial prejudices, the same is true to at least as great an extent when he turns his attention to the lower levels of metropolitan society. The Irish maids, Swedish doormen, the waitresses and typists, the dwellers in the alleys, tenements, and flats of depression Brooklyn are so alien to his attitudes and expectations that it is all but impossible for him to write about them other than satirically. Allowing for Wolfe's far more versatile and subtle rhetorical skills, it is almost as if an Erskine Caldwell bereft of his comic instinct had transferred his attentions from Tobacco Road to Skid Row. In the abstract Wolfe can admire the great city and its citizenry, but when he gets down to particulars what comes out is mostly disgust and despair.

It is true that the magazine version of "The Party at Jack's" does not contain nearly as much of the xenophobia; it is written much more economically and surely. Yet the economy and objectivity are attained in large part at the cost of suppressing the intensity with which George Webber and his autobiographical author-narrator are engaged in the situation. The gain in objectivity is at the expense of vividness; Wolfe's art depends upon the presence of that author-narrator, and without it the fiction tends to be flat and unexciting. So that while the shorter version of "The Party at Jack's" is more focused and compact, it lacks much of the emotional engagement on the author-narrator's part that makes Wolfe's best work, for all its excess, so compelling.

Let me point out at once that when Wolfe turns to the people back home in Asheville—Libya Hill in the George Webber narratives—and describes the commercial opportunism and real-estate mania that brought about the end of the boom there, he is equally as savage in his disapproval. Characters such as Tim Wagner, Rumford Bland, Jarvis Riggs, and Dave Merrit are depicted in terms that are fully as repulsive and denunciatory as those used on the wealthy New Yorkers. Their Anglo-American Protestant credentials do not save them one whit. There is no more withering episode in all of Wolfe's writings than that which portrays the "company man," the two-faced Dave Merrit, all cordiality and good will on the surface, as he savagely browbeats George Webber's friend Randy Shepperson for his failure to meet an ever-increasing sales quota for the Federal Weight, Scales and Computing Company. Libya Hill and its residents are caught in a vicious, inhuman commercial system based on self-delusion and greed: "They had squandered fabulous sums in meaningless streets and bridges. They had torn down ancient buildings and erected new ones large enough to take care of a city of half a million people. They have levelled hills and bored through mountains, making magnificent tunnels paved with double roadways and glittering with shining tiles—tunnels which leaped out on the other side into Arcadian wilderness. They had flung away the earnings of a lifetime, and mortgaged those of a generation to come. They had ruined their city, and in so doing had ruined themselves, their children, and their children's children."

It is a searing indictment of American materialism that Wolfe offers us in *You Can't Go Home Again*—and it is the more convincing because in the instance of Asheville Wolfe is able to understand what had caused it. The get-rich-quick mania had come not merely out of avarice, but a thwarted sacramental energy. The people of Libya Hill wanted "some thrilling and impossible fulfillment, some glorious enrichment and release of their pent lives, some ultimate escape from their own tedium." An emptiness in the condition of their lives, a balked need for love and spiritual growth that was not to be reckoned merely in terms of economic indices and material possessions, had led them to grasp so eagerly and fatally at the chance for easy money and extravagant prosperity.

Wolfe and his autobiographical protagonist understand this, because Wolfe is *of* these people; he could see that what the people of his home city did to themselves came out of much the same needs and hopes that had motivated him to pursue a literary career in the shining city beyond the mountains. No such understanding is exhibited when Wolfe writes of the coming of the depression in the metropolis: the wealthy New Yorkers, the artistic aesthetes of Esther Jack's world, whether bearing Anglo-American or whatever names, are finally alien to Wolfe and to his autobiographical protagonists, and though he tries very hard on occasion to know them, there is a barrier that cannot be overcome. Wolfe's depiction of the city remains that of an outsider, frequently fascinated and as often repelled by what he finds there, but never *of* it. The impact of the Great Depression brought to the fore his political and social outrage, but did not notably increase his understanding. Thus his sympathy is pity rather than compassion, and his anger seems often to be directed as much at the inhabitants of the city for being the kind of people who are to be found in large cities as it is at the symbols of the wealth, privilege, and injustice that helped to cause the crash.

Yet the final judgment of Wolfe's writings about the depression years is one of admiration, qualified but real. For Wolfe did his best to understand his experience; he took no cheap ways out, he did not try to avert his gaze from what he saw. He never ceased in his effort to recreate in language his experience of the world, and he sought always to reveal himself nakedly and honestly, without subterfuge or self-deception. As an artist he did not flinch at revealing what manner of man he was, and this self-revelation, which is his basic technique for writing fiction, does not fail to show the worst as well as the best. And he *learned* as he went along. Even the atavistic xenophobia of the early years must be qualified by the episode entitled "I Have a Thing to Tell You," written after a final visit to Germany in 1936, in which he confronts the evil of Nazism and the world-sickness of the Germans. In C. Hugh Holman's words, "nothing Wolfe ever wrote has greater narrative drive or more straightforward action than this novella." The Wolfe fiction, finally, *works*: it has its flaws, its failures aplenty, but in its particular kind of vision it is unique. Even *You Can't Go Home Again*, filtered through a clumsy and distorting editorial job, is a work of dignity.

But—to repeat—it is not often very effective social criticism as such, and we must ultimately say of Wolfe what has been noted about Caldwell and Agee: that whatever the considerable achievement of the work they wrote about the depression, they do not develop and sustain a believable and consistent artistic indictment of social injustice, whether of tenement or tenant shack, which was what they set out to do.

I have sought to show how in each instance the conscious intention of the author seems to have been severely qualified by other aspects of his literary imagination which impelled his artistic attention elsewhere. In Caldwell it was the reliance upon low comedy, in the long-established tradition of southern poor-white humor. For Agee the intention to write about the degradation of sharecropping moved swiftly into an exploration of *his* experience in attempting to do so, an exploration that led him away from Alabama and back into his own past. For Wolfe the intended indictment of mammon and philistia in the city was fatally compromised by the basic provincial hostility that he brought to bear upon almost all those who inhabit the American metropolis.

Why couldn't these three southern writers deal with the Great Depression in the way they wanted to do?

In Caldwell's instance I read the several assessments of him as an important social critic, and then I go back to the novels, and even so I cannot take them seriously. Caldwell had a genuine talent for a certain sort of low-life humor, and it comes, as I have suggested earlier, out of a longstanding regional literary tradition. The old southwestern humor involved looking down at the rustic primitives from above, with mingled amusement and astonishment. Caldwell mostly omits the genteel narrator customary to the mode, but nonetheless he is looking down from above at every moment along the way. If we grant Caldwell an underlying seriousness of literary purpose (I find it difficult to do so), then it was betrayed by a vision of caste and class that has been characteristic of southern literature almost from its beginnings.[1] For despite his intention to blame the low estate of the Lester family on the workings of economic determinism, what comes out strongest is a moral contempt for their depravity. Jeeter *says* that the town merchants and the absentee landlords are what prevents him from making a crop; but what Caldwell creates for us is a lazy, unregenerate sinner. Caldwell's view of the inhabitants of Tobacco Road is, in defiance of his intentions, historical and Calvinistic. The depiction of unregenerate mankind is much like Jonathan Edwards's: "Thus do all unclean persons, who live in lascivious practices in secret; all malicious persons, all profane persons, that neglect the duties of religion. . . . Thus do tavern-haunters, and frequenters of evil company; and many other kinds that might be mentioned." Unlike Edwards, the Reverend Ira Sylvester Caldwell's son is amused at the uncleanliness and lasciviousness, and he says that the sinfulness is due to the social and economic system. But what he shows is the Mark of the Beast. It is not inappropriate that when the Lesters perish at the end of *Tobacco Road*, they are consumed by fire.

James Agee gives us no such apocalypse. His Gudgers, Ricketts, and Woods are men and women of dignity. But their imaginative significance for him is that they move him backward in time to his origins, to his father's people in the Tennessee mountains:[2] "half my blood is just this; and half my right of speech." The result is "so keen, sad, and precious a nostalgia as I can scarcely otherwise know." What he saw in Alabama is important because of what happened to him twenty years earlier: the death of his father, the abrupt severance of the link with the east Tennessee hill folk.

The past is also the key to much of Wolfe's performance. In linking the materialism and irresponsibility of the wealthy partygoers to his own presence there as a young provincial, Wolfe ties the episode in with the basic pattern of all his work: the flight from the mountain town in North Carolina to the city and the promise of artistic fulfillment, which is the saga of both Eugene Gant and George Webber. He had sought to put down roots in the city, as exemplified in his compulsive searching out of the details of his mistress's family history and the life of turn-of-the-century New York. But it does not work. The party at Esther Jack's is the occasion of his decision to turn his back on the world of Esther and her friends, a decision he says comes because of the materialism and philistinism of that world, but which is also emotionally bound in with the sense that it is alien to him, foreign to the life that had nurtured and shaped his art. Much of the imaginative significance of "The Party at Jack's" thus lies in his own provincial past.

The imaginative importance of the past in Wolfe's work is even more strongly emphasized in the sequence about the collapse of the boom-town economy in Libya Hill. Wolfe and George Webber find the origins of the boom in George Webber's own childhood, in "the barren nighttime streets of the town he had known so well in his boyhood. . . . Yes, it was here, on many a night long past and wearily accomplished, in ten thousand little towns and in ten million little barren streets where all the passion, hope, and hunger of the famished men beat like a great pulse through the fields of darkness—it was there and nowhere else that this madness had been brewed." Their need had been his; in search of fulfillment he had left for the metropolis, while they had remained home and let their frustrated appetite for change and their hunger for meaning overcome their better judgments.

Thus the experience that both Agee and Wolfe looked back to in their effort to understand the depression was that of the movement away from an older, small-town community with small rural ties and into the metropolitan society that both of them knew and, as adults, inhabited. And that experience, registered personally, is nothing more or less than the histori-cal experience of the twentieth-century South. In Agee's instance he did not recognize and begin writing about the past at once, but we have seen that it was what the imaginative response to Alabama sharecroppers in-volved for him. The ultimate result, *A Death in the Family*, was a chronicle of how that separation from the older community occurred and what it meant. In Wolfe's instance the response was more direct.

It has often been noted that the greatest source of strength of southern writing in this century lies in the continuity of its historical imagination. Like Virgie Rainey in Eudora Welty's *The Golden Apples*, the southern writers "saw things in their time." By this is meant not merely the specific history of the South itself (although each of these three authors, including Caldwell, has a very clearly defined notion of southern history). It means a way of looking, an attitude toward the form and meaning of human experi-ence as a process involving a personal, familial identity in historical time.

For the writers we have been examining, this characteristic was not, it seems to me, of notable use in their efforts to write about the social impact of the Great Depression, since it tended to direct their imaginations away from the delineation of the massive phenomenon of the depression itself and toward a scrutiny of personal and family relationships. But when we turn away from the books we have been considering and think about some of the best southern writing of the twentieth century, we realize that precisely this historical sense is what enables the writers to get at the underlying meaning of the depression years. For now that the immediate crisis of the Great Depression has long since become history, we can see in what happened during those years an acceleration of the process leading toward urbanism and industrialism, and the final, conclusive shattering of the insularity and self-sufficiency of the old southern system of caste and class. What seemed at the time to be a breakdown in industrialization, a sudden suspension of progress and prosperity, in reality had precisely the opposite result, in that the depression brought an end to the dominance of subsistence farming and cleared the way for the rapid industrialization and urbanization of the South during and after the Second World War by removing many traditional barriers and hindrances to social and economic change. The depression forced the South to face up to the need for change; the old ways clearly wouldn't suffice.

The single literary "movement" or "program" that any of the important southern writers were involved in during the decade of the 1930s, of course, was Agrarianism. The Nashville Agrarians who in 1930 published the symposium entitled *I'll Take My Stand: The South and the Agrarian Tradition* were not writing as a direct response to the depression; their manifesto was conceived and executed in 1929 and 1930, and was in the process of publication when the depression hit the South. The advent of the economic collapse, however, gave the work an added impact, as well as having the effect (unfortunate, I believe) of making the book appear to be more "practical" and economically prescriptive than it actually was. *I'll Take My Stand*, it seems to me, is best understood not as a treatise on the advantages of a return to a farming existence, but as a humanistic rebuke to the industrializing, centralizing, depersonalizing tendencies of urban America, written in the spirit of *Walden* rather than *Das Kapital*. During the early 1930s some of the Agrarians developed their critique in terms of what was going on with the regional and national economy, but without notable efficacy. The South was bent upon recovering and upon industrializing, and it was not until the 1960s that the region acquired sufficient leisure to be able to recognize the relevance of the warnings that the agrarians were delivering about what was happening to the quality of life within the southern community and in the southern countryside in the wake of the machine age.

Yet the basic impulse of Agrarianism, however programmatically and topically conceived, was identical with that of the better imaginative writers of the 1930s. It was concerned with human change, with the urgency of facing up to the impact of new ways and new demands upon an historical community. It was a response to the breakdown of older and familiar ways of thinking and feeling. Let me briefly suggest how this kind of response to the 1930s manifests itself in a group of four important southern novels, three of them published in the 1930s, the fourth appearing in 1946 but written about events that culminate during the depression decade. In William Faulkner's *Absalom, Absalom!* young Quentin Compson looks back at his relationship to the life and death of Thomas Sutpen, a vigorous, powerful plebian who had come into Quentin's community many years earlier and in his ruthless, single-minded quest for a dynasty had brought suffering and tragedy to all around him. In Margaret Mitchell's *Gone with the Wind*, a work for which I have a qualified but considerable admiration, a strong-willed young woman cannot share in or understand the community pieties, and will not accept the role of Southern Lady that her society assigns to her. She learns to cope with war, change, tradition in ways that appall others but enable her to survive and even flourish. In Allen Tate's *The Fathers* the Buchan family must confront the presence within it of George Posey, who cannot understand the traditional code of manners and behavior. Caught in the impact of war and change, the Buchan family, its northern Virginia home, and the planter civilization it exemplifies are destroyed. The collapse is not only from without but equally from within, as a survivor, young Lacy Buchan, realizes many years later. Finally, in Robert Penn Warren's *All the King's Men* a young man of patrician family takes up with a strong, charismatic upcountry politician who, free of the blinders and the scruples of upper-class complacency, is able to act meaningfully, though recklessly, in the modern twentieth-century world of economic and political forces and broader human needs. In turning to this man as a substitute for the exertion of individual moral choice, however, the young man and others bring disaster to themselves.

Each of these novels, therefore, involves a powerful central figure who both symbolizes and embodies the force of change. Each deals with the inevitable erosion of a tradition before the onslaught of new times and new needs, and each depicts both the agony and the inescapable necessity of being able to cope with such change. In each instance the meaning of what is taking place is perceived by a young person of tradition and breeding— Quentin Compson, Lacy Buchan, Jack Burden, and in the instance of *Gone with the Wind* the very ambivalent and often unconsciously self-revelatory author herself. In each instance the person doing the perceiving both sympathizes with and is repelled by the iconoclastic central figure.

Thus each of these novels seems in its own way to constitute a response to the necessities of change—a problem that was strikingly characteristic of the years during which the novels were being written. For what is involved is the ability to live and function amid profound social change, and the price that must be paid in order to do so. The older, traditional ways—in three of the novels exemplified by the antebellum South—no longer suffice; yet the new ways are perilous. Is not this the situation of the depression South, a community of complex human beings come lately to modernity, impelled to accept and often to welcome new ways of thinking and doing, confronting new crises and new economic, social, and political demands, yet very much the inheritor of a powerfully apprehended traditional order that has embodied much that the community would hope to retain as well as much that must be sloughed off?

In these novels, and in the best work of all the modern southern writers (very much including that of Wolfe and Agee), the historical imagination, rather than acting as a hindrance, makes the artistic achievement possible. From the standpoint of almost a half-century's perspective we recognize that it is in works such as these that we can find mirrored the underlying human meaning of the Great Depression of the 1930s.

The American South was never the same after the Great Depression. If you want to find out why, read the literature.

CHAPTER 7

VICTOR A. KRAMER

The Consciousness of Technique:

THE PROSE METHOD OF JAMES AGEE'S
LET US NOW PRAISE FAMOUS MEN

Let Us Now Praise Famous Men (1941) is a text that resulted from the happy conjunction of James Agee's vast ambition and the specific needs that he saw generated during the 1930s. Looking at the contemporary scene, he could see beyond what many artists saw, and therefore *Famous Men* became a text that goes far beyond the use of particular facts to document observations or support a thesis. This is a text that evokes and honors reality, not uses it.

Agee knew that to contrive a fully adequate technique would be impossible, and he sensed this before he began to write; but five years of energy went into the intricate composition of this, his most problematic book, and the resultant text is, on one level, a record of a struggle with a project about which he could not stop feeling strong emotion. On another level the text gives us one of the most complete pictures of the 1930s, and this seems to be so because manifold purposes support the composition of Agee's ambitious experiment. Its charged rhetoric provides enormous amounts of information both about him and about its ostensible subject matter, tenant farming.

Agee warned readers that this text was an inquiry into "the predicaments of human divinity," while he also stressed that his effort was an attempt to "recognize the stature of a portion of unimagined existence, and to contrive techniques proper to its recording, communication, analysis, and defense."[1] In a notebook, written as the book was composed, he sketched his subject matter and insisted that at the "centre" of the work the following was to be found: "[1] At the centre, every recapturable instant of those eight weeks spent in the middle South; [2] At the centre again: ourselves, and our instruments (both camera and language.) The primary instrument is individual human consciousness; [3] Again at the centre: these three families chosen with such pain to 'represent' their kind."[2]

Such a complexity of intention and determination to provide a means of access to so many facets of a particular experience illuminate both the success and "failure" of Agee's unusual text. He knew that he could not achieve a unity that some writers might desire, nor one that most readers would look for. In his preamble he stated: "No doubt I shall worry myself that I am taking too long getting started, and shall seriously distress myself over my inability to create an organic, mutually sustaining and dependent, and as it were musical form: but I must remind myself that I started with the first word I wrote, and that the centers of my subject are shifty" (p. 10). Above all, he was concerned with recording the sacramental reality of particular lives, and experiences, yet as he reconstructed such facts he knew they expanded outward. He had been thinking about related technical problems for years before this *Fortune* magazine assignment to go to the South.[3] The Alabama assignment provided him with an impetus to develop methods that might begin to catch the rhythm and complexity of the *un*imagined. Agee knew if such stylistic contrivance was to be effective, the technique would have to be severely controlled. (Ultimately he even admitted that the specific trip to Alabama—and the ostensible subject matter—was not of particular significance to him. Most important was this attempt to develop ways of reflecting the dignity of an *un*imagined world.)

Because Agee attempted so many different things within this text, he accomplished various things. The text has been carefully studied in relation to the development of American romanticism. It has been interpreted as the key to Agee's maturation of artistic capability. It has been described as a book about the writing of a book about tenant farming.[4] And each of these approaches is correct. The present essay is an analytical consideration of some of the technical devices "contrived" to evoke the reality of what was observed, remembered, and imagined because of a few weeks' trip to Alabama in 1936. Agee's text has been called a failure.[5] This analysis seeks to clarify the complexity of his method, and to show how it grew out of the particular historical situation of the mid-1930s, a time when Agee was learning to look carefully at the "dignity of actuality" that was part of his contemporary America. But Agee was interested in revealing, not in suggesting solutions. This fact sets his text off from related works.

One of the reasons this text has been so often misunderstood could be that it seems to be composed of so many different components. Agee was aware of its diversity (even incongruity) but he felt if he was going to convey the complexity of his subject, and in a manner appropriate to his vision, his mode of communication would have to be complex. In his preamble he says: "And if there are questions in my mind how to undertake this communication, and there are many, I must let the least of them be, whether I am boring you, or whether I am taking too long getting started, and too clumsily. If I bore you, that is that. If I am clumsy, that may indicate partly the difficulty of my subject, and the seriousness with which I am trying to take what hold I can of it" (p. 10). His subject was the mundane daily life of farmers in middle Alabama. He wanted to retell his experience with them in as truthful a way as possible "without either dissection into science, or digestion into art, but with the whole of consciousness" (p. 11). That he knew it was impossible to accomplish such a task is reflected in the many apologetic statements sprinkled throughout the book.

Writing in the thirties when it was sometimes easiest to think as a member of a group, Agee believed he had first to communicate the fact that he wrote of separate, distinct human beings as apprehended within a unique texture of events. Each person was "a human being, not like any other human being so much as he is like himself" (p. 232). Because each person was respected as distinct and holy, the dignity of the human person serves as the basic recurring motif, providing a dimension of religious awe and celebration through which this dignity is presented.

Language and, even more, obvious external use of religious forms, strengthen this religious motif. Because each person is distinct and therefore to be respected, Agee felt that one of his duties as writer was to suggest how that individuality was brought about. Influences of varying sizes and shapes come into contact with particular individuals, and with each contact some change is made in the person. "It would be our business," Agee wrote, "to show how through every instant of every day of every year of his existence alive he is from all sides streamed inward upon, bombarded, pierced, destroyed by that enormous sleeting of all objects forms and ghosts how great how small no matter, which surround and whom his senses take: in as great and perfect and exact particularity as we can name them" (p. 110).

But while trying to adhere to particularities, he also knew that he had been affected by what he had seen. His perception had acted as contributor to the effect. Agee's aesthetic therefore focuses attention on details remembered but always as remembered (perhaps changed and distorted) by him. Such a method would almost surely insure disfavor among some readers and critics of leftist political persuasions. Agee's consciousness remains central.

That the recorder, Agee himself, was in many ways a poor instrument for the recording of what he relates is considered of prime importance. To judge better about incidents and objects included within the text, Agee felt that the reader had to be given adequate knowledge of the writer. One extreme example of this conviction is the inclusion, under the caption "Intermission: Conversation in the Lobby," of Agee's impulsive answers to a series of questions asked of American writers by the *Partisan Review*:

questions, for instance, about the duties of the writer in the late 1930s, should war develop, seemed an impertinence to Agee, who flippantly answered he had always considered himself to be at war. He wanted his readers to know some of his biases; they might more easily then draw conclusions about other parts of the book. Similarly, this text is replete with remembrances of Agee's childhood and experiences only obliquely related to the tenant material.

But Agee's presence within the text is not only to provide the reader with knowledge of the limitations of the recording instrument but also to indicate that what had happened to him was unique, consequently important, and therefore to be part of an accurately recorded experience. Several explicit statements are made concerning problems that arose in the recording of the experience. Such technical problems were, to Agee's mind, integrated with the whole experience. The actual event, its remembrance, and the problem of how to combine the best of each of these confronted him. He knew that what he hoped finally to accomplish was really beyond the capabilities of language, but at the same time he knew that language possessed distinct qualities separate from other modes of communication and for which it could and should be valued. He stressed that "words could, I believe, be made to do or to tell anything within human conceit. That is more than can be said of the instruments of any other art. . . . It may, however, be added: words like all else are limited by certain laws. To call their achievement crippled in relation to what they have tried to convey may be all very well: but to call them crippled in their completely healthful obedience to their own nature is again a mistake: the same mistake as the accusation of a cow for her unhorsiness" (pp. 236–37).

His doubts about achieving all he desired are reflected throughout his text; primarily these are doubts about how best to handle the technical problems. From the very beginning of the book the writer's attention is divided between the problems that faced him as he tried to write of what had happened and his doubts about his very right to be prying into the lives he writes about: in other words, moral problems. Also in this way Agee's text is a step beyond so many "documentaries" of the 1930s.[6] He labors the point that possibly what he is doing should not be done at all. He opens the book proper by saying, "It seems to me curious, not to say obscene and thoroughly terrifying, that it could occur to an association of human beings drawn together through need and chance and for profit into a company, an organ of journalism, to pry intimately into the lives of an undefended and appallingly damaged group of human beings" (p. 7). At one point he says if it were possible there would be "no writing at all" (p. 13). Yet remembering that Beethoven once said "he who understands my music can never know unhappiness again," Agee writes he must say the same of his perception. If he could have communicated all that he felt, he knew that his moral problems, the doubts about his right to attempt such a book, would be eliminated. Agee's qualification is that "performance is another matter" (p. 16). The fact that he was so aware of such problems is what ultimately makes his text a success. Knowing that he must ultimately fail, he took on the challenge of suggesting what he sensed and wanted to communicate.

The material for *Famous Men* was gathered by living with one family, the Gudgers, for a period of about one month, but close ties were also developed with two other families. It was hoped that in this way a representative idea could be gained about tenant farming in general. Upon these ideas he elaborated and developed broad statements that concerned all tenant farmers. The best example of this type of elaboration is the section entitled "Work," wherein Agee blends his love of those with whom he had lived with a realization that millions are forced to lead lives much like those of the Gudgers, the Woods, and the Ricketts. These three particular families therefore served as a base from which imagination flowed toward all tenant-farm families throughout the South.

The text of the book as a whole finally concerns itself not just with sharecroppers, or even with workers in the United States, but with all who live in the world.[7] In 1938, as he was working on this manuscript, Agee wrote Father James Harold Flye to explain how he was faced with the problem of his whole subject matter "intensifying" itself. "The whole problem and nature of existence"[8] was present within his questioning mind. Thus while the text is a picture of Agee's unique remembrance as he devises procedures appropriate for this retelling, it is as well a commentary about the fragility of man's existence. Many of the more meditative parts of the book suggest no writer more than Thoreau. Thus moving from the particulars of living in Alabama, and framed by his dissatisfaction with much that had been called "documentary," Agee wrote a text that is precise and that radiates outward beyond the particularities of its inspiration.

Famous Men functions like a poem, even though its author clearly urges throughout that a work of "Art" was not intended. Agee had to write of his experience, and because he was so inextricably involved with those about whom he wrote, his basic manner of presentation was lyrical. Intense personal emotion was at the core, even when he wrote about a very plain "object" or "atmosphere." For such "objects and atmospheres have a sufficient intrinsic beauty and stature that it might be well if the describer became more rather than less shameless: if objects and atmospheres for the secret sake of which it is customary to write a story or poem, and which are chronically relegated to a menial level of decoration or at best illumination, were handled and presented on their own merits without either distortion or apology. Since when has a landscape painter apologized for painting landscapes?" (p. 239). It is significant that he notes immediately following this passage that Cocteau had remarked of Picasso that "the subject matter is merely the excuse for the painting, and that Picasso does away with the excuse" (p. 239). Such a comment is an indirect admission by Agee of how important his presence is within the text. That presence is important even when he presents a record of something for its own sake, as when he records all the contents of a particular drawer in the Gudgers' bedroom.

Agee wants his reader to feel as if he too were in a living situation. In the preamble he had suggested that the text might be read aloud; and he indicated that he was striving for a new literary form that would be analogous to music. Ultimately, the form he developed was one that relied upon several basic techniques that flow into one another.

Because of the complexity of the variegated experience that had been undergone, Agee felt that several different techniques would have to be employed to communicate his experience verbally. The point of view with which he approached his writing is reflected in the following passage:

> The whole job may well seem messy to you. But part of my point is that experience offers itself in richness and variety and in many more terms than one and that it may therefore be wise to record it no less variously. Much of the time I shall want to tell of particulars very simply, in their own terms: but from any set of particulars it is possible and perhaps useful to generalize. In any case I am the sort of person who generalizes: and if for your own convenience and mine I left that out, I would be faking and artifacting right from the start. [Pp. 244–45]

Each technique he employed represents an attempt to communicate an absolute "realness," yet the subject matter differs in three basic ways: the first of Agee's "realities" centers around the simple fact that he wrote about what *he* had experienced. What exactly his reaction was, later described within the text, becomes a basic item to be communicated. Second, he wrote about real persons and events. He did not go to Alabama and gather materials for a composite picture of tenant farmers, using bits of many lives and his imagination to fit together a work of "Art." However, there are millions who must face essentially the same problems as those Agee knew, and therefore he had to communicate a third type of reality. To help his reader understand how widespread were the conditions described, he was forced to generalize. Therefore from the particular things that he saw and recorded, his concern and love extended to millions of other humans leading lives similar to those that he knew and described.

Agee himself, in the section "On the Porch" (a part of the book that was written early), spoke of handling the technical problems of recording what he had seen and felt "from four planes." It is possible to demonstrate how each of the sections of *Famous Men* is built on a distinct level.

A study of Agee's concept of planes of writing yields insights into the complexity of *Famous Men*, and, indeed, whole sections can be profitably identified as being consciously crafted with particular planes in mind. But still other methods reflect Agee's consciousness of technique and demonstrate how he moved from the particulars observed to the implications beyond. Both his construction of a "continuum" and his precise use of stylized language emphasizes his reverence for the subject matter. Such techniques also emphasize Agee's vision.

In his development of the continuum the controlled fusion of elements already mentioned takes place. Thus, as Agee writes in a continuum the many "centres" he mentions in his notebook entry begin to move closer together and, by implication, he condemns the easy observations of others. Agee is concerned with the point of view expressed in the following words:

> George Gudger is a man et cetera. But obviously in the effort to tell of him (by example) as truthfully as I can, I am limited. I know him only so far as I know him, and only in those terms in which I know him; and all of that depends as fully on who I am as on who he is.
>
> I am confident of being able to get at a certain form of the truth about him, *only if* I am as faithful as possible to Gudger as I know him, to Gudger as, in his actual flesh and life (but there again always in my mind's and memory's eye) he is . . . I would do just as badly to simplify or eliminate myself from this picture as to simplify or invent character, places or atmospheres. A chain of truths did actually weave itself and run through: it is their texture that I want to represent, not betray, nor pretty up into art. [Pp. 239–40]

We remember that for him the camera was the "central instrument of our time," and Agee's immense respect for the camera has its basis in the fact that it is "incapable of recording anything but absolute dry truth" (pp. 11, 234). With this in mind he admits as he "catalogues" what he saw that a camera might do a better job. Yet language, he believed, has merits distinctly its own. With language as his basic instrument, used as a photographer might use a camera but fused with the poetic imagination, a writer is able to give a sense of an experience as seen with eye *and* mind (both at a particular time and as recalled later as well). For Agee such a fusion can best be presented as a continuum.

A continuum is therefore an extremely successful fusion of many methods employed throughout the text. Indeed, when considered in relationship to Agee's planes, it is evident that this device cannot be separated from his second category, "as it happened," yet it includes regular use of plane three, recall *and* imagination. Looking at specific pages headed "The room beneath the house," we see Agee's attempt to fuse straight description with mental reactions both initially and later. These pages consist of six paragraphs and a prose poem (pp. 147–49). Here an instant of *un*imagined reality is recaptured; but the writer simultaneously reveals himself and places an imagined family in focus through a kind of extended meditation. It is Agee's success in fusing all of these things in his meditation that sets *Let Us Now Praise Famous Men* off as a superior achievement.

The first paragraph is descriptive: "The rear edges of the house rest in part on stacked stones, in part on the dirt . . . forward edges . . . on thick rounded sections of logs." Here the writer attempts to give an accurate description. But the second paragraph shows an immediate shift to metaphor. The dirt beneath the house, a "cold plaque," is compared to a wall against which "a picture has been hung for years." Agee wonders to what other uses this land could have been put. Only by chance is it a home site; it could have been as easily "field, pasture, forest." The second paragraph then is imaginative: yet it is connected closely with the "reality" of a particular instant recalled which brought about the imagined extension.

A step further is taken in the third unit. Here Agee imagines how this house was built: "lumber of other land was brought rattling in yellow wagonloads and caught up between hammers." A house was built to "hold this shape of earth denatured: yet in whose history this house shall have passed soft and casually as a snowflake fallen on black spring ground, which thaws in touching." The construction and decay of all houses is suggested by these sentences, which reveal how the perceiver's mind works. Agee has used what he saw as a means to extend his awareness and to meditate about all men.

The fourth paragraph returns to the immediate scene, and in this long unit there is constant movement from the concrete to the abstract, or from what was almost "verbally photographed" to what was imagined. Here it becomes a matter of Agee's imagining how children of a particular family might act. He says, "There in the chilly and small dust . . . the subtle funnels of doodlebugs whose teasing, of a broomstraw, is one of the patient absorptions of kneeling childhood." The thought of the children is a personal reaction, yet part of the total experience as recalled. Inclusion of such mental reactions helps the reader to see as Agee did. Objects are described in their physical terms; for example: "an emptied and flattened twenty-gauge shotgun shell, its metal green, lettering still visible." But other objects lend themselves well to more imaginative description. For instance, Agee writes that a string of ants was "a long and slender infinitesimally rustling creek and system of ants in their traffic."

The "clean pine underside" of the house looked new to Agee, and this "fresh and bridal" appearance sets the stage for the fifth unit of this short section, the prose-poem. This poem, only a few lines in length, is a meditation about how quickly the expectations of those entering new homes are brought to ruin:

*(O therefore in the cleanly quiet, calm hope, sweet odor, awaiting, of each
new dwelling squared by men on air, be sorrowful, as of the sprung trap, the
slim wrist gnawn, the little disastrous fox:*
    *It stands up in the sun and the bride smiles: quite soon the shelves are
papered: the new forks taste in the food:*
    Ruin, ruin is in our hopes: nor hope, help, any healing:)

The sight of the lumber beneath the house, woven into the total experience, set such thoughts working in Agee's mind. The poem (prayer),
written after the experience, helps to clarify his actual feelings of that time
but also reveals Agee's later reactions. It adds to the understanding of the
writer's intentions throughout the book, one of those being to meditate
about all who must lead lives similar to those of the Gudgers.

His final two paragraphs concern themselves with the house proper and
its relation to the "room beneath." The house is "the flat scarce-lifted
stone, the roof and firmament." This underside, "shelter and graveyard
. . . and meditation space of children," is covered over by a "wide inch-
thick plat of wood, swept with straws and not seldom scrubbed, soaped and
spreaded with warmth of water." In this final paragraph, Agee incorporates
things observed at other times—how, for instance, the floor was cleaned.
Thus the meditation has become (by implication) one about all houses and
all children who play in and under them. Yet above all it remains a
meditation on Agee's original meditation.

Agee approached his subject matter with a devotion akin to traditional
religion as it approaches the worship of God. Erik Wensberg has noted that
an outline of *Famous Men* reads like the program for a Protestant church
service: "The book's design, presented in a kind of program at the front, is
that of a religious service. One moves from Verses (page 5) to Preamble
(page 7) to Inductions (page 359)—which begins, for no explicit reason
(with the Forty-second Psalm) . . . to the signification of the triumphal
recessional."[9]

One goal of *Famous Men* is to stress the writer's reverence for living
persons and existing things, yet Agee knew from the beginning of the
writing that the "texture" of the events that had been experienced must
ultimately remain inexplicable. It is, however, clear that events that are
inexplicable, those that do not shed their mystery, are often "dearer"—in
the words of Emerson—than events "we can see to the end of."[10] Such
inexplicability, Agee's wonder at the events he witnesses, is indirectly
responsible for the ultimate form of his text.

Agee's specialized uses of language are precipitated by the mystery of
the events written about. One might feel that parts of the language of this
text are rhetorical, in the sense of something stylistically added; but Agee's
involvement is always at the core, and that involvement necessitates un-

usual uses of language. Kenneth Burke's observations about the ubiquity of rhetoric in human situations are of assistance in explaining why Agee relied upon such rhetorical uses of language in this text.

Agee saw particular human beings as part of a divided human community. Burke argues that division within any community gives rise to a universal communicative situation, and that therefore rhetoric as such is found in all communicative situations. The more complex a situation is, the greater is the need for rhetorical devices when that situation is communicated. Rhetoric is not merely a calculated use of language and linguistic resources. It is also a means toward achieving social cohesion. Thus, when we read any section of *Famous Men* and are moved by it, the language in that section acts rhetorically. With such rhetoric Agee makes an indirect identification between his readers and subject. (Some parts of his text were first experimentally written in very plain prose that even a child would understand. Agee abandoned that method; however, had he used it, it too would be describable as a "rhetorical" structure.)[11]

Just as there can be courtship only insofar as there is division, so also will there be a need for rhetorical structure in proportion to the division within mankind. Rhetoric, Burke writes, is the mode of appeal essential for bridging the conditions of estrangement natural to society as we know it. Thus the rhetorical element becomes most important in a section such as "Colon: Curtain Speech." In "Colon," a generalized meditation about all who live in situations similar to those of the particular tenant families whom Agee knew, rhetorical structure is relatively more important than in a deliberately antipoetic section such as the "Work" chapter.

Because a rhetorical structure, resulting from unusual language uses, is significant throughout Agee's text and is a means whereby writer indirectly appeals to reader, the questions arises, To what degree may that rhetoric have been consciously planned? In one respect much of the rhetoric in *Famous Men* was not planned at all, for most of the text was *not* constructed in the manner that an orator might plan a speech in order to elicit a response from an audience. Yet as a document of Agee's responses to a particular situation, the text is intricately planned and executed. And while any desire to appeal to his readers may have been unconscious, the method of presenting the experience is a rhetorical one. Also, because Agee wanted to involve the reader as much as possible, the text was written with the possibility of its being read aloud in mind. Alliteration, metaphor, rhythm, and specialized vocabulary: all are facets of a rhetorical structure that resulted because of the writer's desire to suggest for the reader, as closely as verbally possible, the texture of experiences that he underwent. Agee's thoughts and acts were affected by interest in those about whom he wrote. Accordingly his use of language suggests an impassioned involvement with those about whom he wrote. Also because the text was written partly in disgust with a glib, more or less accepted "documentary" style that tended to oversimplify events, Agee's language contains an undercurrent of rebellion that contributes to its rhetorical appeal.

Agee was sure that most documentary writers did not become deeply enough involved (and such an accusation would apply to much of the writing that he himself had done for *Fortune* magazine). An example is relevant. If a person's pet is killed violently, the effect of the death upon that person is a fantastically complex event that ultimately cannot be adequately transformed into language. Especially the feelings of the owner are inexplicable; the death remains for him a mystery.[12]

A fundamental fact of *Famous Men* is Agee's personal involvement. Generally, the more intensely personal his insights (and accordingly the more difficult to verbalize), the more often there is a highly structured presentation. Burke suggests that often events such as those described by Agee must remain mysteries, only to be communicated by means of "incantation." Even then only a suggestion of the complexity of the felt emotions can be attained. Thus as a situation is more intensely felt, the need arises for a more comprehensive means of expressing that feeling; but unfortunately as the feeling increases the difficulty of communicating it increases also. Probably Agee did not feel as strongly about making an appeal to his readers (suggesting an identification between his reactions and the potential readers of the book, although that element is present) as he felt the need of making an identification with those about whom he wrote.

Identification in its simplest terms is a deliberate device, as used for instance by a politician. Franklin Roosevelt said, "You are farmers: I am a farmer myself." Agee ironically placed that quotation at the beginning of his "precis" about "Money," implying that identification is vastly more complicated when one is emotionally involved. Identification can be an end, "as when people earnestly yearn to identify themselves with some group or other." With such identification there is a partially idealistic motive, "somewhat compensatory to real differences or division, which the rhetoric of identification would transcend." It appears that such an idealistic motive was part of Agee's intent. In Burke's language, when one identifies himself with another, he becomes consubstantial with that person (or thing). In a written discourse a writer is faced with the problem of making the identification with another person or event clear, or at least apparent. Agee wants to suggest his identification with these farmers; yet he also (at least unconsciously) wants to set up an identification between himself and the other "intellectuals" who would read his text. For Burke, all structure as we know it, whether in speech or story, is a mode of identification. And such structure is a (possibly unconscious) appeal to the needs of a potential audience.[13] This is to say that while Agee had made a strong identification with the sharecroppers, the mystery of what he beheld, and the partly unconscious desire to establish an identification for the reader as well, also contributed to the rhetorical structure. Agee's method then had to become complex.

Because his impressions and imaginative wanderings are central, the text must ultimately be approached as poetry. The most obvious instance of Agee's radically subjective language being simultaneously factual, lyrical, and rhetorical is found in his "Colon: Curtain Speech." This section is an extended meditation about how each tenant farmer's consciousness is formed from a complexity of sensations. Written like an interior monologue, the prose of the speech is tightly organized, and highly formal at times. The rhythms of the passage are those of a pulpit delivery, and what contributes to the pleasure of reading it is its predictability of sentence structure. Key words and phrases tie the passage together, and in addition there is a constantly recurring pitch and stress pattern. However, the basic device employed to convey the number of items impinging upon human consciousness is, as noted earlier, a poetic one, the extended use of metaphor. Five dominant images recur throughout this passage: crucifixion, flower, prison, water, and star. These different images are woven together in an evocation of Agee's feelings about these tenant farmers. Agee's experiments, which began with the reality, the desire to get at the facts, to be *un*imaginative, finally make it absolutely necessary that he also include the facts of his own imagination. That too is a reality, a fact.

Despite flaws, which are in most instances the extensions of merits, Agee's elaborate text, above all, manifests the dignity of particular tenant farmers, holy individuals, as beheld and imagined by the writer. What he experienced (even as he composed the text) Agee attempted to give back to his readers. With a combination of poetic imagination and a disciplined technique, he evokes the reality of what had been experienced, but in a much more complex way than others might have been willing to attempt.

A comment made by Agee several years after *Famous Men* had been published serves well as summary of what his intentions must have been as he wrote this text. Indeed, it could be used as a summary of his artistic philosophy: "I dislike allegory and symbolism which are imposed on and denature reality as much as I love both when they bloom forth and exalt reality."[14] *Famous Men* is a successful demonstration of the controlled use of many diverse approaches including near–verbal photography as well as the use of imagination to clarify and honor reality as experienced and remembered. Agee's decision to include his reactions and feelings within the text provides the necessary framework. That presence is what finally makes this image of tenant farming accurate, and of lasting value. It is a portrait of a time and the times of composition, and it is timeless.

CHAPTER 8

JACK B. MOORE

The View from the Broom Closet
of the Regency Hyatt:
RICHARD WRIGHT AS A SOUTHERN WRITER

In his entertaining, illuminating, and authoritative essay, "The View from
the Regency Hyatt," my former mentor and the distinguished southern
literary historian C. Hugh Holman corrects those critics whose cultural
blinders permit them to see only one main strand in southern literature
and who treat that strand as though it were some primary fiber binding
together the remarkable fabric of southern writing.[1] Holman surveys and
briefly describes the various partial, "absolutist" views in turn and mentions a few writers who best or most popularly embody the particular kind
of literature that presumably dominates the southern literary terrain.

His point is that though each cadre of interpreters posits a single,
"monolithic" South that southern literature is most typically or essentially
about, no agreement exists among critics recognizing which one of these
Souths is preeminent. Some see only the "aristocratic South of broad lawns
and happy banjo-strumming Negroes," the South of Thomas Nelson Page
and Margaret Mitchell. Others have eyes only for the South of "apocalyptic
vision" dreamed first by abolitionist societies and not too long ago by
Robert Penn Warren in *Band of Angels*. "There is a South of industrialization, liberalism, and the middleclass democratic virtues . . . announced by
Henry Grady of Atlanta and documented by Howard Odum and his
cohorts . . . a South that is a degenerate, poverty-stricken world . . . the
South of Mark Twain's river towns. . . . And there is also a South which is a
lost paradise of order and stability, of honor and a religious view of
man . . . the South of the Vanderbilt Agrarians."

There is further a South rendered with joy through a "highly sophisticated and self-conscious literary technique" by Joyceans whom Holman
admires; but as a pluralist himself, in this excellent essay he counterbal-
ances the Joyceans with a group of less esoterically inclined social critics—
T. S. Stribling, Thomas Wolfe, Erskine Caldwell, and Flannery O'Connor.

Holman's essay is significant, I feel, not only because it provides such a witty, solid, and magisterial overview of southern literature but because in discussing some of the figures who dot the literary landscape of the South he mentions not one black writer. He clearly states the centrality of the black experience in the South, its cruelty, and the ways several white writers have to their credit treated it, but he refers to no black writers at all. I relate this omission not to berate Holman—who is perhaps the most perceptive of literary critics of the South, and who is furthermore a sensitive analyst of southern social conditions—but to note the typical invisibility of black writers in literary explorations of the region where black inhabitants have been politically and socially of extreme importance. One often finds in discussions of the southern literary heritage or of the southern culture, especially in the older, mellower reports of traditions such as southern hospitality and patrician rhetorical styles, strangely Nixonian gaps in the cultural record, caused by the assumption that southern traditions are white traditions. What southern blacks have accomplished has been cropped from the white picture, just as what might have been, say, their critique of southern hospitality has been rarely considered.

The black writer I wish to discuss in terms of his contribution to southern literature is Richard Wright, because I feel he wrote during the thirties fiction of high quality about the South and because much of the fiction he wrote during this period was set down when he was a Communist or Marxist and therefore offers a doubly special perspective on the South. I do not claim that my study presents the official black Marxist view of the South. Analysis of other black Marxist perceptions might very well yield other results, but I do suspect that my findings may suggest some modifications in standard views toward aspects of southern culture. For example, again using Holman's essay as a handy and quite orthodox source, I find that Henry Grady of Atlanta supposedly represented in his day "industrialization, liberalism, and all the middle-class democratic virtues." Yet W. E. B. Du Bois, another black Marxist who lived several decades in Grady's Atlanta, characterized Grady as at heart a conspiratorially reactionary oligarch, a fascist, and a racist.[2]

But it is with Wright's vision and artistic techniques that I will concern myself. I would like to start my analysis of Wright with how he presents the South in his stories, and how the ways in which he employs the South cast light upon the nature of his work during what was perhaps the most successfully productive period of his career. I will focus on seven pieces of long and short fiction he published in book form in *Uncle Tom's Children* and *Eight Men*,[3] stories he wrote during the years 1935–37, almost a decade after he moved to Chicago "taking a part of the South," as he recollected in *Black Boy*, "to transplant in alien soil."

Wright's South is stripped of the richness of subregional delineation often associated with southern literature. A cliché of southern studies is that there is not one South but many Souths, revealed in densely and disparately localized literary regions such as Faulkner's Yoknapatawpha, Wolfe's Asheville and his mountains, Warren's Louisiana, Cabell's or Styron's Virginia, each area a distinct place often with its own evocative history, possessing its own presumable mimetic resonance. An often stark and danger-filled land stretches throughout most of Wright's stories, but points on it are unrelated to each other except by sharing horror. The landscapes in Wright's stories do not suggest for the reader a continuous region. The land seems to exist only in each story unconnected to the land of other stories, ready to disappear, as so many of the characters in the stories depart or die and are unheard of again. Once, in "Bright and Morning Star," the "rich black earth" is referred to, and in that story and in several others the clayey soil and patches of trees are mentioned, but nothing distinctly regional seems to bind the land together to give it continuity, to distinguish it from other southern regions whose clay bakes under a ferocious sun. Place names either real or made up are rare, and it is with surprise that the reader finds Memphis alluded to in "Bright and Morning Star," for it is one of the few points on the map localizing Wright's southern world.

Along with their disconnected geography, the stories are genealogically thin. Each story is about a different character in a different place, living with a different family, with few memories of the past. The younger characters have mothers and fathers and in "Down by the Riverside" there is a grandmother (another grandmother is mentioned in "Long Black Song" but does not appear in the story), but no deep pool of family experience appears to exist that individual characters can tap or contribute to. None of the stories contains the sense of sustained family and personal history that, for instance, lends such substantiality to Katherine Anne Porter's linked episodes in "The Old Order." Wright's stories tend to spotlight brief periods in the lives of people with only a very limited and personal sense of the past. His characters, black and white, also exist totally outside the plantation world that seems to serve as a focal symbol, either in glory or decay, for so many of the "monolithic" views of southern life Professor Holman describes. Wright's blacks don't try to destroy the plantation, his whites don't exist in the shadow of its decay or mock its aristocratic gentility, and no one reminisces about its follies or grandeur, as in Lillian Hellman's plays. The plantation myth is simply irrelevant to everyone's existence.

What connects the stories to each other and to the South that Wright insists he is describing in them? One recurrent image is the hot sun, which glows pleasantly and briefly in "Big Boy Leaves Home" when the black boys horsing around let it shine squarely in their faces and against their softly closed lids. But more often the sun is hostile, as it glares "pitilessly" later in the same story on the boys who are now sick with fear. In "Fire and Cloud" the "dying" sun smears a window bloody red. Rain beats down as often as the sun in Wright's South, though rarely does it nourish life. It rots seeds in "Down by the Riverside," causes floods in the same story and in "Silt," collects discomfortingly in "Big Boy Leaves Home" and "Bright and Morning Star."

Southern food is a more pleasant part of the traditional South, providing a slender but distinct connection between Wright's stories. Food is not plentiful, in fact in "Fire and Cloud" it is so hard to come by that poor whites and blacks are ready to demonstrate to obtain it from the government. Yet food is socially important to Wright's South since it is one clear way characters in the culture achieve emotional communication with each other. People want other people to eat well so that for a time in the middle of trouble the other will have been satisfied, in part physically but more importantly emotionally: food given is a sign of affection. The meals eaten are spare but substantial, filled with blackeyed peas, heaping plates of greens, buttermilk, fat meat, salty ribs, cornbread, peach cobbler, and plenty of molasses. The preparing and eating of food is a way family members communicate their caring, so it seems appropriate that in "Fire and Cloud" whites join blacks protesting for the food that shows their common need.

Each of Wright's southern stories presents a single critical moment in the life of one black person who clearly belongs if not to a distinctly delineated region, then to a particular family made up of parents or a husband and wife and children. The central character relates strongly to the family nexus even when, as in "Long Black Song," the story concerns the betrayal of one family member by another, or when, as in "Big Boy Leaves Home" or "Down by the Riverside" or "Almos' a Man," the protagonist must leave his family. Each story focuses on one family and there is little connection between families within a story and none from one story to another. In several stories, such as "Silt" and "Long Black Song," the central family unit is totally isolated from other families.

The southern world of Richard Wright's stories is a world of people in family constellations whose relationships to the inimical land on which they live is shallow, not simply in the sense that they do not belong intensely to the land but in the sense that there is not much in or on the land for them to belong to. The land is no foundation for them. Their dreams have never blossomed in the land, have never accumulated into something grand or substantial. These people have never been able to get much from the land or put much that is lasting into it. Their roots have driven deeply no place into the soil of a distant region. When the young men of this land leave their homes as Big Boy does or the protagonist of "Almos' a Man," they leave with no regrets, and one senses the land will not miss them. The inhabitants of the land in these stories, especially the young men, are easily displaced persons. Sometimes they displace themselves.

The force containing the black people of Wright's region is oppressive white society. All the stories show black men or women attempting to grow up or live decently and instead banging into the white world that bounds their black existence, tightly restricting them. In the seven stories under study, perhaps only three white characters act justly toward the blacks, or with integrity, and these characters are very sketchily described. At least one of them, the Communist in "Fire and Cloud," is probably not from the South, and two are poor whites. Without exception all seven stories deal with situations where whites exploit or kill blacks.

One critically unnoticed technique Wright uses to emphasize the split between southern blacks and whites is the way he treats dialogue. The blacks in Wright's southern stories all speak the same somewhat phonetically spelled dialect that identifies them as black and southern but not as belonging to any particular subregion. The whites more often than not speak in no dialect. For example, in "Almos' a Man" the young black protagonist and his family speak in the same generally southern or perhaps generally southern black accent. The whites in the story—the shop owner who sells the protagonist the gun that he hopes is to make him a man, and the farmer whose mule the young black boy kills, practicing, he thinks, to be a man—do not speak in accent though they are from the same region. The linguistic difference is especially apparent in "Down by the Riverside," where all the blacks speak in dialect and all the whites regardless of class or occupation talk in the same bland, standard fashion. All the whites control all the blacks; so all white masters speak the same. The usual absence of a white dialect coupled with the special accent of the blacks further emphasizes the separateness of the two races, and also suggests that the whites are aliens to the region the blacks inhabit since they do not speak the language of the land.

This land the whites dominate and within which they attempt to crush black prosperity or even survival sometimes, is rural land. Only one story, "Fire and Cloud," seems to take place in a community of any size. The way of life shown as taking place in this rural and plantationless land offers nothing to reinforce any decent agrarian myth for white people or black. It is a mean way of life squeezed dry of justice or art. There is little support in Wright's stories for Robert Penn Warren's old claim in *I'll Take My Stand* that "the small town and farm . . . is where [the Negro] still chiefly belongs by temperament and capacity; there he has less the character of a 'problem' and more the status of a human being who is likely to find in agricultural and domestic pursuits the happiness that his good nature and easy ways incline him to as an ordinary function of his being." The "South of the Vanderbilt Agrarians," which Holman states "has been magnificently celebrated in some of the best poetry and fiction of the region as a repository of the finest traditions of the old South," is not celebrated in Wright's fiction. Of the three black small-farm owners in these stories, two are killed by whites and the other is led off like a slave by the white man to whom he owes more money than he will ever be able to repay. In this last story, "Silt," the exploitation of the black farmer is made sharply tragic by being played off against the biblical myth of the Flood. The black farmer finds no new start possible in his flooded-out world. All of Wright's chief black characters are poor or killed, and some are both, in this rural or (in one instance) small-town land. Those who are farmers find no profit and no fine traditions in the land. No aristocratic or guilt-ridden gentlefolk or petit bourgeois lawyers try to help the blacks achieve justice, as they do in Faulkner's South or Harper Lee's.

Nowhere in Wright's fiction of this period with the possible exception of "Bright and Morning Star" can one find white farmers characterized as they are in the Vanderbilt Agrarian myth. Wright need not have been responding directly to *I'll Take My Stand*, though that work was under constant attack from the left as he was creating his images of the South. Sporadic shots from the guerilla warfare between the Agrarians and the left front crackled around Wright throughout the decade. As a black southerner and as a Marxist he could only have viewed the Agrarian's Last Stand as some other version of the pastoral. Claims such as John Crowe Ransom's that "the farmers are the freest citizens in this country; the most whole, therefore the most wholesome" seem like cruel mendacities when placed beside Wright's depiction of hard and cunning white farmers in "Silt" and "Almos' a Man." Ransom's statement is from his May 1936 rebuttal in *Scribner's* to V. F. Calverton's article in the same magazine titled "The Bankruptcy of Southern Culture." Ransom goes on to say that the southern farmers are "the perfect examples of the propertied man . . . whose business relations are personal, moral, and neighborly." In the South, he says, they constitute the most "real bulwark against those revolutionaries under which men surrender their general integrity and become pure functions, or abstractions, or soldiers in an army," the Communists and Socialists. Wright's fiction clearly and violently contradicts this assertion, offering in its place a white farmer's world of hard bargains, exploitation, and murder.

If the glories of some real or imagined agrarian tradition seem lacking from Wright's South, the sustaining potential of religion, certainly as much a staple of southern life as fatback, blackeyed peas, and sowbelly, is not. As a black man of the thirties trying to understand black history, and as a Marxist, Wright was unfixed in his attitude toward black religion. In his "Blueprint for Negro Literature," one version of which appeared in 1937, in the short-lived periodical *New Challenge*, he called attention to the

Negro church as one of the two cultural forces (the other was Negro folklore) which "helped to clarify his consciousness" as a Negro and to "create emotional attitudes which are conducive to action." The struggle for religion "on the plantation between 1820–60 was nothing short of a struggle for human rights." This struggle, he asserted, was progressive "until religion began to ameliorate and assuage suffering and denial." Even in his own day of the thirties the ambivalent Wright had to admit there were "millions of Negroes . . . whose only guide to personal dignity comes through the archaic morphology of Christian salvation." Thus the black church could sustain and contort at the same time, aiding the race in its fight for survival but also conditioning it to passivity and acceptance of earthly conditions, producing a strong but stunted sense of self.

When the black victim of "Down by the Riverside" starts his ordeal and thinks "nobody but God could see him through this," we know Wright is either being hideously ironic by suggesting that only God could stomach such a terrible experience, or we suspect that Wright is simply demonstrating that reliance on God is the response of a fool, that reliance on God is reliance on nothing. The grandmother in this same story also verbalizes her dependence upon God, praying sincerely along with Elder Murray's empty and formulaic prayers. We know throughout the scene that no succor is on its way; the sucker is the black man who relies on God.

A number of critics have mentioned that many Negro hymns, what Du Bois called the sorrow songs, are sung or alluded to in Wright's southern stories. In "Bright and Morning Star" and "Fire and Cloud" they emphatically bring images of strength and hope in their words, but the symbolic value of individual songs needs to be examined carefully in the context of individual stories. In "Big Boy Leaves Home" joyous black boys happily chant "Dis train bound for glory" at the start of their day. Soon three of the boys will be dead with no glory and the fourth will be bound for Chicago in a truck. The hymn in the story is followed immediately by one boy's fart and another boy's remark, "Jeeesus, tha sho stinks!" So much for the religious life of the young.

The reliance upon religion of both Reverend Taylor in "Fire and Cloud" and the mother called "Sue" or "Aunt Sue" in "Bright and Morning Star" is another, more complicated matter. Both these older characters are strongly religious, and clearly their religion has enabled them to develop strong self and race consciousness. But both seem to transcend if not totally to shed their Christian heritage when they finally take political stands. Sue, for example, thinks, as she is about to participate in the great militant political sacrifice of her life, that though it had been a "great boon . . . to cling to [Christ] . . . and suffer without a mumbling word," that because of a "new and terrible vision . . . the wrongs and sufferings of black men had taken the place of Him nailed to the cross." She yearns to test her newly annealed political faith through an act of martyrdom. Reverend Taylor's Christianity in "Fire and Cloud" leads him similarly beyond Christian meekness. "Freedom belongs to the strong," the story concludes, which is another way of saying "the strong shall inherit the earth." Taylor is a fictional precursor of Martin Luther King in his militant and aggressive pacifism, and "Fire and Cloud" seems far more realistic now in showing the force of assertive religious-political action than perhaps it was when originally written.

Finally, in this general discussion of what Wright's imagined South looked like and what kind of people inhabited it, I should point out that the one constant overriding emotion felt by the black characters in it is not hope or pride but rather fear, sometimes overcome, sometimes not, but invariably experienced. Eleanor Roosevelt once wrote in a review that *Uncle Tom's Children* was about the "tragedy of fear," and she was correct. No protagonist in any of the stories is free from fear. The strongest subdue it and sometimes die as a result or continue to fight for justice anyway. Still Wright's South is a land of fear.

I would like now to examine several of Wright's southern stories briefly, in order to comment concerning what they reveal about the nature of Wright's South and about the art that created it.

Most interpretations of "Big Boy Leaves Home" focus upon it as an initiation rite, and indeed the boys' ritual withdrawal into the woods and their trip to the deep pool beyond a barbed wire fence, together with numerous other details, reveal Wright consciously or unconsciously following almost step by step the initiatory monomyth described by Joseph Campbell in *The Hero with a Thousand Faces*. But the black boys lolling naked in the sunshine warming their blood who suddenly see a white woman who has almost magically appeared on the other side of their swimming hole's bank, are not inexperienced innocents—they immediately know their danger. When they see the woman "poised" opposite them, "her hair lit by the sun," they cover their genitals with their hands, one suspects not so much to shield their nakedness as to protect themselves from castration. The seductive and dangerous white woman backs slowly out of sight and shortly after, when Big Boy goes after his clothes, suddenly reappears much closer to him. Her disappearance had been complete and sudden and so is her reappearance, and the prose of this passage makes her movements very strange, almost mysterious. She is the "White Witch" that James Weldon Johnson (another black southerner often omitted from literary discussions of the South) warned black children about in his poem about her, an attractive but diabolic wraith, a white *belle dame sans merci*. She is the white woman that black boys were trained by the society around them to fear and to be attracted to, for does she not, as depicted in Wright's

"The Ethics of Living Jim Crow," appear to possess great beauty and secret, forbidden sexual powers? She is inevitable in the lives of the boys, an inescapable fact of their existence. They were destined to meet her and to be punished for it. Three of the boys are killed for her.

While running away from the white mob pursuing him Big Boy lives in a cave, a kiln dug in the hillside where he hopes he can wait until the next day for a ride. While hiding he is forced to watch in silence his friend Bobo's lynching. Wright's South is an unremittingly violent land filled not only with sudden racial murder but with slow tortures and beatings, old women kicked senseless, a son's eardrums popped in front of his mother, a minister flogged, a young black man's leg cracked by a crowbar. Lynching seems the ultimate violence, however, because it is a communal act practiced quite openly as really a political technique—much like a rally with attendant fun and ritualized hoopla—insuring while dramatizing the white-controlled social order of the South and providing rewards for the party faithful. It is of course a staple of southern fiction and by no means unique to Wright's fictive world.

It might be illuminating very briefly to compare Wright's lynch scene to examples from two other southern writers of his day, William Faulkner and Erskine Caldwell. One major difference between Faulkner's "Dry September," Caldwell's "Saturday Afternoon," and "Big Boy Leaves Home" is that the two white writers focus on their white characters, the victimizers, and Wright focuses on the victimized black. The other chief difference is that Wright describes the actual lynching in painful detail whereas Faulkner and Caldwell omit close particulars. Faulkner's story focuses successively upon a white barber who would like to prevent the story's lynching but cannot; the white woman who has been supposedly "attacked, insulted, frightened" by a black man; and McLendon, the white racist who organizes and presides at the lynching, which is, however, not described. The two sections of the story devoted exclusively to the experiences of the white woman and the three sections in which McLendon functions make these two characters much more substantial in the story than is the accused and lynched black man, Will Mayes, who becomes a minor character compared to the whites.

Caldwell's "Saturday Afternoon" is a work of remarkably powerful social criticism—exactly what Holman commends Caldwell for in the "The View from the Regency Hyatt." Caldwell communicates the horror of lynching through indirect means, mainly through describing the day of a butcher named Tom Denny, who attends the lynching and who on the day of the event is first shown napping on a meatblock with a "cool hunk of rump steak" under his head, sometimes spitting tobacco juice into a cigar box full of sawdust. The actual lynching is described sketchily in a short paragraph whose brevity results not from the reticence of the narrator, who represents a communal point of view, but from his lack of concern at this point. The story ends with Tom back again chopping meat at the meat block.

The angle of narration of the lynching in "Big Boy Leaves Home" is Big Boy himself, confronting the reader with an agonized and trapped Negro who is in hiding, watching another Negro with whom he closely identifies being tortured, while he himself is utterly powerless. Wright describes the carnival atmosphere of the lynching as does Caldwell, while Faulkner isolates his lynching from the community and makes it an act perpetrated by a carful of white men acting secretly. Only Wright closely describes the lynching itself, impressionistically through Big Boy's eyes, noting how the hot tar smells, how Bobo's body twitches while still alive, how the flames shoot from Bobo's body, how Bobo writhes, how his screams rise one on top of the other "each shriller and shorter than the last." And only Wright describes women participating in the lynch ritual, showing several at the scene including the mysterious and attractive white woman who precipitated the affair. This inclusion makes more perverse the white community's corruption and underscores the sick sexuality inherent in the politics of lynching.

At the conclusion of Wright's story Big Boy escapes from his hiding place in a truck. Dan McCall suggests in his very helpful book *The Example of Richard Wright* that Big Boy is heading for Chicago where he "will become Bigger [Thomas]".[4] This is doubtful because Big Boy is neither as ignorant of whites nor as insecure as Bigger Thomas. He is the product of social conditions different from those producing Bigger. Big Boy has a strong and competent mother and father who help his escape, he has a strong sense of self, and he has had the experience of the black community wholeheartedly aiding him to escape. He does not appear to hate blacks as does Bigger at least in the first section of *Native Son*.

Though born in the South Bigger has no experience of the South: he has lived a northern, urban existence. His connection to the South is highly tenuous. Bigger tells Jan Erlone he was born in Mississippi and that he attended southern schools through the sixth grade, but he does not employ the southern dialect Wright devised for his black southerners in the short stories. He possesses no memories of the South beyond his remark to Jan that when he was a "kid" his father was killed in a riot "in the South." And he does not even say what kind of riot. One would assume it was racial, but he gives no further information about it to Jan or, later, to Max, who would assuredly have used the detail in his peroration had he known it. When Max digs into Bigger's life to find the reasons for his behavior, he treats Bigger as a product of the Black Belt, but it is Chicago's Black Belt, not Mississippi's. The "dazzling" civilization Max refers to that allures and taunts blacks in a crippling double bind that so often breaks into violence is the civilization of America's "urban centers." A newspaper in Jackson offers evidence of Bigger's life in the South, but the supposed facts it gives are clearly spurious. Wright probably made Bigger southern to add demographic verisimilitude to the novel, but the texture of Bigger's relationship to the South is noticeably thin compared to the dense and deadly environment that surrounds him in the urban North. Big Boy is hunted by whites, but he is not haunted by whites, as is Bigger. Big Boy kills three times—a man, a snake, and a dog—but each time for necessity and self-defense and not from panic and hate, as does Bigger twice. "Big Boy Leaves Home" is a story of the South and its terrors, not of the North.

"Down by the Riverside," the second story in *Uncle Tom's Children*, is often criticized for what McCall calls its "serious plotting difficulties." Edward Margolies also says that "the plot becomes too contrived; coincidence is piled on coincidence, and the inevitability of his protagonist's doom does not ring quite true."[5] Here I believe is an instance where viewing Wright in the context of southern literature may illuminate the value of his work. A strong element of southern fiction is its tendency toward what Richard Chase called the romance, toward the fabulous, toward the grotesque. Wright's early work is usually described as naturalistic, which it is, but only if the fabulous and grotesque conclusion to a novel such as Norris's *McTeague* is considered quintessentially naturalistic. Wright, like Faulkner in *Sanctuary* or Carson McCullers in *Reflections in a Golden Eye*, often employs expressionistic techniques in his fiction. The characters and objects and events in his stories—in a story such as "Down by the Riverside"—are manipulated and distorted and contorted to suggest an inner reality that the surface of the world he describes masks. The outer world projects and symbolizes an inner world. This is as typical of the technique of the romance as it is of the expressionistic play—for example, one such as O'Neill's *The Emperor Jones*, which is also a highly contrived tale of inescapable black destruction. "Down by the Riverside" displays the inside of one black human being's South, a world that is completely perverse, where only the worst that can possibly happen will happen. The plot is contrived because it reflects the black existence Wright portrays as absolutely rigged in the South, the victim's doom does not quite ring true because there is no reason for it—beyond the victim's blackness.

At one point in the story the narrative explicitly states that the victim sees real objects "like dim figures in a sick dream." The entire story could be seen as a sick dream, a dream that distorts while it reveals reality. Mann—the victim—and his wife are trapped by a flood. Mann sends a friend out to buy a boat but the friend can't—instead he steals a white boat from one of the most notorious white bigots in town. Here the long reach of coincidence seems to exceed Wright's artistic grasp only if you ignore the inevitability of the doom awaiting black Mann in his southern land, if you forget that disaster will meet him at every turn for no rational reason at all.

Mann rows through a totally confusing, dark and flooded nightmarish world that he is trapped in and will not be able to leave because this too is inevitable for him, born a victim: "To all sides of Mann the flood rustled, gurgled, droned, glistening blackly like an ocean of bubbling oil. Above his head the sky was streaked with faint grey light. . . . All around he was ringed in by walls of solid darkness."

Mann's wife is pregnant, but her body carries death and not life: she and her baby both die. Nothing happens as it should in the story. Seeds rot in the wet ground. When Mann tries to escape from the flood, his stolen boat bumps into the house of the racist to whom the boat belongs, and Mann kills him. At the hospital Mann is forced to serve on a gang shoring up a levee until it breaks, and then he must help rescue other flooded-out white families. After this work is done he is told one more white family remains in the dark, and inevitably it is the family of the racist Mann has killed. Compelled against his desires to rescue this family, Mann is taken to them by another obsessionally helpful Negro. He is recognized by the dead man's son (whose life he saves), ultimately accused, and condemned. Relentlessly at point after point in his dream of life Mann is battered closer to his doom. Born a victim, a loser, he cannot even get a drink of water in the midst of a flood.

Mann acts out dreams within dreams, for example the white dream of the black savior. Handed a piece of damp paper by a white colonel and told, "That's the address of a woman with two children who called in for help. . . . If you and that [black] boy think you can save 'em, do what you can," Mann functions as the trusty retainer asked to bail out missy once more. Mann carries an axe into the room where the woman huddles against a wall, "her arms about her two children. Her eyes closed. Her little girl's head lay on her lap." He looms over the trio with his axe raised, his body taut, a potent black man ready to kill innocent white womanhood and innocent white babes: this nightmare is as old as the early Indian captivity and escape narratives and was redreamed by some of the more virulent antiabolitionists. Typically, the woman's husband is powerless to come to her aid: here, he is dead. Ironically, posters for the filmed version of *Native Son* would later depict a variant, related dream: black Bigger (played by Wright!) carrying Mary Dalton, limp as Fay Wray in King Kong's arms, down the cellar to her destruction.

Mann is himself killed without a trial by the whites he had saved from the flood. One commentary says he then "chooses to try to escape" and thereby finally rebels like an existential hero,[6] but I feel he chooses nothing in the story, that all choice is beyond his control. He runs away from soldiers about to execute him the way a person runs from any enemy in a dream—futilely, not really moving out of range at all. When life is out of control, you can't escape your fate. The worst will happen for life has contrived it so, this story says. Life is fixed against the victim and Mann is the victim. One may object and say but it isn't always that way, just as one can complain that the whites in this story are incredibly bad, wicked in a way that all whites never are. But these objections miss the expressionistic depiction Wright aims at in the story, which is true to the nightmare reality of Mann's southern existence.

I have tried to suggest some benefits that can be derived from viewing the bulk of Wright's short fiction during the thirties as a product of his southern black heritage, by analyzing some of the subjects and techniques he employed to communicate his vision of the South. Examining his short fiction as a prelude to his longer works or as steps along the way of his disenchantment with communism or his attraction to existentialism yields definite insights into his artistry. But these ways of treating Wright's work are also illuminated by recognizing the southern tradition out of which he emerged, which he left in the early forties but to which he returned in *The Long Dream*, published in 1958.

His later works feature many and complicated portraits of women characters (Bigger's mother, Mary Dalton, Mrs. Dalton, and Bessie in *Native Son* alone) that might for critical profit be placed alongside the equally fascinating gallery of southern black women in these early stories, just as his southern black women could be compared to a number of similar black and white women created by white southern writers. It would be interesting to compare languid, sleepy, sensuous Sarah in "Long Black Song," with her dream of white men killing black and black killing white, and her other dream of black and white men gladly together on green fields, to Eula Varner or Lena Grove, two other earth mothers. Sue in "Bright and Morning Star" seems a black Amazon compared to Berenice in McCullers's *Member of the Wedding* (who was played in the film version, revealingly enough, by an unthreatening Ethel Waters). Killing one white Judas and aiding her black son to sacrifice himself in his attempt to achieve a new society, Sue seems also almost a conscious counterfoil to Faulkner's Dilsey, who, as characterized by Addison Gayle, "attempts to hold the white family together . . . [and is] the foundation of a dying institution. While suffering insult and abuse, she survives by virtue of patience and submissiveness."[7] Sue also contrasts with Wright's own mother as he described her in "The Ethics of Living Jim Crow," who beat her son Richard with a barrel stave to teach him to submit to whites and stay alive. Sue is very much in the tradition of Sojourner Truth and Harriet Tubman. Both Sue and Reverend Taylor in "Bright and Morning Star" are also precursors of real southern black men and women like Martin Luther King and Fannie Lou Hamer who employed a militant black Christianity as part of their political strategy.

The political analysis of Wright's fiction gains greatly from being seen in its southern context. Much has been written about the supposedly super-imposed or obtrusive emphasis upon the Communist party in "Bright and Morning Star" and "Fire and Cloud," and upon the way in each story that Wright portrays a black-white union that does not seem historically justi-fied: Rickels and Rickels say in their book on Wright that in " 'Fire and Cloud' . . . the forces that create the black-white coalition at the end come from outside the world of the story."[8] The endings to these stories seem clearly more prophetic than realistic, suggesting a possible strategy to be employed later. Wright's vision of black and white together, overcoming oppression, could be seen in the South of the sixties, although white labor was not at that time in the forefront of the justice parade as he hoped it would be. At any rate the emphasis on the Communist party in each story is rather slight. The party functions more as a generalized force fighting for equality and advancing toward the goal of poor black and white unity than as a doctrinaire political organization with a clearly articulated political economic plan. The party is what brings blacks and poor whites together, but it represents for neither group a call for collectivization or for the expropriation of land. The party is a biracial force seeking Christian stan-dards of humanity as the basis for southern life but disavowing the sup-posedly Christian call for passivity in combating injustice. The party is more a spiritual or moral symbol than a fully developed political reality in these stories. The Reverend Taylor and Sue become party adherents by traveling the black Christian path and going beyond it—but not by totally rejecting it. They know neither Karl Marx nor Earl Browder. To confuse the party as it existed in the thirties with the party as Wright employs it in these stories is to mistake a real institution for the symbol it has become in a work of art. My point here is not to draw away from Wright as a Marxist but to draw closer to him as an artist—a southern artist.

Wright wrote the stories that I have been discussing while he was a member of the Communist party, but I would like to stress that in his southern fiction Wright created as an artist first and not as a party member. Indeed as a good party member this seemed his primary task. As Earl Browder stated to the assembled members of the First American Writers' Conference (16 April 1935)—which Wright attended and participated in— "the first demand of the Party upon its writer members is that they shall be good writers, constantly better writers so they can really serve the Party. We do not want to take good writers and make bad strike leaders of them." But a more powerful influence upon Wright, because he had the authority that derives from being recognized as a distinguished writer, was James T. Farrell, who seems to have served Wright as a model of the engaged and yet objective artist. Farrell aided Wright in many personal and immediate ways, and he was also persistent during these exciting years in campaigning for the right of the revolutionary artist to remain true to his craft despite the often shrill and shifting demands of his ideological comrades. Farrell also spoke at the First Writers' Conference, and according to Michel Fabre in *The Unfinished Quest of Richard Wright*[9] talked about the revolutionary story, defending art against propaganda. Wright was impressed by what he heard, and Fabre conjectures that he revised some of his fiction in light of Farrell's remarks. But Fabre also states that Wright revised parts of "Big Boy Leaves Home" and "Down by the Riverside" after reading Henry James's *Prefaces*. Considering what Farrell says about James as an interpreter of morals in *Literature and Morality*, I am not certain he would have approved. But the point is that Wright during the thirties at the height of his involvement with communism was primarily a writer and not an ideologue, so that one should not go to his works expecting to find worked out any doctrinaire program defining the revolutionary potential of blacks in the South. Like Farrell, Wright wished to report with artistry what he saw, avoiding what Farrell called in an article appearing in the 18 August 1936 *New Masses* "revolutionary sentimentalism" and "mechanically applied materialism."

At the same time I would not want to discount Wright's involvement with Marxism and the Communist party. I think he was personally fortunate in forming the link he did in his Chicago years with the party, and clearly, radical thought provided him with important insights and theories that he would weave throughout his career into his work along with his own particular brand of political thought.

Moreover, Wright's southern stories skillfully probed a problem vexing radical theorists still today, and the depth of his probing is possible, I think, because he was an artist and a southerner and a Marxist. The problem, very simply and even crudely stated, is whether, in the struggle to overcome capitalistic oppression in the United States, to treat blacks as a separate nation within the nation with distinct and exceptional—even unique— difficulties, or whether to identify the black struggle for liberation precisely with the class struggle and to treat black workers essentially as members of the mass of proletariat.

In his classic 1935 study *Black Reconstruction*, W. E. B. Du Bois constantly referred to the freed slaves who inhabited the southern rural land as "black proletariat," thus suggesting that their situation was strongly analogous to that of the white proletariat, though not necessarily identically the same. Du Bois at this time saw black liberation as an aspect of the proletariat's class struggle. Wright instead viewed many of the blacks in his southern stories as representatives of the peasantry, or as descended from and conditioned to a peasant class. One hears much of the proletarian writers of the thirties, but in works such as "Silt" and "Long Black Song" and "Down by the Riverside," Wright was dealing with a peasant class, which is a different revolutionary matter altogether. The black peasants he describes are diffused throughout rural areas, possess political rights more limited than those of the proletariat, are not a part of the concentration of workers in urban industrial centers, live a less technologically oriented life than the city proletariat, work with simple tools and occasionally but rarely with machines they therefore could neither stop nor seize control of, and generally have a more limited political awareness, partly due to the physical difficulty of organizing them or disseminating information to them.

The black rural world Wright described in his fiction of the midthirties was the southern world he had seen at closest hand early in the twenties when he took a swing through Mississippi with an insurance salesman–itinerant preacher named W. Mance. This world of black peasantry existed in America only in the South and only a southern writer would have firsthand knowledge of it. Unmechanized and feudal, the world had not changed at all in the thirties, as statistics showing the number of black tenant- and cropper-operated farms reveals, together with figures demonstrating the low degree of mechanization on southern farms during the twenties and thirties.[10] Now there is a black proletariat in the South, in the cities and on farms, but not when Wright wrote.

Wright noted in *Twelve Million Black Voices* that life in the Black Belt was in many respects like a feudal system, so it is only logical that he would depict many of its black inhabitants as peasantry. In an explanation of "Long Black Song" he explicitly stated that this work was to be a "social comment . . . an indictment of the conditions of the south." Sarah, the woman in the story, he said he saw as a "simple peasant."[11] He was not using this term peasant as a pejorative, but as a way to place people in a specific political-economic category, which is dissimilar to the category of proletariat. It turns out, incidentally, that in viewing the southern rural blacks as peasants he was following the thought of Karl Marx, who in his letter to Frederick Engels dated 11 January 1860, compared southern blacks to serfs. He follows also Lenin, who in his "Capitalism in Agriculture in the United States" (1915) examined the black masses engaged in tenant farming or sharecropping in the Black Belt as a social phenomenon parallel to the feudal "labor service" system which existed in tsarist Russia. Wright seems to have read neither of these analyses and appears to have derived his conclusions from his immediate experience around the Delta during the early twenties. So that in treating many of his southern blacks as peasantry, he operated as an artist basing his perception upon personal observation, and not as a theoretician.

Wright was early a southern writer, and his early fiction is part of the southern tradition. He underscored the regionalism of his fiction by including as an epigraph to *Uncle Tom's Children* a verse from the popular song

"Is It True What They Say about Dixie?" which in the context of the stories that follow becomes one of the most hilariously and hideously ironic songs ever written. Wright turns the song into the cruelest possible parody of what it supposedly glorifies, in much the same way Jimi Hendrix would later churn "The Star Spangled Banner" into the frightening sound of a murderous bomber detonating its explosives and strafing with machine guns. "Is it true what they say about Dixie?" the song asks innocently. "Does the sun really shine all the time? / Do sweet magnolias blossom at everybody's door, / Do the folks keep eating possum, till they can't eat no more? / Is it true what they say about Swanee? / Is a dream by that stream so sublime? / Do they laugh, do they love, like they say in ev'ry song? . . . If it's true that's where I belong."

Well, the sun doesn't shine all the time in Wright's Dixie, and when it shines chances are it is shining either pitilessly or it is a dying sun spreading its bloody rays. The magnolias don't always blossom but the trees do bear strange hanging fruit sometimes. Stomachs aren't often filled with possum and the river's flooding or has dead bodies in it. The dreams by the stream are sour with defeat and death, and there isn't much time or opportunity to love. "If it's true, that's where I belong," the song says. Wright did not belong in the white-dominated South, could not stomach it and could not be stomached by it. Black southern writers from Frederick Douglass to John A. Williams have often left their Dixie homeland and have rarely gone home again. Wright went to Chicago and then left that city for New York, and left New York for foreign exile. One cannot blame him. The South of his day would have been a dangerous place for him, and the North, while less overt about its bigotry, was also a land of constant humiliation: during his lifetime he could never get his hair cut in Manhattan.

He was nonetheless at one time a southern writer. With the exception of *Native Son*, his most consistently good work is contained in his stories of the South. His art was nourished in some strange ways by his southern connection, just as his art fed back, though often unacknowledged, into the mainstream of southern writing. The South is there in him and he is in it, like it or not. When he was searching for his roots in black Africa, in Ghana, he was plagued by the feeling that he was being treated like an American by the people he wanted to be his brothers. In a weird meeting I had years ago in Africa with a Ghanian citizen who was a subchief in Aburi and had been a high official in Kwame Nkrumah's government and in the military government that replaced it, and who was also originally British, as fat and white as Sydney Greenstreet in *The Maltese Falcon*, I was told about the stomach sickness Wright experienced during his stay in the then Gold Coast. "He didn't like Kenkie," the London chief told me, chuckling. Kenkie is the local staple food, thick and glutinous and tasting like a cross between sour tamale dough and mahogany. "He didn't like Kenkie—he preferred his pork chops and gravy." I could understand. Pork chops and gravy and blackeyed peas and cornbread and molasses—sorghum molasses. Even in Ghana in 1953, Richard Wright belonged a little bit to the South. That he could not live there and that as a major artist he wrote so comparatively little of it is unfortunate. But he did write of the American South; and what he did write in the thirties as a southerner exiled or exiling himself from his people's land should be acknowledged as belonging to the southern tradition and valued for what it is really worth.

CHAPTER 9

GLENDA HOBBS

Starting Out in the Thirties:

HARRIETTE ARNOW'S LITERARY GENESIS

The surging of interest in the southern rural poor during the 1930s was a mixed blessing for fledgling writer Harriette Simpson Arnow, whose fascination with Kentucky hill people predated the depression years. The revival of southern letters now termed a renaissance coincided with Americans' riveting attention on poor whites, whose perennial poverty made them likely symbols of a failed economic system. Writers with varying talents and intentions depicted their plight; most, like Erskine Caldwell and John Steinbeck, attempted in different ways to document their degradation, evoke anger and thereby inspire change. Harriette Arnow had no such wish. She sought only to tell stories about people who had stimulated her interest as far back as her memory reached, when as a child she glanced toward the hills from her Kentucky home and wondered about life deep in the hollows. Her chosen subject was in one way lucky, for editors and publishers shared her curiosity about the rural poor, but their prejudices and preconceptions would affect both the form and the content of her work and prove partially responsible for one novel's short (though successful) life and another's never reaching print. Had Arnow's first published work appeared before or after the 1930s, she might be known as more than the author of *The Dollmaker*. But however dissociated she was from the political agitations that marked the depression years, she found the 1930s an anxious and a strenuous decade for one determined to try to make it as a writer.

By 1930 there existed a firm literary tradition of southern Appalachian hill people depicted by local colorists who most often were genteel outsiders making tours to the hills in search of quaint and picturesque material.[1] Moonshining, feuding "mountaineers" were frequently portrayed as ignorant, lazy, suspicious, and maniacally violent—alien creatures to be ridiculed or pitied. Mary Murfree's influential *In the Tennessee Mountains* (1884) helped to establish and to popularize this genre of "mountain fiction." It achieved twenty editions in just a few years, and reprints of her other twenty-four books, which also patronizingly pointed out the "humanity" and the "dignity" of this strange breed, were common into the early twentieth century. By the late nineteenth century there developed a subgenre of mountain fiction that survived well into the 1930s: stories of city women traveling to the rural South as teachers or social workers eager to improve the lives of the "underprivileged" mountaineers. In these sentimental, condescending tales, the urban heroines persuade the mountaineers that their feuds are foolish and that only science and reason have value. All these novels, many written by the popular Lucy Furman and Charles Neville Buck, depict the teacher "uplifting" the ignorant country folk and convincing them to lay down their arms and settle their differences peacefully.[2]

Arnow's own experience, rather than any affinity for the literary tradition, inspired her both to focus her autobiographically rooted first novel, *Mountain Path*, on a schoolteacher marooned in feud country and to break with conventions entrenched in the genre. Arnow's heroine, Louisa (Arnow's middle name), travels to a remote corner of Kentucky, as Arnow herself had done in 1926, to board with a hill family and teach in a one-room schoolhouse. Forced to quit college and earn enough money to return, both heroine and author reluctantly committed themselves to a seven-month term. In her initial resentment of the hill people Louisa differs from other fictional heroines, who journeyed to the hills willingly, even enthusiastically, fired with a missionary zeal to help the unfortunate "hillbillies." Unlike her smug predecessors, Louisa learns more than she teaches. Rather than educating her host family, the Calhouns, about "good sense" and "reason," she learns from them the value of hope, patience, and love. Other differences result more from Arnow's imagination than from her experiences. Louisa is unable to stop the Calhouns from feuding, as her literary forebears had so easily done. Instead she grows to understand the emotions that perpetuate the feud and even to share, at the end, their desire for vengeance. In this realistic dramatization of the bitter anguish feuding families feel over their perceived obligation to kill neighbors, Arnow demonstrates the difficulty of uprooting imbedded values.

But the stereotype of the comic hillbilly, affectionately mocked or sentimentally pitied, continued in the 1930s to dominate mountain fiction, which drew the attention of varying groups seeking to further their own ends. Caldwell developed the strain to its extreme, presenting a sordid picture of degraded, ludicrous people exploited to the point of dehumanization. Though Caldwell's aim may have been to demonstrate the evils of an economic system that could so destroy poor farmers, he exasperated

guardians of the literary left wing searching for a native proletariat wholesome enough to deserve radical change.[3] Southern highlanders, poor even
in the booming twenties, were looked to as a possible source for the masses
destined to become enlightened. Another self-conscious group in the
1930s, the agrarians, also looked to the southern farmer as a source of
hope—of a different kind. In their defensive attack on industrialism and
capitalism, the agrarians preached the value of a life tied to nature and to
God, a creed that forced them to ignore the poverty and debasement of
tenant farmers and sharecroppers. Advocates of proletarian and agrarian
literature looked to the poor white to vindicate their views. Thus budding
young writers composing the flowering of southern letters were often up
against the preconceptions of editors and publishers searching for propaganda for various causes as well as for talent. Even those not affiliated with
a particular group were enough infected with political fever to be carriers of
one strain or another. The turbulence of the decade even affected expectations and judgments about literary form. Experimentation lessened at a
time when people felt the need to define themselves politically; writers and
readers alike nervously edged books into categories. Such a climate would
alternately frustrate and anger neophyte novelist Harriette Arnow, whose
pride in the individualism she attributes to her Appalachian heritage would
cause her to take issue with advice on how to make it as a writer in the
fervent 1930s.

Her first assertive act in pursuing her goal was moving in the fall of 1934
from her family's home in Wayne County, Kentucky to a furnished room in
Cincinnati near the main library, where she could read the "great novels"
and try to write. Harriette's flight scandalized her parents and puzzled or
outraged friends and relatives in her native community. Writing during
one's free time was appropriate for a college student or a teacher, but as a
profession it was risky and morally suspect. Harriette was undaunted. At
twenty-six she had just had her first taste of a life committed to writing.
After several years of trying to write while teaching, she was given a cottage
at a Michigan resort rent-free for a few weeks, where she began a collection
of sketches of hill life she called *Path*. The experience was exhilarating.
Harriette was on her way to fulfilling a childhood wish kindled by her
father's and grandmothers' stories—one day to tell her own stories, or write
fiction.

Supporting herself with part-time jobs—typist, saleswoman, waitress—
Harriette completed *Path*, then turned to short stories about her native
Kentucky. "Marigolds and Mules," her first published story, appeared in
the February-March 1935 *Kosmos: Dynamic Stories of Today*, one of the
many short-lived little magazines that flourished in the 1930s. Focusing on
the explosion of a mule-drawn wagonload of nitroglycerin en route to a
Kentucky oil field, "Marigolds and Mules" is a story of shocking violence

that juxtaposes natural beauty with industrial ugliness; it dramatizes a young hill boy's painful recognition that mangled human and animal flesh can coexist in God's world with luxurious blooming flowers. The story inspired several editors to ask Harriette to submit stories to their magazines. Her next published story, "A Mess of Pork," appeared a few months later in the *New Talent*. In this terse, suspenseful vignette, a Kentucky hill woman avenges her husband's murder by sending his killers unsuspecting into a valley of wild hogs. *New Talent* received more appreciative letters for this story in a fortnight than it had for any other piece of fiction to appear in that publication. Harold Strauss, then editor at Covici Friede, saw the story and wrote to the author, praising her for its "remarkable vigor and purity of style" and calling it a "unique piece of dramatization."[4] The story so impressed him that he asked Arnow to send him a novel if she had one. Elated, Harriette sent him the book begun in the Michigan resort and finished, or so she thought, in her Cincinnati roominghouse.

Harriette had been encouraged by a commendatory letter from MacMillan editors, who ultimately rejected the book. Now she welcomed the help of an editor from another press who was favorably disposed to her writing. Reading the manuscript confirmed Strauss's belief in Arnow's talent: "The book as a whole is one of those rare volumes which, as the MacMillan people say, belongs in no regular class but have such extraordinary quality of their own as to be completely self-justifying."[5] Unfortunately, Strauss felt that if the book were to survive in the marketplace, it must be salable rather than self-justifying.

Path's resisting classification proved a liability in the 1930s, which did not continue the preoccupation with artistic form and experimentation that characterized the 1920s. Clearly demarcated action with an exposition, a development, and a solution better suited a decade geared more for action than for analysis.[6] Voicing the wisdom of the time, Harold Strauss advised Arnow to decrease her heroine's introspection and to build a firmer line of "narrative continuity" with the customary "complication, crisis and resolution." Arnow was urged to turn what Strauss viewed as a collection of meditative sketches into an easily recognizable novel. The young writer, eager to become a novelist and sure that she could preserve the poetic evocation of a land and its people that distinguished her volume, bowed to her editor's experience and judgment.

Strauss's suggestion of a structure for the "thread of central action" likewise derived from his acquaintance with merchandising rather than his literary sensibility. The stock material of mountain fiction had proven successful. He wagered that even a "conventional melodrama of mountain feuds, of bigoted suppresssion of normal sexual desire, or some such other theme would not harm the delicacy and beauty of your gallery of portraits and would without question be of enormous help to us in selling your book." Although the draft Strauss read is no longer extant, it is likely that the feud existing both in the manuscript Arnow resubmitted to him after receiving his letter and in the novel's final published form was incorporated at his suggestion.

Arnow accepted Strauss's advice because she felt that doing so would not impair the book's integrity. And she knew something of the emotions attending mountain feuds. During her 1926 stay with the hill family in a remote corner of Pulaski County, Kentucky, Arnow recalls several families not speaking over ancient grievances, though she remembers no mention of feuding deaths. The aspiring writer rightly felt that she could demonstrate her heroine's growing understanding of the mountain people's lives by her gradual, unwitting participation in their feud. At first Louisa feels most alien from her host family, the Calhouns, when they speak of their running feud with the neighboring Barnetts; more than anything else the feud persuades her that the hill people can never be "her own kind." But after the Barnetts murder Chris, the hill man she has grown to love, she can comprehend their demands for vengeance; she is shocked to hear herself begging the Calhoun men to gun down Chris's killers. Mountain fiction had portrayed the feud as the most exotic and colorful aspect of picturesque life deep in the hollows; in Arnow's novel it is used to demonstrate the horrifying tragedy of a practice too deeply rooted and grisly to be viewed as a quaint custom.

The nearly unqualified rave reviews of Arnow's novel, now called *Mountain Path*, found fault with its one departure from assured originality—the feud. Astute critics such as Alfred Kazin, who reviewed the book for the *New York Herald Tribune Books* shortly after Covici Friede published it in August of 1936, wondered why every "Kentucky novel" must include a feud. He discerned, though, with other perceptive critics, that the heroine's self-appraisals, not the feud, make up the novel's heart.[7] He observed that Arnow's apparent closeness to the heroine gave the book its "intimate revelation and occasional power." Kazin's praise of the novel was enthusiastic. He judged *Mountain Path* one of the few novels "of its type" to avoid condescension toward the rural poor and a "spurious lyricism" in evoking the landscape. He applauded Arnow for her solid commitment to character. But Kazin's praise, however wholehearted, was tempered by his assumptions about novels of this "type"—"southern regional novels" and, because of the feud, "Kentucky novels." He implied that they are by definition limited in design and appeal. Hence the novel Strauss judged as belonging to "no regular class" was labeled a specialized variety within a minor mode.

Though Arnow had capitulated on an aesthetic point that harmed her novel's reputation, and possibly its quality, she was not tempted, as were many untested writers at that time, to achieve some measure of acceptance by using fiction to proselytize for a political cause or an economic system. As she confessed to Harold Strauss, "I can't think there is any one best way of life."[8] The proletarian novel had no attraction for her. "During my years in Cincinnati," she later recalls,

> I read considerable proletarian "literature" partly because I was pushed on by the hope I could find a novel which I could respect; there was also the push of the critics; high praise was heaped on works now forgotten. On the other hand I did enjoy and admire the earlier works of John Steinbeck, most of Gorki, Malraux and a few others, but these rose above the level of the average proletarian novel so busy with its "message" and bemoaning the state of a faceless proletariat, little else came through; most seemed unable to create realistic characters.[9]

Arnow wrote *Mountain Path* because the characters demanded expression, not because she wanted to examine how a segment of society managed to make a living. In *Mountain Path* she does not try to point out the evil of an economic system that leaves the small farmers indigent or the good in an alternative political system. She never distorts or sensationalizes the farmers' degradation, as Caldwell does in *Tobacco Road* and elsewhere, or maps out, as Steinbeck does in *The Grapes of Wrath*, a solution to the exploitation in a mystical brotherhood transcending politics. Neither did Arnow set out to write an "agrarian" novel celebrating rural life, though *Mountain Path* evokes the benefits and the joys of a life vitally connected to the land. She acknowledges the occasional boredom of the Calhouns' routine as well as the vexations and trials their poverty causes. Arnow doesn't "recall thinking of Agrarians at all during the thirties. I believe I first read their manifesto, *I'll Take My Stand . . .* sometime in the nineteen fifties."[10]

Arnow's distance from the 1930s political movements and groups does not, however, betray an apolitical sensibility. Her own words, if taken literally, can be misleading. Speaking of *Mountain Path*, she says that she sought only "to tell a story" about the community she imagined as a child in the "other world" behind the hills.[11] If Arnow's motivation is merely to tell stories depicting credible characters who have engaged her imagination, her social-political consciousness is so deep that these threads are woven into the fabric of her tales.

She objects to proletarian novels designed to preach. But she cannot ignore injustice in her fiction because it is part of the world she sees and imagines. Throughout her career Arnow has been particularly drawn to stories involving a character's struggle against social pressures or political, economic, and religious forces that threaten one's integrity or freedom, even one's life. From her earliest short stories in the 1930s, such as "White Collar Woman," which chronicles a newspaper's retaliatory measures against union organizers, to *The Weedkiller's Daughter* in 1970, which sympathetically depicts a teenage girl's attempts to free her mind of the hysteria and hate McCarthyism engendered in the 1950s, Arnow has repeatedly dramatized stories most readers would regard as political. But her fiction shows these injustices as they affect individual characters, not as points to be underlined. Unlike many proletarian novelists whose politics are superimposed on skeletal characters, Arnow begins with a character whose "story" often involves a political or a social confrontation that tests his or her grit.

Arnow's fiction succeeds in sharpening the reader's political conscience even more than proletarian novels bemoaning a "faceless proletariat" because readers care what happens to her fully realized characters. We are incensed by the moonshine laws that make Kentucky farmers criminals in *Mountain Path*, and by the Flint, Michigan, factory in *The Dollmaker* that breeds distrust among the workers and subjects them to hazardous labor conditions. Thus it is neither surprising nor inconsistent that Arnow can call herself only a storyteller and yet admire Gorki, Malraux, even Zola. At their best they accomplish what Arnow perhaps less consciously achieves: awakening the reader's social-political consciousness by telling a story that embodies the author's full range of concerns and values.

Readers and critics across the political spectrum heaped encomiums on *Mountain Path*, probably because they responded to the full humanity of Arnow's characters. Some saw it as an excellent novel of the "soil" that demonstrated the dignity of the rural poor. Admirers of proletarian literature appreciated the wholesomeness of Arnow's rural characters, though they never come to an awareness of oppression or desire to incite a radical change. Arnow's characters at least testify to the existence of a native proletariat meriting a life free of poverty and shame. Agrarian sympathizers, too, would welcome Arnow's positive view of a hill family living in harmony with the land. While Arnow concedes the limitations of such a life, her characters are fully rounded persons leading lives attractive enough to inspire Louisa, a city-bred intellectual, to relinquish creature comforts and a career to begin life anew among them. In a time of polarized politics, Arnow found common ground by focusing on a character and a story.

Despite *Mountain Path*'s enthusiastic reception, many readers and all reviewers misread Arnow's book, a fate that proved helpful to its short-term success but fatal to its longevity. The climate of the 1930s, especially the widespread fascination with the poor that crossed all political lines—the tendency to view them through a romantic haze—encouraged this misreading. All reviewers saw it as a *Bildungsroman* of the highest order, probably because they shared Louisa's perceptions of poor whites. They described Louisa's remarkable change from aloofness and resentment to acceptance and understanding of the Calhouns, praising her recognition of the values preserved in the "primitive mountain life." Many exposed their own condescending regard for the poor white when they applauded Louisa's discovery that the mountain people are after all "human beings like herself" with a "sullen dignity." One reviewer admired the Calhouns for being "child-like" and "strangely wise"; another noted the "mystery, charm, nobility, and heroic qualities" of these "contemporary ancestors" who "walked with fortitude, courting danger."[12] Although some reviewers—Kazin and Margaret Wallace of the *New York Times*—perceived that *Mountain Path* departed from several conventions of sentimental mountain fiction, not one detected that Arnow was in her novel indicting and exposing those enlightened 1930s citizens who felt they could understand and "empathize" with the rural poor white. Readers were too moved by *Mountain Path* to notice that Arnow was criticizing a genre rather than producing another example of it.

The novel only begins as a conventional mountain tale about a city schoolteacher educating the illiterate poor. When Louisa arrives at her new home she is emotionally vacant. Devoting her life to the development of her superior intellect, she has "never loved anything": she couldn't remember her parents, had never held a baby or cared for a man in her twenty years: "Heretofore all people she had known were but adjunctive to the cultivation of her mind."[13] She sees the seven-month term teaching school as an unpleasant interruption of her education and her career. Though she promises herself she will forget the Calhouns as soon as her miserable job is finished, against her will she begins to feel affection for them. The children's mother provides a lesson not available in the university: "She learned things from Corie that she had never found in books—not information. Louisa had never been grateful for anything, but from Corie she learned gratefulness and thankfulness for all things: dry wood, rain when the spring was low, cold snaps that cured up colds and made a spell for killing hogs, sunshiny days, snowy days (that meant good crops), hard frozen bare ground—for it was then that the children did not wet their feet or ruin their shoes" (pp. 214–15). From Chris, a cousin of the Calhouns, Louisa learns love. When she becomes aware of her newly awakened emotions and body, she wants them to remain alive; in a decision that reviewers saw as demonstrating her growth, she decides to stay in the hills, marry Chris, have his children, and "learn the things that Corie knew" (p. 368). The feud is the last barrier between Louisa and the Calhouns; she cannot reconcile herself to senseless hatred and violence. Finally she surmounts even that obstacle. When Chris is shot in retribution for another feuding death, hatred no longer seems senseless: she pleads with the Calhoun men to avenge his death. Her emotional awakening is complete as she feels loathing and ire for the first time. In her grief she became "a body attached to an emotion that destroyed her reason and her senses" (p. 371). She finds it deeply disconcerting to hear herself voicing support for a practice she judges archaic and uncivilized.

But the novel does not end with Louisa's realization of how deeply she has slipped into that "other world." She glances at the callus on her third finger, made by pencils scratching out figures and mechanical drawings, and notices that in seven months this symbol of her dedication to her mind has not gone away. After Chris dies she proclaims, "It would never go away—now. She would spend the next few years of her life in making it bigger; pencils and pens and test tubes—her finger and a little of her brain" (p. 374). What of the newly awakened emotions and body? Thinking of her lost lover, Louisa observes, "The rest of her would die. It was dead already" (p. 374). Her inability to weep is a sign of her return to the emotional emptiness of her past life. Arnow underlines Louisa's resuming the emotional insulation that characterizes her arrival at the Calhouns' by ending the novel as it began: with Louisa determining to "forget them all" as soon as she returns to the city.

The novel's circular ending is not the only indication that Louisa is fundamentally unchanged. Although before Chris dies she decides to give up her career and stay in the hills, her perception of her choices is never altered. In her mind city and country are irrevocably divided as the dwelling places of reason and emotion respectively. When she chooses Chris, she resolves to allow her mind to die, and when he is killed she is convinced that her emotions die with him. She never tries to envision a life in either place that combines her physical and emotional needs with her ambitions; she sees the two as mutually exclusive. Even when she chooses the hills, she perceives relinquishing the university and giving in to her emotions as signs of weakness rather than strength. Shortly before Chris is shot, Arnow discloses that Louisa "pitied the weakness in her that made this man's pleasures and displeasures matter so, that made her too glad when he smiled" (p. 206). When Louisa resolves to marry him she is momentarily overcome by emotions that "destroyed her reason and her senses"; she never reconciles emotion with reason or acknowledges that a mountain hollow can be a suitable replacement for a chemistry laboratory.

All reviewers not only missed striking evidence that Louisa's "growth" is short-lived; they also failed to note suggestions throughout that it is stunted. Her affection for the Calhouns and her appreciation of their emotional vitality notwithstanding, Louisa never sees her mountain friends as peers. She cannot regard them dissociated from their poverty and illiteracy. She would of course be upset at any disruption of her career, but she is alarmed that uneducated hill people are the ones to stimulate her dormant emotions and thereby threaten her plans. She is angry at herself for being touched by a hungry child who refuses her offer of food: "Respect for a dirty child in a single rag was an unpleasantly disturbing thing" (p. 136). At other times she betrays a sanctimonious pride when admitting to being stirred by her students' kindness to her: "She was happy. Happier than she could remember ever having been before, and all because a handful of people, their illiteracy exceeded only by their poverty, had this day shown that they liked her and were pleased that she was among them" (p. 265). No reviewer noted the superiority that prompts Louisa alternately to criticize and to admire herself for letting them into her life. Most, in fact, made a point of applauding her complete transformation, her enlightened perception of them, the *New York Times* affirmed, as more than "pitiful" and "picturesque."

It is likely that the liberal concern for the poor that characterized the depression years clouded the perceptions of even the most discerning reviewers, blinding them to Louisa's unwitting patronizing of the Calhouns. Louisa's yearning to have children and thereby to become a "woman" rather than a "professor"—a touch that might have been prompted by Strauss's suggestion to insert a theme describing the "suppression of normal sexual desire"—evoked sympathy from 1930s readers eager to shed the accouterments of learning and experience life raw and unvarnished, as they imagined the uneducated might. Few could then discern Steinbeck's sometimes embarrassing efforts to poeticize the Joads in *The Grapes of Wrath*, or Agee's less pervasive but noticeable straining to appreciate and to express the tenant farmers' humanity in *Let Us Now Praise Famous Men*. A painful, often guilty awareness of the gap between authors and their subjects accounts for much of the effusiveness of their portraits of the rural poor. To write of the poor unselfconsciously was an impossible task for most writers in the 1930s. Those who succeeded best were most often members of the class they portrayed in their writing.

Though Arnow was not of the class she fictionalized, from experience she knew the nearly insurmountable barrier education could create between persons otherwise congenial. In an early draft of *Mountain Path* Louisa asks herself whether any outsider can ever really know the hill people. The spirit of that question pervades the published version. In both drafts this distance is underlined in letters Louisa receives from her aunt, a well-intentioned lady who asks Louisa how she can bear living in such poverty, however delightful the "Elizabethan speech" spoken by the "pure-blooded Anglo-Saxons" she must encounter daily. Her aunt's passionate concern for the Harlan coal miners, who attracted the attention of *engagé* Americans in the early 1930s, is likewise tinged with condescension. The reader should detect in Louisa the superiority Louisa observes in her aunt.

How, then, does one explain Arnow's own apparent understanding of lives she describes as forever obscure to outsiders? Perhaps she could achieve in seven months what Louisa could not because Louisa is less sensitive, less imaginative, less eager to share their lives than Harriette, whose curiosity was sparked years before her trek to the hollow school when she became acquainted with hill farmers coming for supplies and company to the small Kentucky town just beyond her hillside home. Arnow's pointed, unsentimental descriptions of the Calhouns and their neighbors indicate that the author perceived them accurately; attention is drawn to their "quaint" speech or "picturesque" customs only when Louisa analyzes her feelings about them. In such moments Arnow conveys her disdain for Louisa's initial aloofness and for the condescending identification that replaces it at the end. Hence in depicting the limitations of many a city-dweller's excursion into "Appalachia," Arnow condemns what she was thought to support, a conclusion strengthened by her admission that she "could never abide" Louisa.[14]

Readers in the 1930s seemed to admire Louisa's metamorphosis as much as reviewers. The first edition sold out shortly after its printing, and it won favorable mention in the Book of the Month Club; Covici Friede went bankrupt soon afterward. Yet *Mountain Path* is nearly unknown today, perhaps for many of the reasons it was acclaimed in its time. When the country began to recover from the depression and readers became less preoccupied with the perpetually poor, Arnow's book disappeared with the breadlines.

The novel is usually either lost or misplaced in literary histories. In *Renaissance in the South*, John M. Bradbury credits Arnow's "fine novel," along with Jesse Stuart's *Man with a Bull-Tongue Plow*, with stimulating mountain fiction's burst of popularity in the late 1930s. He praises the "honest objectivism" of Arnow's portrait of the hill poor as well as the "clean, unified narrative development" of her story.[15] Whether he means to praise Louisa's compassion or Arnow's criticism of it is unclear. But he does the book a disservice when he calls it an example of "mountain fiction." This diminution is probably unintentional as he discusses Arnow's novel in a chapter subtitled "A Miscellany," recalling Strauss's judgment that the book belongs to "no regular class." The novel Bradbury judges superior both to *Hunter's Horn* (1949) and *The Dollmaker* (1954) thus died with the fashion for mountain fiction. Its one reissue in 1963 was by the Council of the Southern Mountains at Berea College in Kentucky, a group dedicated to preserving the culture of the southern Appalachian mountain region. An aesthetic reassessment is overdue.

Pressure on Arnow from editors, and now an agent, did not end with the publication of *Mountain Path*. An agent urged Arnow to take advantage of the book's success by seeking publicity. In a decade that searched for a "Shakespeare in overalls," Arnow was asked to pose in her waitress's uniform for a picture accompanying a Cincinnati newspaper article head-lined "Waitress Writes Book."[16] Determined not to be manipulated, and upset over her family's reaction to her notoriety, she refused. Her parents, who found nothing praiseworthy in being either a waitress or a writer, were afraid people would think Harriette had fallen in love with a moonshining murderer. When she made clear her refusal to be marketed as a member of the enlightened working class, she was urged to take a job with a newspaper or a publishing house to gain training in the writer's trade. But Arnow considered hours spent reading (or writing) mediocre journalism a waste of time and refused that too. She ignored suggestions that it wouldn't hurt to befriend reporters, to take an occasional drink with some of the more influential among them.

Her agent was more insistent that Arnow publish as many short stories as possible to keep herself in the public's mind until the release of her second novel. The young writer still in search of her best material was advised to demonstrate her "range" by varying her subjects. The number of letters urging Arnow to select different subjects and the absence of any response among her papers suggests that she may have silently refused to write on order. Most of the stories written at this time focus on hill men and women dreaming and battling for their integrity or survival. Only two take place in a city, where Arnow lived during the writing. "White Collar Woman" depicts the struggle of newspaper guild workers to organize and to receive fair treatment from the management. "Almost Two Thousand Years" movingly chronicles a child's losing battle with frostbite and bitterness as he sits beneath a snow-covered wagon and cleans fruits and vegetables for Italian street vendors. The assured, unself-conscious writing of these un-published stories suggests that this material was as much her own as the tales evoking the lives of Kentucky highlanders at home in the hills and hollows. These two stories of city life, though different in setting from the others, are actually close kin to their country cousins. All depict persons of unusual mettle facing economic ruin or spiritual exhaustion. These are Arnow's subjects in her greatest novel, *The Dollmaker*, written in her artistic maturity. (In fact strikes and the plight of children and Italian fruit vendors reappear in that novel.) The emotional complexity of Arnow's characters rather than the number of settings attests to her power and range as a fiction writer.

While Arnow was on her way to discovering that her writing was most authentic when she focused on the emotional and spiritual lives of poor people hoping and striving for more than subsistence living, other writers were finding it fashionable and lucrative, if not always a genuine interest of theirs. Thus many of the magazines that received Arnow's stories—*Atlantic Monthly, American Prefaces, Scribners*—reported having an abundance of stories "with a rural flavor" and regretted being unable to print them.

Occasionally an editor judged a story too "somber" for his magazine or said he had a plethora of "death" stories. Magazine editors apparently wanted to avoid further "depressing" readers already concerned over the hardships of the rural poor; they wanted happy endings or stories so exaggerating the characters' debasement that they were unrecognizable as real persons. Arnow's fully rounded hill people are depicted in situations exposing their poverty as realistically as their joys and dreams. All editors praised the high literary quality of the stories they rejected for nonliterary reasons. Several editors trying to reduce a backlog asked Arnow to resubmit stories in a few months; by then she was hard at work revising her second novel to please Harold Strauss, who offered to help her find a publisher. Of these stories, only one more was published in the 1930s. The *Southern Review*, then edited by Robert Penn Warren, printed "The Washerwoman's Day," her best and most anthologized short story, in the winter 1936 issue. In it she depicts the frustration and anger one can feel living in a poor yet proud mountain community.

The nature and subject of her second novel derived from Arnow's developing recognition of her most compelling themes and characters; the published writer was also better able to dismiss uncongenial subjects and modes with authority. Although she knew that radical novels easily found their way into print at that time, Arnow recognized her own aversion to pamphleteering: "I can't take refuge in any one camp such as writing for the commustic [sic] cause or writing to save the conscitution [sic], for from the time that I was very young and half way able to see a few of the things that went on about me, I knew that I should never deliberately attempt to change people for good or for evil or better or worse, and that I would never make promises to do thus and so or believe thus and so."[17] Coal mining fascinated Arnow, but she stifled a wish to write of a subject she knew little about: "Sometime during the thirties Zola, most especially *Germinal*, set me on fire: I wanted to do a manuscript on the then troubled Eastern Kentucky coalfields; men were being killed and children starving. Sanity returned to me: I had never been in a coalfield and knew no miners."[18]

Arnow did know hill farmers at home and in the city—those who stayed on the farm, and those who migrated in hope of a better life. She decided "simply to write of two people who wanted different things"—a farmer who loves working his land and his wife who yearns for the conveniences and the excitement of city life.[19] Both of their goals would be valid but unacceptable to the other. She wanted to focus not on their everyday realities, but on their dreams, "to make it beautiful, not revolting, but heartbreakingly sad."[20] She would meet more resistance on this venture than she had with *Mountain Path*.

Harold Strauss cautioned Arnow not to write another "hillbilly novel." Some had thus termed her first novel, and he feared she would be tagged a "hillbilly writer" if she stayed with the same characters. He regretted advising her to incorporate the feud in *Mountain Path*. Strauss might have learned from this regret not to interfere with a talented writer's designs; what he did learn was to be yet more mindful of the market rather than the writer's evolving sensibility. This time Arnow was secure enough to hold firm to her plan to write of the people who had held her interest since childhood. The result was *Between the Flowers*, a beautifully written novel dramatizing the developing emotional gulf between a hill farmer happy with his occupation and his dissatisfied wife, who views farming as an endless round of grime and boredom.

Perhaps Strauss felt that Arnow would be accepted as a mainstream, not a hillbilly, writer if she eschewed the affection and gentleness of her portraits and drew them more severely—as exploited laborers living wasted, unfulfilled lives. The market, which Strauss felt compelled to consider, would welcome a novel documenting a farmer's incessant toil. Though again he judged Arnow's evocation of emotions exquisite, he felt that she should write with a harsher "realism"—that seedy god lurking around depression lunchcounters and sharecroppers' shacks.

Since she was trying to get into the mind of Marsh, her farmer, Arnow agreed to turn for direction to male "realist" writers who had "worked with their hands." After reading Vardis Fisher, Meyer Levin, James T. Farrell, and Jack Conroy, she wrote Strauss an eloquent letter detailing her disgust and heartsickness.

Her first complaint is that by dwelling on objective reality and omitting the nonmaterial—emotions, dreams—some realists create a distorted picture of life: "Though they may be Realism," she argues, "they are not necessarily true."[21] Arnow most hated their exaggerations of the seaminess and weariness of farm life. In a letter to Strauss, she proclaims that when she goes among farmers, "I hear little talk of drudgery, and not all of them are stupid and stolid, but people with a great capacity for thinking and loving and hating." She confesses wishing that the literature of the time would balance its presentation of farming:

It is foolish to go on crying that all farmers are failures and that life on a farm is a dreary waste of ugliness and manure. Sometimes I get a little out of patience with all the pity that is expended on working men; I wish that *New Masses* and such would now and then mix a little glorification with their pity. I know that all things are not as they should be among the farmers and laboring classes but I am sick to my death of hearing them always made weak and pitiful or studied as if they were hardly human beings. However, such seems to be the fashion, and I know the safest thing is to stick to it. I would if I could.[22]

Arnow then assures Strauss, "It was never my intention to preach that a farmer's life or life in a small community was good for people in wholesale quantities"; she judges Delph's, the wife's, case to be "just as strong" as Marsh's. But it is crucial to Arnow's vision of the novel that Marsh love farming; otherwise he would have abandoned it and moved to the city to please his wife. Arnow does not intend to "sentimentalize or slop or gush or picture the man [Marsh] as being too conscious of himself"; she seeks only to show "how much land and crops can mean in the life of a man." Admitting that she'll never be a "real realist," Arnow insists on focusing on the couple's loving and dreaming rather than on their "belches and oaths," which in her view preoccupy too many contemporary writers. Tired of what she considers the "literary man's conception of the working man," she argues that Marsh more closely resembles farmers she has known than the "weak, pitiful beings, dissatisfied with their work" that crowd the covers of many a "realistic" book.[23]

The manuscript of this novel, whose title, *Between the Flowers*, Strauss thought to have "many sales assets," persuaded him that Arnow should indeed concentrate on "loving and dreaming." He writes: "All my hopes for you—now well on their way to being fulfilled, are grounded on the fact that you are one of the few who dare today, when the sophisticates think it unseemly to show much emotion, to write about loving and dreaming. . . . You should go on to search for poetry wherever you find it, and to make your songs without worrying about 'realism.' " His elation notwithstanding, Strauss could not refrain from cautioning her once again against a spare plot. He inserts, "That does not mean that you can go back to writing meditative little sketches, as you did in the first version of *Mountain Path*."[24] As with her first novel, clearly developed action was a point of dispute in her second.

Finding the "narrative line" of *Between the Flowers* weak, Strauss asked Arnow to "point and repoint" the plot. Wishing to write novels rather than sketches, she revised the manuscript to suit his wishes and resubmitted a novel that persuaded him she was a "major talent":

> It is a long time since I have been moved by a novel as deeply as I was by yours. . . . The last hundred pages swept me off my feet. You seem suddenly to have broken loose, to have lost all self-consciousness, to have mastered your characters so thoroughly that you have lived with them and in them. That is what makes them so real and what happens to them so effective. . . . It is only lesser talents who pour their characters into rigid moulds; a major talent permits its characters to live according to the inexorable laws of their own natures. You have done that.

He then adds: "There is nothing more that I can tell you about writing novels. You have passed beyond me, and must explore for yourself.

Instinctively you know better than to attempt the strident, ugly realism of Farrell, just as you know better than to imitate Virginia Woolf or Thomas Wolfe, who, as you say, tend to use words as an end in themselves." This disclaimer follows his one criticism of the novel—that the beginning is "perhaps in spots a little too slow-moving, because of your painstaking adherence to my suggestion that you point and repoint the conflict between Marsh and Delph." This admission that revisions executed at his suggestion impair the final product is painfully reminiscent of his judgment of the completed *Mountain Path*. It is just that measured movement, the obviousness of the narrative thread, that troubled the Covici Friede editorial board and convinced them to turn down the novel.[25]

Strauss later agreed with their decision and explained that in the revised version he had looked only for the strengthened plot and failed to see that the fullness of her previous characterizations had been "sacrificed to the architecture."[26] After the demise of Covici Friede, Strauss sent *Between the Flowers* to several other publishers, though it is unclear which version he sent because editors complained either that the characters or the plot needed fleshing out. More than one shared Stackpole and Sons' opinion that while it went "beyond 'soil novels,' " Arnow would need to add "story value" to the "poetic qualities" if she were to produce a truly "fine novel."[27]

That happy combination of full characters and a clean narrative she easily achieved in her short stories and in her later novels, *Hunter's Horn* and *The Dollmaker*. Perhaps these novels testify to Arnow's ripened talent, as yet unseasoned during the writing of *Mountain Path* and *Between the Flowers*. Or perhaps in these early years Arnow showed signs of developing into the kind of writer temporarily out of fashion in the 1930s—one who had mastered, as had Sarah Orne Jewett, the delicate rendering of natural beauty and the full humanity of the countryside dwellers, and one who perceived fiction as the revelation of a particular people at home in a distinctive place rather than the movement of a hero or a heroine through a crisis and its resolution. *Mountain Path* or *Between the Flowers* might have been an Appalachian *Country of the Pointed Firs*, but the demand for novelistic conventions outweighed any appreciation of a perfectly evoked and peopled time and place.

If Arnow were indeed redirected toward what she called "real realism," readers should not merely lament what might have been. Her remarkable talent for telling stories and depicting action, especially grisly violence, was evident even in her earliest stories, "Marigolds and Mules" and "A Mess of Pork." In the first the fragmented parts of a mule and a man hang from trees after they explode with a wagon carrying nitroglycerine; the second ends with the sound of wild hogs crunching on the bones of screaming men, the revenge of a crazed widow bent on justice. Descriptions of bullets ripping through the bodies of the feuding men in *Mountain Path* are amazingly fresh and immediate even in the early version. Arnow's skill at such descriptions developed as she matured. Few novels convey the frenzy of a drunken brawl more visually (or more comically) than *Hunter's Horn*. And few fictional renderings of horrifying violence match Clovis's beating and Cassie's death in *The Dollmaker*. Whatever the fictional mode, Arnow has always been as adept at depicting action and violence as she is at delicate evocations of the land. Violent, realistic vignettes are as much her forte as characterizations and poetry.

The strenuous decade ended for Arnow in March of 1939, when she married newspaperman Harold Arnow and moved to a 160-acre abandoned farm in southern Kentucky in an effort to "get away from it all." A few more short stories and several pamphlets on Cincinnati done for the Federal Writers' Project were Arnow's last literary efforts during these early years. The 1940s would bring more plaudits for short stories published in *Esquire* and the *Atlantic Monthly* and critical accolades for the best-selling *Hunter's Horn* in 1949. Now that the fashion for depictions of the poor white had run its course, editors were no longer bombarded with stories with a "rural flavor"; while they were no longer "disposed" toward hill characters, they would print distinguished stories on any well-treated subject. The 1950s would finally bring Arnow national recognition as the creator of a master-work, *The Dollmaker*, written in Detroit, where Arnow moved in 1945, and in Ann Arbor, her home since 1950.

Arnow's eschewing her hill characters in her 1970 novel about suburban middle America, *The Weedkiller's Daughter*, is partly a result of her determination not to be labeled, whether that be regionalist, realist, transcendentalist, Marxist, or feminist.[28] In her dislike of tags she resembles Josephine Herbst, who thought the label "proletarian," often attached to her 1930s trilogy, damaged her reputation. Unlike Herbst, Arnow temporarily relinquished the material she treated so well in her own trilogy about Kentucky poor whites and found herself on fallow ground. She was to come closer to the power of her earlier fiction when she returned to writing about her native Kentuckians in her most recent novel, *The Kentucky Trace: A Novel of the American Revolution* (1974).

If luck and justice are on her side, Arnow will someday be credited more publicly with what the most discerning readers of her fiction have perceived—what Malcolm Cowley noted about *Hunter's Horn*: that it defies categorization. Any label, Cowley argues in *The Literary Situation*, fails to suggest "the special quality of the novel, which is partly a poetry of earth, partly a sense of community, and partly a sort of in-feeling for the characters, especially the women, that hadn't appeared in any other novel about Kentucky hill people since Elizabeth Madox Roberts's *The Time of Man*."[29] Like several other notable American writers starting out or making it in the

1930s—Zora Neale Hurston, most notably—Arnow wrote from no ideological preconceptions. If matching novels with decades were trustworthy, one would place *The Dollmaker* rather than *Mountain Path* in the 1930s. Its depiction of union organizers and strikers, industry's neglect of workers, the fanatical radio priest based on Father Charles Coughlin, and the general economic struggles of the laboring classes suggest the social and political consciousness that marked that decade. In this 1954 novel's gritty, realistic portrayal of the trials of poor whites it resembles Steinbeck's *The Grapes of Wrath*, Conroy's *The Disinherited*, and Roth's *Call It Sleep*. Yet Arnow never proselytizes: her presentations of bosses and laborers are fair-minded and balanced. In beauty of language, fullness of original characters, and depiction of the intimate connection between the poor and their land, Arnow most closely resembles Hurston, another female novelist who started out in the 1930s and did not make it until long after the turbulence of that frightened and frightening decade had settled and allowed readers to see clearly the poetry that makes hardship bearable.

CHAPTER 10

HUGH KENNER

Oppen, Zukofsky, and the Poem as Lens

It was a bleak year, 1931, the breadlines hardly moving. "The world,"
George Oppen wrote at about that time, ". . . the world, weather-swept,
with which one shares the century."[1] It was a world in which someone
approaching the window "as if to see / what really was going on" saw rain
falling. All of which seems easy, pictorial, the Pathetic Fallacy in fact: a
rainy day as emblem for a rainy time. Oppen's poem, though, encloses the
falling rain amid many syntactic qualifications, and our first sense of it is apt
to be not of an image but of a single sentence so intricate we're never quite
sure we've grasped it whole.

> The knowledge not of sorrow, you were
>   saying, but of boredom
> Is—aside from reading speaking
>   smoking——
> Of what, Maude Blessingbourne it was,
>   wished to know when, having risen,
> "approached the window as if to see
>   what really was going on";
> And saw rain falling, in the distance
>   more slowly,
> The road clear from her past the window-
>   glass——
> Of the world, weather-swept, with which
>   one shares the century.

This is the untitled first poem in Oppen's *Discrete Series* which the
Objectivist Press published in 1934, and having just carefully copied it out
I'm aware anew that it's virtually impossible to reproduce it from memory
with perfect accuracy, although it clings to the memory. It is full of
seemingly arbitrary decisions. How many lines has it? Seven? Fourteen? I

was about to say it had seven capital letters, making the other seven elements look like runovers, but even that isn't true, since "approached," in a flush-left position, lacks a capital. And the dash after "Is," like an open parenthesis, promises a mate it never finds, the poem's other two dashes being twice as lengthy. We may eventually want to elide all the poem's middle, and read for its kernel sentence just the first twelve words and the last ten:

> The knowledge not of sorrow, you were
> saying, but of boredom
> Is . . .
> Of the world, weather-swept, with which
> one shares the century.

When we do that we're aware of three persons, the speaker, "you," and "one," to which cast of characters the elided middle section adds a fourth, Maude Blessingbourne (someone we know?—perhaps) and even a fifth, whoever spoke the words, carefully attributed by quotation marks, that say how Maude moved, having risen. To be told that Maude Blessingbourne is to be found in Henry James's "The Story in It" makes less difference than you'd expect.

I'll not labor this, though I could linger on the syntax, its careful engineering, its look of improvisation. I'll say only in summary that more and more comes out of the poem as we linger with it, and that though at first glance it's apt to seem built around a glimpse of someone at the window glimpsing emblematic rain, it turns out to create a populous, complex, difficult world for its gray mood to pervade. A Discrete Series, Oppen later explained, is a series of numbers wherein no rule permits one to guess the next term; his example was 14, 18, 23, 27, 33, which looks arbitrary but in fact corresponds to the stops of the uptown Manhattan subway: the numbers, you see, dictated not by numerical laws but by history, by long-forgotten accidents of city planning. So the poem's words, this analogy implies, are specified neither by prosodic laws nor by syntactic, but by a complex reality to which it is faithful. And this is why it is so difficult to memorize its local accuracies, since mnemonic systems are guided by poetic symmetries this poem invokes only to evade them.

The February 1931 *Poetry* printed Louis Zukofsky's "Sincerity and Objectification," with its homemade lexicography:

> *An Objective: (Optics)—The lens bringing the rays*
> *from an object to a focus. That which is aimed at.*
> *(Use extended to poetry)—Desire for what is objectively*
> *perfect, inextricably the direction of historic*
> *and contemporary particulars.*

This is worded to guide future dictionaries, and among other things states that the poem deals with particulars, among which the historic and the contemporary are inextricable, like those forgotten Manhattan determinations, commercial, social, architectural, which today's subway stops register.

"Each word," Zukofsky went on to say, "in itself is an arrangement, . . . each word possesses objectification to a powerful degree." A one-word poem, even, seems thinkable, and not the least strange moment in that anthology of strangenesses, Zukofsky's long poem "A," is the appearance, after fifteen movements spread through several hundred pages, of a sixteenth movement that has only four words, carefully disposed on white space.[2] "The objectification which is a poem, or a unit of structural prose, may exist in a line or very few lines," Zukofsky had written in 1931; still, "the facts carried by one word are, in view of the preponderance of facts carried by combinations of words, not sufficiently explicit to warrant a realization of rested totality such as might be designated an art form." That nevertheless the one-word poem is a thinkable lower limit is a fact to remind us that words, one by one, encapsulate "historic and contemporary particulars." Speaking of his collected short poems, Zukofsky said, "The words are my life." And he said in the same statement that the poet's form "is never an imposition of history, but the desirability of making order out of history as it is felt and conceived."

For the endlessly surprising thing about Zukofsky and Oppen, ministering to the bewilderment that has attended them from their first publication until now, is their balance between verbal algebra and the demands of what they could not pretend to control. The predominantly verbal poet, of whose ways Swinburne may serve as example, feels obligated to no such balance, writing for instance "in a land of sand and ruin and gold" with no need to imagine that land, its time, its name, its geography, content so that word leads into word, offsets word. On the other hand, writing enthralled by a subject's particularities may be graceless, settling for lurid fact: "The blown-up millions—spatter of their brains / And writhing of their bowels and so forth." (That is Browning.) Still, either convention is clear and gives readers no difficulty. The exacting objectivist ambition was to keep the poem open to the entire domain of fact, and simultaneously to keep it a thing made of words, which have their own laws.

The domain of fact, moreover, had received its exegete in Karl Marx, and of nothing were Zukofsky and Oppen more fully persuaded in 1931 than of the pertinence of dialectical materialism to all human experience. They had what hindsight discloses to be complementary but classic revolutionary backgrounds. Oppen (who had the money for a while to grubstake their publishing activities) was born in 1908 into a family sufficiently affluent for repudiating affluence to seem a matter of conscience, while

Zukofsky was born in 1904 into a working-class, Russian Jewish family—its only member to be born in America—and in due course got radicalized at Columbia College in the 1920s. He was close to Whittaker Chambers, in whose *Witness* he figures as "the guy with the eyebrows," after the suicide of Chambers's brother "Ricky" wrote an elegy that is now the third movement of "*A*," and was recruited by Chambers for the party.

There followed a Keatonian comedy. He was taken to a meeting like a scout for induction and aroused the suspicions of shrewd Ma Bloor herself. She had vehement doubts of his proletarian credentials ("My father pressed pants all his life," he would interject, telling the story). He was a bourgeois intellectual, was her verdict. Willow-slim, pulled forward as if by the weight of his own eyebrows, he seemed an implausible stormer of any moneyed Bastille, not even a forcible pusher of leaflets. Ma Bloor's verdict was final, and Zukofsky, debarred from membership, soon cooled in fervor though he retained a lifelong respect for Marx's intelligence. As for Oppen, after *Discrete Series* (1934) he dropped poetry for a third of a century, organized workers, also moved to Mexico, where he lived as a cabinet worker and tool and die maker.

Anyhow reality, for these young men when they were in their twenties, was dialectical materialist reality: the sensible, physical world interacting with physical brains. How to make poems from that? Hymns to The Worker might have been acceptable, but bombardment of the senses by particulars disclosed no apotheosizable Worker—what Walter Lippman, in a genial gibe at John Reed, had called "a fine statuesque giant who stands on a high hill facing the sun." Poetry, moreover, existed, like all things, in history, which by 1931 had disclosed certain things about its nature.

Words move, exist, in time; and the formal problem of the poem may be described in this way: How may a work strung out in time justify its beginning, its ending, and its progress from its first word to its last? There appear to be several main ways. The poet can tell a story, like Homer or Wordsworth. He can construct an argument, like Lucretius or Donne. He can follow the promptings of a tune, like Sappho or Swinburne.

A fourth, less canonical way is to make as if to describe a picture, as Rossetti did in "The Blessed Damozel"; continue till its detail is accounted for; then stop. This had been a satirical mode; it is related to the ancient convention of the character sketch and underlies Chaucer's portraiture in the General Prologue. More than one satire of Marvell's is headed, "Instructions to a Painter."

The story, the argument, the tune, the picture. But novels had long since preempted the story, making versified stories seem quaint (one senses that Edwin Arlington Robinson in *Tristram* is struggling with a dead convention). And the knack of interesting argument in verse was long ago lost, perhaps with the mathematicization of argument, which made verbal equivalents seem either cumbersome or slick. Music—the tune—had been Ezra Pound's recourse, the poem prolonged till it fills out and resolves a melodic figure its first words imply, and in the long run it was to be Louis Zukofsky's guiding analogy likewise. But in 1931 he pointed out what was to be the underlying procedure for the short "Objectivist" poem, writing "An Objective (Optics)—The lens bringing the rays from an object to a focus." As the first great decade of social photography opened, the decade of Dorothea Lange, Walker Evans, Margaret Bourke-White, the poem was directed to work, with leisured sophistication, like the photograph.

This seems, in retrospect, a natural development of the dominant verbal movement of two decades before, so-called imagism, in 1931 only eighteen years in the past. "An Image," Pound had said, "an intellectual or emotional complex in an instant of time." He had probably not been thinking of the snapshot, but nothing in his formulation precludes it. Imagism, William Carlos Williams was to remark, had, however, "no formal necessity implicit in it." By the 1930s it had long since "dribbled off into so-called 'free verse,'" and the poem had become "formally non extant," stopping arbitrarily after being shaped haphazardly.[3]

To think of rays being brought to a focus, though, is to think of a necessary configuration, its geometry obligated by physical laws. Through the lens stream photons responsive to the randomness of the physical world, the world that is simply *there*: "historic and contemporary particulars." They impinge on the plate, arriving (if all is well) at a focus when they are just where the plate is. Not all of the random given world is entailed, only what the geometry of circular ray-cone and rectangular plate can comprise together. And the resultant image, fixed in chemicals, drained of color, is arrayed in massed patterns of monochrome, with, however trivial the subject, the special authority of law. And, for the camera as not for the painter, there are no trivial subjects: it receives all equally, accords equal status to all. And resolving the patterns of monochrome into a "picture" is a culturally learned skill: savages cannot do it, and typically see in photos "of" themselves about what the casual reader sees in a Zukofsky poem.

The "image" of imagism, for Pound an almost mystical perception, was apt in lesser hands to degenerate into a picture. Objectivist intuition forfended that particular degeneration—Zukofsky is the least pictorial poet one can think of—because its analogy for the poem was not the photograph but the photographic process, recreated in slow motion. This process is restricted to today's world (there were no photographs before there were cameras), and today's world's prime realities, though technological, may receive mysterious inflection from human presence: you can tell an Oppen poem as you can tell a Dorothea Lange photograph, though neither Oppen nor Lange in the old declaiming way has made a statement, and Lange's kind of camera is available to anyone much as Oppen's brain is anatomically indistinguishable from anyone else's ("nerves, glandular facilities, electrical cranial charges," wrote Zukofsky of the organism—his own—that shaped the words we are reading about it).

Photographs introduced representational art to a new theme, the indifference of the subject. Zukofsky's "To my wash-stand" (1932) is a sharp-focus monochromatic study of something that would no more, once, have attracted poets than a plumbing fixture would have attracted painters:

> To my wash-stand
> in which I wash
>   my left hand
> and my right hand
>
>   To my wash-stand
> whose base is Greek
>   whose shaft
> is marble and is fluted
>
>   To my wash-stand
> whose wash-bowl
>   is an oval
> in a square
>
>   To my wash-stand
> whose square is marble
>   and inscribes two
> smaller ovals to left and right for soap . . .

We can imagine all that in a fine glossy black-and-white eight-by-ten: it is part of the new sensibility of the 1930s. And so is the close-up of a cracked tile that can look like a face:

>   . . . so my wash-stand
> in one particular breaking of the
>   tile at which I have
> looked and looked
>
>   has opposed to my head
> the inscription of a head
>   whose coinage is the
> coinage of the poor
>
>   observant in waiting
> in their getting up mornings
>   and in their waiting
> going to bed

```
        carefully attentive
to what they have
        and to what they do not
            have . . .
```

The poem ends,

```
        an age in a wash-stand
and in their own heads
```

—"inextricably the direction of historic and contemporary particulars."
Neither the poem nor the fugue of attention it reenacts would have been
thinkable before that decade: a decade partly characterized by poor folk
who rise and go to bed and have maybe no amenity for keeping themselves
clean—not even anything as simple as that. This wash-stand comes to seem
a luxury, even, and one operative word, emphatic as early as the first line,
is "my." Zukofsky's cosmos pivots on little worlds.

Oppen in *Discrete Series* was less hermetic if not less subtle; the poems
go by like snapshots in an album.

```
Bad times:
The cars pass
By the elevated posts
And the movie sign.
A man sells post-cards.
```

And:

```
It brightens up into the branches
And against the same buildings
A morning:
His job is as regular.
```

And:

```
Town, a town,
But location
Over which the sun as it comes to it;
Which cools, houses and lamp-posts,
    during the night, with the roads——
Inhabited partly by those
Who have been born here,
Houses built——. From a train one sees
    him in the morning, his morning;
Him in the afternoon, straightening——
People everywhere, time and the work
    pauseless:
```

One moves between reading and re-reading,
The shape is a moment.
From a crowd a white powdered face,
Eyes and mouth making three——
Awaited—locally—a date.

These glimpses, carefully composed and accented, enforce nothing save a certain emptiness. Men exist in the physical world, always have: but exist now aimlessly, going as their machines go, their images going as their glass surfaces go:

Closed car—closed in glass——
At the curb,
Unapplied and empty:
A thing among others
Over which clouds pass and the
                    alteration of lighting,

An overstatement
Hardly an exterior.
Moving in traffic
This thing is less strange——
Tho the face, still within it,
Between glasses—place, over which
                    time passes—a false light.

That was how it was; and as to how the poems were, they bespoke the 1930s in a certain necessary thrift, using every word impartially, notably the little monosyllables: *place, over, which, time, passes, a, false, light.* . . . That semantic monotone declares a decade, marking such poems off sharply from the shaggy diction of Williams a decade earlier, with his "reddish, purplish, forked, upstanding / twiggy stuff of branches and small trees," much as their lenslike objectivity has replaced Williams's brio and zest.

Small words of course were part of the young century's mystique. Perhaps remembering how Stephen Dedalus feared "those big words which make us so unhappy," Ernest Hemingway made his Lt. Henry declare that words such as *glory, honor, courage, hallow,* were obscene. Hemingway implied that small words were more honest because closer to the testimony of the senses. Oppen thought rather that little words were potent because we are sure what we all agree about when we use them: without them, he has said, we really are unable to exist. "I believe that consciousness exists and that it is consciousness of something," and we share consciousness most fully in words like *sun* and *stone* and *grass.* He wrote in the 1960s of how we manage with less substantive words, making do as we always must:

The steel worker on the girder
Learned not to look down, and does his work
And there are words we have learned
not to look at,
Not to look for substance
Below them. But we are on the verge

Of vertigo.

There are words that mean nothing
But there is something to mean.
Not a declaration which is truth
But a thing
Which is. It is the business of the poet
"To suffer the things of the world
And to speak them and himself out."

"But there is something to mean:" yes: and Oppen is always accessible because some substantial perceived thing is always there. Zukofsky, more philosophically inclined by far, a lifelong reader of Spinoza and in later years a connoisseur of the spiky Wittgenstein, was fascinated by the little words that do not even name: the prepositions, the articles. "To my washstand:" *my* is a pivot word, and so is *to*, commencing as in "An Ode to . . . " and altering its import part way through the poem. At twenty-three, perhaps remembering that Pound had begun the *Cantos* with "And," Zukofsky wrote "Poem beginning 'The' " and got Pound to publish it in the *Exile*. That was perhaps a mite cheeky. But his lifelong work called "A," a poem fascinated for close to fifty years by the intimate processes of language, pours the public and private events of half a century—"inextricably the direction of historic and contemporary particulars"—through an intricate grid of rules as austere as Euclid's, dominated by the taxonomies of the indefinite article, which says of everything that it is "a" something, itself yet one of a kind. As late as 1938 Marx was still supplying "A" with materials, but by then no hope lingered, if there had ever been any, that the poem would make a difference to the masses. Zukofsky had by then become the most hermetic poet in the American language: as hermetic as Mallarmé: an odd destiny for a poetic that had once meant to register objectively the social and material world of the dialectic. Oppen's poetry, though less difficult, has no more hortatory relevance. When he turned full time to activism he simply gave writing up, for decades.[4]

How poetic language may be related to social change remains an unsolved question. It may be that there is no such thing as social change, that such a phrase gets uttered only in the throes of romantic dream, that only details can change, and techniques, and formulations. Still, Ma Bloor was clearly right to reject the guy with the eyebrows, and Oppen to choose years of silence. The only American poetry that had its roots in the 1930s brought the premises of the decade—objectivity, comprehensiveness, literature exact as science—to conclusions no one intuited any better than Ma Bloor, and that histories still pass over in baffled silence.

Part III

CRITICISM AND THE 1930s:
TRIALS OF THE MIND

But it is not only the old
Bolsheviks who are on trial
in Moscow--we too, all of
us, are in the prisoners'
dock. These are trials of
the mind and of the human
spirit. Their meanings
encompass the age.
         Philip Rahv,
         <u>Partisan</u>
         <u>Review</u>,
         <u>1938</u>

CHAPTER 11

DANIEL AARON

Edmund Wilson's Political Decade

From time to time throughout his life, Edmund Wilson would step down from his critic's pulpit and speak in a matter-of-fact way about himself. Such a personal statement—"the case of the author"—appears at the end of his book, *The American Jitters* (1932), Wilson's report of depression America between October 1930 and October 1931. It explains, among other things, how it was that a bourgeois liberal writer could end up believing in Karl Marx's prophecies. His family, he informs the reader, had "never departed very far from the old American life of the country side and the provincial cities" and had "never really broken in to the life of machinery and enormous profits." Yet he had been a beneficiary of the general prosperity. Thanks to his social connections and a small inheritance, he had been allowed "a margin for classical reading, liquor, and general irresponsibility." Later his war experiences taught him that "class antagonisms, conflicts, and injustices" were real, and although he did his best to enjoy himself in the boom years, his disgust with the owning class (as well as with his own efforts to rationalize his acceptance of capitalism and its culture) made him receptive to the "convinced and cool-headed revolutionists" when the crash brought down the fatuous world of bond salesmen, bankers, and businessmen.[1]

Wilson's identification with the working class at this moment and his admiring references to the Russian Communist leaders ("men of superior brains," he called them, "who have triumphed over the ignorance, the stupidity and the shortsighted selfishness of the mass"[2]) came after a year's investigation of his own demoralized country. These, and comparable statements he made about the same time, led to the widely held notion that he had become an "enthusiast for communism and a defender of Stalin,"[3] if not a party member, in the early 1930s and that he remained a supporter until roughly the Russian treason trials of 1935–36. This summary of his political involvement, however, grossly simplified his position vis-à-vis communism and his complex and ambivalent attitudes toward the left in general. Nor can it be reconciled with the detached witness of the 1930s whose sympathy with the lower orders was maintained from a considerable social distance.

Even before the decade opened with the sound of collapsing institutions, Wilson's political and social philosophy was already pretty well formed. The execution of Sacco and Vanzetti had helped to focus his rather unspecific anticapitalist biases, and he was on the lookout for any intellectual system that conceived of literature, history, politics, and everyday life as parts of a single content. In 1930, humanism—however much he scorned its parochialism, its intolerance of human frailty, and its "incomprehension of art"—seemed to him the only "systematic attempt in sight to deal with large political, social, moral and aesthetic questions, in relation to each other, in a monumental and logical way." Socialism and communism, humanism's only rival systems, struck him at this time as foreign and somehow inapplicable to a still comparatively well-off society unsusceptible to new ideas and wanting the brains and courage to formulate them. As for himself, he wrote to Allen Tate in 1930, he was going further left all the time and likened his efforts to get converted to communism (Wilson's friends were well aware of his antireligious animus) to Eliot's "efforts to be converted to Anglo-Catholicism." But until he began his investigations of public events for the *New Republic*, communism seemed pretty remote from American life. Then it dawned upon him that America was passing through a "profound psychological change," that the "money-making ideal" was "about played out" and "the country ripe for something new." Out of his reports of trials, riots, and strikes, his descriptions of cities and landscape, his interviews and meditations came *The American Jitters*, an attempt, as he put it, "to write a sort of fragmentary history of what is happening here." It was admittedly spotty and left out a good many important facts, but in the act of writing it he became convinced that a decisive battle was looming between capitalism and communism and that America's expansionist period had come to an end. The Beards' *The Rise of American Civilization* illuminated the historical background of what he was seeing with his own eyes. So did the thrilling disclosures of Marx and Trotsky, which he took pains to distinguish from the secular religious dogma of Stalinism and likened to "the literature of the Enlightenment before the French and American Revolutions."[4]

Wilson's independence and aloofness irritated many radicals, but they respected both his integrity and his reputation and were eager to have him firmly planted in the leftist camp. Wilson watchers speculated on the depth of his "conversion" and looked for signs of a deepening commitment to

Marxism in every piece he wrote. For many, his kaleidoscopic view of a sick America proved that he had been politically and socially reborn. According to Clifton Fadiman (not yet the book reviewer of the *New Yorker* and master of ceremonies for popular radio programs), Wilson's new socioeconomic awareness had communicated to his prose style "a force, a clarity and a bitter wit" it had previously lacked.[5]

This kind of comment was typical of the period when fellow-travelers like Fadiman and Malcolm Cowley and other bourgeois converts to the movement constantly reminded writers still hanging in the liberal limbo between communism and capitalism that Marxism was not only morally uplifting and scientifically and intellectually clarifying but that it also made better artists. Prose style, after all, was intimately related to the writer's comprehension of the world around him. That was why popular bourgeois writers like Thornton Wilder and Willa Cather, Fadiman declared, were no longer readable—even granting the supposition that their craftsmanship remained unimpaired. In a literal sense, his argument went, these writers did not *know* or *see* what they were writing about. Either they distorted American life to conform to their preconceptions, or they fled from it toward some fantasy world.

An analogous charge would soon be brought against the proletarian writers, but in 1931–32, many intellectuals, including Wilson (and Ezra Pound, for that matter), were saying that communism had created a literary as well as political culture and that Trotsky and Lenin, if not literary men, were creators of a new literary style. In Wilson's words, "Communism had forged its own instrument—accurate, impersonal, lucid, compelling, without the ostentation of the professional logic of the schools from which Marx was by no means free, stripped of the romantic rhetoric which had obfuscated bourgeois radicalism, a perfectly functioning means to an end."[6] Given the obfuscations of the Communist party's official jargon, Wilson's comment reads rather strangely, but it fits the notion, current then, that the Soviets were technicians and engineers. An accurate revolutionary analysis required the writer to look intently at reality with unglazed eyes.

What made Wilson such an important catch for the left was his possible serviceableness as a kind of bellwether for "the growing class of bourgeois intellectuals" outside the revolutionary movement, disowned by the ruling class and deserted by the culture class. "As the strain of economic struggle tightens," wrote Fadiman, "the so-called middle class vanguard immediately reveals its essential moral weakness and particularly its intellectual poverty, thinly coated by a veneer of artistic sophistication." Wilson's "burningly clear" depictions of reality might make these sentimental, cynical middle-class liberals really *see* for the first time. *The American Jitters* was important not simply because Wilson himself was a "potentially important personality in the revolutionary movement," but also because by temperament and training, he was "splendidly equipped to open the eyes of those members of his own class who are lagging behind."[7]

It is now time to turn to the man whose alleged "conversion" touched off these remarks.

In the spring of 1932 there occurred one of those seriocomic episodes, not uncommon during the depression decade, which says something about Wilson's political uncertainties at this time. It had to do with a manifesto sponsored jointly by Lewis Mumford, Waldo Frank, John Dos Passos, Sherwood Anderson, and Wilson "without collaboration or knowledge of the Communists." It called the political and economic state of affairs a "crisis of human culture," denounced the present capitalistic system and the corrupt "ruling caste," demanded a "temporary dictatorship of the class-conscious workers," affirmed the signers' identity with workers and farmers, and summoned writers, artists, teachers, engineers, "and intellectuals of every kind" to join the workers' cause. Much to Waldo Frank's annoyance, Wilson procrastinated six weeks before sending out the manifesto to other writers. Finally, largely on account of Dos Passos's and Mumford's objection to its language and tone (especially the phrase about the "dictatorship" of the manual workers) and its failure to emphasize the mutual interests of the proletariat and the petty bourgeoisie, Wilson recommended that everyone write his own manifesto or sign the pamphlet drafted by the Communist party for the coming presidential election.[8]

Wilson did both. He issued his own statement on why he intended to vote for the Communist candidates and signed the party's open letter to writers and professional groups, *Culture and Crisis*. But his own document discloses his opinions about communism and the Communist party far more clearly than the open letter.

In brief, Wilson invidiously contrasts the lacklustre Socialists and the energetic self-confident Communists, lists the iniquities and inequities of capitalism, and approves the goal of a classless society—the renunciation of "the rewards of bourgeois success" and the repudiation of "the standards of respectability." At the same time, he concedes that until now the American Communists haven't pursued their policies "with a maximum of wisdom or skill." Even worse, they have followed the line of the Russian-dominated Communist International, which has tended to make them "mere parrots of the Russian party and yes-men for Stalin." There is nothing, he insists, "intrinsically Russian about Communism," and cites Trotsky as his authority. In time the American Communist leaders will discard their "narrow and wrongheaded policies" without abandoning the discipline necessary to carry out the socialist program. When socialism finally supplants capitalism in the United States, he concludes, "it may not be under Communist leadership," but its aims will be Communist aims.

For Wilson the Communists were (and remained) "the Communist element"—never "comrades." Just how gingerly he collaborated with them was dramatically and half-humorously illustrated by the episode of the Writers' Solidarity Delegation to Pineville, Kentucky, in February 1932.[9]

The fullest account of Wilson's response to that ill-fated excursion is contained in his diary, *The Thirties*.[10] In it he tells of his journey to Kentucky (he brought copies of *Hard Times* and *Progress and Poverty* for train reading) and of the split that immediately developed between the Communists, who expected to use the occasion to spread the gospel, and the "liberal-radicals" who only wanted to dispense food to the striking coal miners as a way of demonstrating their sympathy. Wilson's notes are breezy and facetious. He mentions Waldo Frank's boast to the unimpressed Pineville mayor that his delegation of famous writers would spread the Pineville story across the United States, and he describes the arrival of the "demoniacal-looking deputy with gray hair bristling straight up from crown, black peering eyes which seemed to gleam with fiendish delight at his work and head thrust down and forward and comically stealthy tread" who at first appalled but who turned out "quite amiable." To Wilson the diarist, the locals were not monsters—merely provincial people deeply suspicious of "foreigners," Jews, and Communists. But despite his sardonic asides about jolly jailers and "vulturine" detectives, the Harlan County caper had its serious side, which he duly noted. The authorities arrested two of the party for making inflammatory speeches; the food trucks were overturned, and while the delegation was being forcibly ridden out of the state, Allen Taub, a Communist lawyer, and Waldo Frank had their heads bloodied by the gun butts of the deputies.

Wilson, the "liberal-radical," liked Frank (who was to become his neighbor on Cape Cod and a good friend) and described him to Dos Passos as playing "his role with great sang-froid and tact." But Wilson, the reporter, could put himself in the place of the "infuriated Kentuckians" and the southern whites of Chattanooga during the Scottsboro trial, outnumbered six to one by the blacks and frightened by the propaganda of the Communists. If the South seemed to him a less threatening part of the world than it did to most urban intellectuals of the Northeast, it was because it was part of an older America he savored, and because he sympathized with the soft-spoken locals who didn't quite know how to take the radical northern visitors, who vacillated between kindliness and ferocity, and who warned him, "don't ever come back to Kentucky again." He didn't want a "Russian" revolution any more than they did. The revolution he wanted (and the same could be said for his fellow writers of the manifesto, Mumford and Brooks) had to be rooted in the values of the American Revolution.[11]

Wilson's musings about the Kentucky delegates indicate his mixed feelings about them and the cause they represented. All in all, he didn't like them much. Some were his own kind of people, liberals like Mary Heaton Vorse, Quincy Howe, Malcolm Cowley "who were going in for the thing out of curiosity, exhibitionism or desire for drama." Or they were "queer equivocal anomalous people—mongrel negroes and Jews, thyroid women—who didn't make any sense anyway—also Communists, etc., finally putting it over on you—leading you like lambs to the slaughter." At moments, a "common feeling" of "solidarity" would come over him. It did not last very long. His mood darkened when he returned to New York and went to a dinner at a speakeasy where everyone accused "each other of not being far enough to the left." He noted the Communists smiling furtively like bootleggers, the "deformed people at the Communist headquarters— hunchback running the elevator, dwarf woman with glasses, woman with part of face discolored as if by a burn but with a protruding growth of some kind from the discolored part."

The attitude implicit in Wilson's musings and shared by many of the old-stock American intellectuals is seldom considered by historians of the radical movement, but given our sensitiveness these days to anything smacking of ethnocentrism or religious bigotry or "racism" (a term loosely applied and rarely defined) it needs to be considered in the context of the times.

Liberals and radicals of old-stock antecedents were often not entirely comfortable with their Jewish, ethnic, or black associates whose back-grounds and culture differed markedly from their own, and they found it hard on occasion to divest themselves of social prejudices they had ac-quired from their families and schools. The 1930s, one suspects, consti-tuted for them a kind of takeover by the aliens whose looks, dress, man-ners, and personalities (not so much their politics or aesthetic preferences) might seem distasteful or embarrassing. And this response may help to account for the reluctance of many old-stock American writers to grant a deeper intimacy even to those "alien" types they admired. They might deprecate, as Wilson did, the bigotry of relatives and classmates. But they *knew* these people in the sense that they never knew the "aliens" and were at least socially in tune with them. It might be plausibly argued, too, that they covertly resented the first- or second-generation American's enthusias-tic appropriation of the Sacred Ground, his assumption that sharing their political and cultural iconoclasm automatically admitted him to their coterie.

The ethnic and especially the Jewish radicals sensed this diffidence or shrinking on the part of the middle-class white American Protestants, and a few of them (the names of Michael Gold and Edward Dahlberg come to mind) had sardonic things to say about what they chose to regard as the snobbishness of Wilson and his circle. None to my knowledge quite appreciated the ambivalence of Wilson, Dos Passos, and other leftward-moving bourgeois writers toward the class they had ostensibly abandoned and the proprietary feeling toward the America of their fathers. What the critic Robert M. Adams says of Wilson in a recent review applies equally well, I think, to some of his friends: "Though theoretically sympathetic, he had no real feeling for black culture . . . or for the Jewish consciousness that was to flower during his lifetime into so important a part of American fiction."[12]

One would have to add, all the same, that in Wilson's case this unresponsiveness to black literature and the Jewish consciousness was balanced by his fascination with exotic cultures and with the experience of people whose lives seemed freer and less inhibited than those of his parents and friends. He could identify himself with the Jewish Communists he encountered in the 1930s, because they possessed what he regarded as the Jewish devotion to high ideals and the "foreigner's advantage of being able to see things objectively." And yet the Jew appeared to him at the same time a stranger "already secretive, half-alien, a member of an opposition, a member of a minority, at cross purposes with the community he lives in," alert to the revolt of the urban industrial workers but with no grasp of the "American revolutionary tradition created by our farmers." Wilson, too, felt himself an alien, as all middle-class radicals did to a degree (later he would even say that he belonged to a minority), but by the accident of birth he also belonged to a group or class whose best traditions he honored and tried to adhere to and whose gaucheries he could tolerate if not condone.

One can't imagine him writing Archibald MacLeish's "Frescoes for Mr. Rockefeller's City" with its genteel slur against readers of the *New York Daily Worker*, but it says something about him and his literary friends during the 1920s and 1930s that they could quite innocently refer among themselves to "Chinks," "wops," "Japs," "dagoes," and "niggers." This is the same man, it goes without saying, who went out of his way to befriend and aid people (Edward Dahlberg[13] or Michael Gold, for example) he did not always find congenial. If his 1930s diary is filled with references to Jews, it is largely because some of his friends and relatives he quarreled with over politics were anti-Semitic and because he was trying to record objectively his impressions of a sort of person whose anti-Jewish feelings, he surmised, had surfaced with Hitler's rise to power. He was pained to discover a trace of the virus even in his mentor, Christian Gauss, but he tended to regard the anti-Semitism of his peers as a bourgeois disease, and he behaved rather in the manner of John Jay Chapman, whom he once described as frequenting the Porcellian Club while complaining constantly of its snobbery.

In approaching this witness of the 1930s, then, it is well to keep in mind the engaged reporter, alternately angry, curious, bemused by retaining his manner of the well-born, well-bred democrat looking downward, whether he was interviewing labor organizers or the hirelings of industry. Working-class types fascinated him, and there is something almost perverse in his explorations into areas remote from the social milieu of the jittery sophisti-cates he made fun of in his fiction and plays, as if somewhere in the streets and factories and mean dwellings lay an answer to his psychic needs. He overheard the "obscene and shocking" talk of the kindly well-to-do as they responded to the depression in the clichés of the times: *private charity is better than public because there is less graft; the only sound government is monarchy; we must return to the ways of our fathers; we must learn better use for our leisure; or workers will have to do without cars and radios; I keep a red flag in my attic*. He observed the would-be aristocracy, vacuous and irresponsible, "despising the business and industrial world which had made their culture and education possible"; the intelligent and sensitive who had to devote their talents to writing advertising or selling bonds; and the scions of the rich, some of them decent admirable people, who pos-sessed no real power.

In New York City he could watch the scavengers on East Fifty-third Street foraging in garbage cans for food and old shoes. He was invited to a swank dressmaker's party where the models wore frocks named after events and slogans and personalities of the times: "Five Year Plan," "Viva Mexico," "Diego Rivera," "Nazi," "Amkino," "Public Enemy Number One," "Three Point Two," "Prosperity Is Just around the Corner," "The Yellow Peril," "Gold Standard," "The Happy Warrior," "A New Deal." He attended a symposium at the Whitney Museum and reported the move-ment to reject abstract for social painting. At Washington parties, he met administration officials and gathered gossip about the White House. "Washington," he wrote, "is really a hollow shell which holds the liberal-ism of the New Deal as easily as the crooks and thugs of the Harding administration—no trouble to clean it out everynight and put something else in the past administration's place." The movie Communists he had been introduced to in Hollywood, he quotes Mrs. John Dos Passos as saying, were bitter against "social fascists" who deserved "to be stood up against the wall and shot." One of them did his part for the cause by secretly arranging publicity against the antistrike film he had worked on; two highly paid script writers donated half their poker earnings to the party.

Wilson's main purpose in making notations of this sort was to collect material for novels and plays. More and more, history seemed to be taking on the character of fiction, and what he especially relished in the *U.S.A.* trilogy of his friend, Dos Passos, was the excitement of "perceiving the drama of which the characters are unaware" through the educated social vision of the author. Like Shaw (Wilson thought), Dos Passos held his characters "at arm's length." And one feels something comparable in Wilson's treatment of the human procession passing through his diary and of the specimens he exhibits in his reportage.

In *The American Jitters*, depression America is refracted through the eye of an observer offended by the baseness of a propertied class that has evaded its stewardly function. The observer presents himself as less a partisan than a "case." He refrains from taking sides too obviously.

For example, in the chapter "Communists and Cops," the city administration is portrayed as inept rather than sinister. The seedy people—the ghetto Jews and blacks—are observed as if they were some kind of unattractive growth in an urban jungle. He treats them with respect, but they are not really a part of the America he knows or cares about. The Communists are "mostly small scrubby zealous people wearing red neckties, red hats or red dresses. A good many of the women have glasses." One of the rioters is "a small plump sharp-beaked Jewess in red—great wrath in a tiny body like one of Virgil's bees." Some of the attending policemen are cheerful young fellows, some "mobilizable brutes," but none is a "cossack" of the *Daily Worker* variety. A characteristic Wilson touch is his comment that the black cops "have almost the same Prussian military stature, the same square faces and mail-slot mouths as their white fellow officers."[14]

Yet this ostensibly objective account of a radical demonstration, for all its icy commentary and scientific air, is carefully contrived and slanted. The book is a series of staged encounters, the "characters" (mostly real people, a few invented) representative types: Exploiter and Exploited; the Energetic and Progressive Minority who resist the Men of Power and seek to rally the Cowed and the Defeated. Wilson's pen portraits resemble stage directions: Hamilton Fish "is a man of immense stature, in a dark blue suit and a very tall stiff white collar. He has coarse features, broad shoulders and a slightly finicking manner and looks like Hannibal turned tailor's dummy or blank-eyed vacuous Bashan bull." And Rep. Bachman of West Virginia "is by way of being the caricaturist's ideal of the lower orders of congressmen: he is pot-gutted and greasy-looking, with small black pig eyes and a long pointed nose. He talks with a cigar in his mouth tilted up at a self-confident angle, and he questions Mr. Foster with a persistent and almost pathetic stupidity which he tried to conceal with a great air of cunning." In contrast, the Communists are drawn attractively. Sensitive and tenacious William Z. Foster, the Communist party's presidential candidate, "has blue eyes, a bald crown, a finely modeled brow and nose, a small mobile Irish mouth and a plebeian Irish lantern jaw." Israel Amter (eventually to be immortalized in Allen Ginsburg's nostalgic poem, "America") is "a dark, intense, and fine-looking Jew. . . . He was formerly a professional violinist and has intelligent liquid black eyes."[15]

Obviously Wilson admired these dedicated and energetic Reds whose only future was the jail, but he found the Russian idiom employed by the American Communists foreign-sounding, even vaguely menacing: "Foster to-day always deals in 'ideologies' instead of 'ideas,' and he is always talking about 'liquidating' things. 'Liquidating' something means getting rid of it. In Russia, they liquidated the *kulaks*, they liquidated the Church—and the Soviet prosecutor has recently demanded that the traitorous engineers be liquidated—in other words, shot."[16] Three years later after his first and only visit to the Soviet Union, he would have more to say about "the constraint of the official terror"[17] in the USSR.

He had received what he liked to call a "Googleheim" fellowship in April 1935, "alleging," as he told Dos Passos, "that I want to work in the Marx-Engels Institute in Moscow." Given his reputed Trotskyist connections (his name was on the masthead of V. F. Calverton's *Modern Monthly*) it took a bit of nerve for him to seek Earl Browder's aid in obtaining a visa, but the visa came through, and he happily took off for Europe. He was "fed up and disgusted with New York" and "full of the rancorous rankling of unproduced plays and uncompleted books."[18]

A diary entry made some time around "this sordid period" (as he put it) may refer indirectly to at least one of the uncompleted books and suggest an ulterior reason for the Russian journey. The thought had occurred to him that nobody had "ever presented in intelligible human terms the development of Marxism and other phases of the modern idea of history." He weighed the costs of undertaking such a work (he would have to learn German and Russian and put aside his putative novel) and decided to plunge ahead on what was to prove, as his letters show, a most demanding task: the writing of *To the Finland Station* (1940). Presumably the four-month trip to the land of Lenin and Trotsky would enrich the Russian chapters of his book and give him a firsthand glimpse of the Great Experiment.

Travels in Two Democracies (1936)[19]—Wilson's composite journal of "U.S.A., November, 1932–May, 1934" and "U.S.S.R., May–October, 1935"—satisfied neither the pro- nor anti-Soviet factions in the United States. The latter thought him too apologetic about the new society taking form under Soviet leadership; the former considered him hardly more than a spokesman for William Randolph Hearst. Robert Cantwell, the novelist and critic, probably did not speak for the majority of readers when he commended Wilson for his refusal to play down those aspects of Communist society that rasped his sensibilities. This outspokenness, Cantwell wrote, made Wilson's Russian impression "more interesting and more real—and thus more understandable and attractive—than the writing of those visitors who, returning, have been unable to communicate much except their enthusiasm or their hatred." Friends of the Soviet Union, of course, felt otherwise. Why, asked Malcolm Cowley, "did Wilson have to emphasize his admiration for Lenin by asserting a contempt for Lenin's countrymen?" The "stoic, end-of-the-epoch tone" of Wilson's book signified to Isidor Schneider (on occasion one of the Party's more perspicuous critics) that Wilson was still "emotionally a part of the dissolving order," still distrustful of the masses, still enduringly suspicious "of Communist repression of intellectual freedom." On the other hand, as another *New Masses* reviewer pointed out, those pages in Wilson's volume which called for "stringent polemical reply" were balanced by pages of artistic observation which evinced genuine sympathy for the Russian people and were untainted by slanderous anti-Stalinist speculation.[20]

But the class-enemy showed his spots not long after the publication of his book. Wilson announced what was implicit in his travel volume: that the Stalinist regime was "pretty hopelessly reactionary and corrupt." After telling Dos Passos that politically nonactive writers ought not to get involved in any political group, he found himself caught up in the Trotsky Defense Committee, badgered by "Trotskyists and Stalinists in every mail and telephone," and convinced that nothing was left of international socialism. Stalinists vilified Trotsky because he kept in view the contradictions of Soviet communism ("Trotsky in the Soviet Union is simply what the Jew is to the Nazis"), but Wilson was not blind to "Trotsky's deficiencies." In the spring of 1937 he declared the whole left movement, literary and political, "completely demoralized" and hoped the Stalinist-Trotsky struggle might ultimately clear the air and make people "think for themselves" instead of relying upon the poison pens of the nonthinking, nonwriting character assassins who hung on Stalin's mustache and Trotsky's whiskers.[21]

As the decade advanced, Wilson confined himself more and more to literary subjects, and his writing about persons and places, increasingly reflective, failed to convey the exultant sense of historical discovery which his none too extensive familiarity with Marxism had momentarily provided him. Writing about Flaubert in *The Triple Thinkers* (1938), he sourly remarked: "Nothing exasperated him more—and we may sympathise with him today—than the idea that the soul is saved by the profession of correct political opinions." And it seems more than likely that in the same essay Wilson was agreeing with Flaubert when the latter blamed "the evolution of the socialist into a proletarian-persecuting policeman" not on the bourgeoisie but on the authoritarianism implicit in socialism itself.[22] The urgency and confidence that marked the style of *The American Jitters* had diminished with his growing skepticism about the possibility of any satisfactory social arrangement. Certainly the writers held no answers for him. Even great ones like Dante were often quite mistaken in their political ideas.[23] In fact "one of the prime errors of recent radical criticism," he wrote apropos of Shaw, "had been the assumption that great novels and plays must necessarily be written by people who have everything clear in their minds."[24]

To be sure, Wilson's diary and letters show that he had many other matters on his mind than political infighting and the detritus of the depression. During the 1930s, as Kenneth Burke once observed, personal ambitions, sexual anxieties, and metaphysical yearnings were often objectified in political forms.[25] And among the literary and artistic set there were a good many breakdown and bursts of self-destructive behavior. Wilson was sturdy and curious enough not to collapse like the hero of his 1932 play, *Beppo and Beth*, who complained that neither he nor his friends belonged to the "natural world" and shared "the same solitude, the same insecurity, the same straining for something to hang on to!"[26] But the death of his second wife in 1932 after two years of marriage haunted him throughout the remainder of the 1930s. There seems to have been no diminution from the 1920s in his drinking and lovemaking, and the personal affairs of his family and friends, as well as his own, preoccupied him more than unemployment and the New Deal.

In retrospect the 1930s appeared to him as a period not without its idealism but subversive to the Republic of Letters. The 1920s were the years he came to prefer. People were freer than they were during the depression to travel and stay up all night and do and write as they wanted to and be amusing and interesting. For all of the irresponsibility and wasted talent, it had been a good time to be a writer, "The idea of the death of a society had not yet begun working on people to paralyze their response to experience." When the depression hit, people began to watch their ideological p's and q's, "preoccupied," in Wilson's words, "with making sure their positions were correct in relation to the capitalist system and the imminence or non-imminence of a social revolution." Many writers lost confidence and stopped writing or compromised their beliefs for reasons of prudence or turned to teaching.[27]

Wilson had felt almost refreshed when the financial machinery went smash in 1929, because he still believed in the resilience of America and took pleasure in what seemed to him the downfall of humbuggery and incompetence. For a time, he thought it might be possible to domesticate Marx and achieve a democratic socialism. But he was too good and honest an observer to palliate depressing facts, too bent upon defending literature and carrying on his rigorous routine of writing and reading to throw himself into the tiresome sectarian battles of the period. He remained at the end of the decade what he had been at its beginning—the uncommitted and determinedly independent witness.

CHAPTER 12

ALAN WALD

Revolutionary Intellectuals:

PARTISAN REVIEW IN THE 1930s

> What distinguished *Partisan Review* from the *New Masses* was our struggle to free revolutionary literature from domination by the immediate strategy of a political party.—William Phillips and Philip Rahv, Letter, *New Masses*, 1937

> But it is not only the old Bolsheviks who are on trial [in Moscow]—we too, all of us, are in the prisoners' dock. These are trials of the mind and of the human spirit. Their meanings encompass the age.—Philip Rahv, *Partisan Review*, 1938

In the third decade of this century, a generation of young American writers and critics began to turn from introverted immersion in the experimental forms and esoteric sensibilities of the years following the First World War to the political-literary activism of the early 1930s. Yet this was a far less sweeping and unqualified process than might appear from our vista in the 1970s because the achievements of the 1920s were considerable and could not be ignored. The disillusioned exiles and individualistic aesthetes of the postwar decade had technically revolutionized and thematically internationalized American literature. Furthermore, the disciples of Pound, Eliot, Joyce, and Stein—despite the apolitical and sometimes reactionary social views of these figures—established themselves, against twentieth-century alienation and commercialism, as an *avant garde* in literary protest. To most writers galvanized into political activity by the 1929 crash and subse-

A shorter version of this essay appeared in *Occident* 8 (Spring 1974). At that time I received valuable assistance from Leonard Michaels, David Reid, Michael Folsom, and James Gilbert. The new version has benefited from critical readings by George Novack and Henry Nash Smith and from comments about the original from Felix Morrow, Meyer Schapiro, Lionel Trilling, and other veterans of the 1930s. Some of the original research for the study was made possible by a travel grant from the University of California at Berkeley, which enabled me to interview F. W. Dupee, James T. Farrell, Dwight Macdonald, and William Phillips.

quent depression, the legacy of Eliot and the others appeared insufficient; but to certain of the newly radicalized literary intellectuals, the 1920s were an important component of a cultural tradition that required assimilation.

It was in part their preoccupation with the work of the previous decade—its innovations in technique and sensibility, its Europeanization of American culture, its absorption with the estrangement of the intelligentsia—that distinguished William Phillips and Philip Rahv from most of the young writers attracted to the Communist party's literary wing and its John Reed clubs. Their preoccupation would later account significantly for the development of *Partisan Review*, when the two editors broke with the Communist party after assessing historical events in the Soviet Union, Spain, and Germany and after witnessing the failure of the proletarian cultural movement. At the end of 1937 Phillips and Rahv emerged as leaders in an independent Marxist, but anti-Stalinist, literary left, whose mark on American intellectual and cultural development remains evident today.[1]

Born in 1908 in the Ukraine, Philip Rahv came to the United States at the age of fourteen. He arrived in New York City ten years later, in 1932, having nourished an interest in literature while working in advertising on the West Coast. He joined the Communist movement and became active in its literary affiliates, *Prolit Folio* magazine and Jack Conroy's Rebel Poets group.

William Phillips was born in New York City of an immigrant family. In 1976 he recalled that

> I myself had come from the poor boy's land, from the Bronx and City College, then graduate work at NYU and Columbia. Despite the lack of money and worldliness, I had managed to avoid radicalization—or, indeed, politicization of any kind. On the contrary, my literary and intellectual development was rooted in the 20s, in the experience of modernism: my world was bounded on all sides by Eliot, Pound, Joyce, the Cubists, Mondrian, etc. It was only in the depth of the Depression—in the 30s—that I began to take any interest in social themes and movements.[2]

Phillips and Rahv met in the New York chapter of the John Reed Club, and, in 1933, together with other members, they conceived a plan for their own magazine. With the support and assistance of established Communist cultural leaders like Joseph Freeman and Mike Gold—and with funds raised through a lecture by John Strachey—the new journal was launched. Recollections still conflict as to who did what in initiating the magazine, but early editorials indicate an agreement that *Partisan Review* would concentrate primarily on literary and critical questions, leaving the *New Masses* (the central organ of the Communist intellectuals) free to turn increasingly to political matters.[3]

From the journal's inception, the articles of Phillips and Rahv demonstrated three objectives: a desire that proletarian fiction and criticism should incorporate certain aspects of the literary achievements of the 1920s; an opposition to schematic, sectarian and reductive applications of Marxism; and a concern with developing a full Marxist aesthetic that acknowledged the special needs of radical intellectuals.

In collaborative articles such as "Criticism," and in "A Season in Heaven" by Rahv, T. S. Eliot's contribution was positively assessed. The *Partisan Review* critics maintained that despite evidence of Eliot's fascist leanings, his writing had sociopolitical criticisms of contemporary life that transcended his own peculiar views. Phillips's "Three Generations," which discussed trends in American literary tradition and their impact on the new generation of left-wing writers, lauded Eliot for his technical proficiency. Searching for a "usable past," Phillips noted that the only successful school of American writers had been the movement analogous to that of Zola in French literature: the realism-naturalism stream of Dreiser/Anderson/ Lewis/Robinson/Sandburg. The Lost Generation writers who rejected this heritage were in turn rejected by the older radical writers (Joseph Freeman, Mike Gold, and Joshua Kunitz). "Nevertheless," Phillips concluded, "the spirit of the twenties is part of our heritage, and many of the younger revolutionary generations are acutely conscious of this."[4]

Rahv's and Phillips's campaign against mechanically applied Marxism (to which they assigned Lenin's epithet of "leftism"), was the hallmark of their criticism.[5] Of course, both gave allegiance to the Communist International's call for a consciously proletarian literature and art. They also believed in building an organized movement of anticapitalist and pro-Soviet intellectuals. "The profile of the Bolshevik is emerging in America," they said, "heroic class battles are developing, new human types and relations are budding in and around the Communist Party." As revolutionaries, they asserted that the writer's assimilation of this new material could not occur by passive observation, but only through active participation in the working-class struggle. The task was to guard the revolutionary aims and direction of the burgeoning revolutionary cultural movement: "The critic is the ideologist of the literary movement, and any ideologist, as Lenin pointed out, 'is worthy of that name only when he marches ahead of the spontaneous movement, points out the real road, and when he is able, ahead of all others, to solve all the theoretical, political and tactical questions which the "material elements" of the movement spontaneously encounter. It is necessary to be critical of it [the movement], to point out its dangers and defects and to aspire to *elevate* spontaneity to consciousness.' "[6]

These early articles, in fact, constitute one long catalogue of the dangers of a mechanical and a sectarian application of Marxist theory to the writing and criticism of literature. In 1934 Phillips and Rahv asserted that the most widespread error in leftism occurs when "zeal to steep literature overnight in the political program of Communism results in . . . sloganized and inorganic writing." To view the writer's goal as merely "discovering" the class struggle for the reader was to renege on one's creative responsibility—which is to assimilate the political context imaginatively. Literature, they affirmed, was not so much a medium of abstract conceptualization as one "steeped in sensory experience" that requires the transformation of the class struggle into "images of physical life."[7]

One year later Phillips and Rahv echoed the same points in a jointly written discussion article on the eve of the 1935 American Writers' Congress. Now they took issue with a long list of Stalinist literary shibboleths. (Ironically, the Communist party itself was starting a new "respectable" political turn to the right, which would result in the jettisoning of the proletarian cultural orientation altogether.) Among other things, Phillips and Rahv questioned the slogan Art Is a Weapon, because this weapon's range was limited to those susceptible to art. Using Faulkner and Proust as examples, they challenged an equation of a nonproletarian attitude in individual writers with the ideological perspective of the bourgeoisie. They concluded, "Revolutionary literature is not the literature of a sect, like surrealism or objectivism; it is the product of an emerging civilization, and will contain the wealth and diversity which any cultural range offers."[8]

The search for a truly Marxist aesthetic concerned Phillips and Rahv throughout the thirties; they never accepted the slogans of the Communist International as a sufficient guide for revolutionary writers and critics. Early in 1935, attempting to apply Marxist dialectics to critical theory, Phillips discussed the relationship of literary form and content. Examining the views of Plato, Plotinus, Kant, Hegel, Croce, and Dewey, Phillips argued that any separation of form and content was simply false. Hamlet's soliloquy, he explained, is banal in its content but achieves aesthetic cogency through its integration in a form. Phillips cited the writings of Sidney Hook and Robert Cantwell as representative of contemporary misunderstandings of this dialectical unity. Likewise, in a review of Joseph Wood Krutch's *The Modern Temper*, Philip Rahv related historical materialism to the theory of tragedy, concluding that the modern recrudescence of tragedy had a material basis in the heroic struggle of the industrial working class.[9]

Despite their evolving critique of the Communist party's exploitation of the proletarian literary movement, Phillips and Rahv remained an integral part of the movement until the demise of the first *Partisan Review* in the fall of 1936. Their criticisms of leftism were balanced with warnings against the "right danger" (writers who "seek to assimilate the Joyce-Eliot sensibility without a clear revolutionary purpose"); and *Partisan Review* contained denunciations of renegades, as well as subtle accolades for Stalinist grandees. Also, Rahv and Phillips wrote as if anticipating an imminent renaissance of proletarian writers and literature: "This last year has seen a quickening in the growth of revolutionary literature in America. The maturing of labor struggles and the increase of Communist influence have given the impetus and created a receptive atmosphere for this literature. As was to be expected, the novel—which is the major literary form of today—has taken the lead. Cantwell, Rollins, Conroy and Armstrong have steered fiction into proletarian patterns of struggle."[10]

By the beginning of 1935 a switch in Communist party policy was becoming visible. Not only had the expected proletarian cultural renaissance failed to materialize, but the Communist International was at the point of a historic political shift away from its ultrarevolutionary Third Period policies of 1928–33. With the disastrous consolidation of Hitlerism, facilitated by the Stalinists' sectarian refusal to seek unity in action with the German Social Democrats against the brown shirts, a process of defensive rapprochement with liberal and "progressive" capitalist forces was under way. The John Reed clubs, founded as organizations of workers and proletarianized intellectuals who were openly anticapitalist and partisans of the Soviet Union, were peremptorily liquidated by the party in deference to structures like the American Writers' Congress and the League of American Writers that had a wider appeal for the liberals among the academics and literati. As Malcolm Cowley recounted, the Comintern's literary and political turnabouts went hand in hand: "Dimitrov called for the People's Front on August 2, 1935, which was some months after the [American Writers'] Congress. But the premonitory rumblings of the People's Front were already spreading over the world."[11]

Before the American Writers' Congress was even held, most of the John Reed clubs were dissolved, which effectually eliminated much of the material support for *Partisan Review* and its copublications. The doubts of Phillips and Rahv regarding the Communist party's relation to the radical literary movement were now becoming certainties. With the end of the John Reed clubs, *Partisan Review* became organizationally independent, although it still remained under the guidance of its three main editors— Phillips and Rahv, who then worked for the Federal Writers Project, and Alan Calmer, employed by International Publishers. It drifted in the direction of the new League of American Writers, which from the 1935 congress until late 1936 considered making *Partisan Review* its organ. Failing to get organizational support, financial difficulties increased and *Partisan Review* merged with Jack Conroy's publication, *Anvil*, in early 1936. When *Partisan Review and Anvil* was forced to close down altogether at the end of that year, Phillips and Rahv continued their search for the reason why the proletarian literary movement had failed—with particular reference to the Communist party's authoritarian interventions.[12]

The two-year interlude between the Communist party's first and second American Writers' congresses (1935 and 1937) was the turning point for Phillips and Rahv. By the time of the Second Congress, Communist party policy had undergone such a complete transformation that not only had the proletarian literary movement been abandoned, but, in accordance with the new Popular Front strategy of alliances with "progressive capitalism," the party's cultural commissars even hailed literary patriotism, the new nationalism of Van Wyck Brooks, and the commercialism of Hollywood. Both the literary and political sensibilities of Phillips and Rahv were outraged. The fraudulent Moscow trials (1936–38) were commencing, and, simultaneously, reports emanated from Spain that the Stalinists had crushed the centrist POUM and other left-wing forces.[13]

Thus Phillips and Rahv arrived at a new assessment of the relationship of revolutionary politics and radical literature. Above all, they concluded that writers and critics must be free of all partisan political and organizational pressure. But they also felt that they had been duped by the appealing simplicity of the notion that writers must ally themselves with the revolutionary working class. As a substitute for a genuine aesthetic, this formula tended to merge politics and literature; it equated the personal views of a writer in specific circumstances with historical class objectives; and it led to the evaluation of a writer's merit and achievements and relation to the working class through his or her support for policies of a particular Marxist party. In a 1940 analysis Rahv concluded, "Within the brief space of a few years the term 'proletarian literature' was transformed into a euphemism for a Communist Party literature which tenaciously upheld a fanatical faith identifying the party with the working class, Stalinism with Marxism, and the Soviet Union with socialism."[14]

In June of 1937, at the Second American Writers' Congress, all ties between the former *Partisan Review* editors and the official Communist movement dissolved. Rahv and Phillips attended the literary-criticism workshop with a little band that included Dwight Macdonald, Mary McCarthy, F. W. Dupee, and Eleanor Clark. Granville Hicks, who was chairing the session, stood helplessly by as Rahv delivered an eloquent speech on the history of freedom and human thought. Dwight Macdonald discussed Trotsky's prose style, emphasizing that its brilliance must be acknowledged even by those who do not agree with Trotsky's politics.[15] Afterwards both Dupee and Rahv were expelled from the party; and, when it became known that a reorganized and politically independent *Partisan Review* was to be launched in the fall, the editors were traduced with a fusillade of invective from Gold, Hicks, and V. J. Jerome in the *New Masses* and *Daily Worker*.

The editorial board of the new *Partisan Review* included several additional names. Three of these—F. W. Dupee, Dwight Macdonald, and

George L. K. Morris—had been friends at Yale. Macdonald and Dupee had edited *Miscellany* in the early 1930s. Then Macdonald joined the staff of *Fortune*, where he was moved increasingly to the left by the bowdlerization of articles. Dupee joined the Communist party in 1936, working with a waterfront unit and serving briefly as literary editor of the *New Masses*. Morris, who provided financial backing for the new journal, was an artist and not as politically involved.

In 1976 William Phillips wrote about how he and Rahv deflected Macdonald's gravitation toward the Communists and won him to their new project, partly through an intense debate:

> We arranged to get together at my house one Sunday—which we referred to for a long time as "Bloody Sunday." As I recall, we were at it all day long; and I still have in my mind a picture of Rahv and myself backing Macdonald up against a wall, knocking down his arguments, firing questions without giving him time to answer, and constantly outshouting him. . . . the result [was] that at the end of the day we were all agreed we should revive *Partisan Review* as an independent radical literary journal.[16]

In a personal interview in 1973, Dupee explained that his own association with *Partisan Review* grew out of a progressive disaffection from the Communist party that somewhat paralleled the experiences of Phillips and Rahv. Dupee started work on the *New Masses* in February 1936. It was here that he first met Philip Rahv, who walked into the office one day. In this same period Dupee also read Leon Trotsky's *History of the Russian Revolution*. He agreed with it, just as he had agreed with Trotsky's *Literature and Revolution*, which he had read earlier. He saw Trotsky's *History* as in part an attack on the Stalinist destruction of the October Revolution.

In the *New Masses* office Dupee became friends with Robert Bendiner, who would later write the book *Just around the Corner* about the depression years. Together they discussed their unhappiness with the Communist party and engaged in attempts to liberalize the policy of the *New Masses*. However, their proposals were rejected and the situation only grew worse. After the Moscow trials began, Theodore Draper, who also worked in the office and was at that time a loyal Stalinist, started listing to Dupee the names of people they had to "get" in the magazine—such as Herbert Solow, a radical journalist known to be sympathetic to Trotsky.

At the same time Dupee was in touch with James Burnham, a professor of philosophy at New York University who was a leader of the Trotskyist political party. Burnham would phone Dupee up at the *New Masses* office to call his attention to the criminal absurdity of the trials. In addition, Rahv introduced Dupee to Phillips and began to involve him in the idea of starting *Partisan Review* up again, on an independent basis. Soon it became clear that the only reason Dupee was staying on the *New Masses* was that Rahv and Phillips thought it was tactically better to remain there right up until they were ready to launch the new magazine; it would make the announcement more dramatic. But not long afterwards the American Committee for the Defense of Leon Trotsky was established and the tensions became too great for Dupee to persist on the Stalinist publication: "The Committee, started while I was still on the *New Masses*, galvanized the radical movement by polarizing it. Like other *New Masses* editors, I was assigned a list of people on the Trotsky Defense Committee and told to contact them and try to persuade them to get off it. Reluctantly I tried one person on my list—Mary McCarthy—and got only a howl of laughter. I then desisted, and was soon out of the picture altogether."[17]

Mary McCarthy captured some of the atmosphere in the New York literary left at this time in her story "Portrait of the Intellectual as a Yale Man," and she wrote about her experiences with the Trotsky defense committee in the memoir "My Confession."[18] In addition, when interviewed by the *Paris Review* in 1961, she described her association with the revamped *Partisan Review* as "a sort of fifth wheel—there may have been more than that—but in any case as a kind of appendage of *Partisan Review*." In her recollection, Phillips and Rahv regarded her as "a sort of gay, good-time girl, from their point of view. And they were men of the thirties. Very serious. That's why my position was so insecure on *Partisan Review;* it wasn't exactly insecure, but . . . lowly. I mean, in *fact*. And that was why they let me write about the theater, because they thought the theater was of absolutely no consequence."[19]

The second half of James Burkhart Gilbert's *Writers and Partisans* describes the association of the five editors as well as McCarthy with the second *Partisan Review*. Gilbert admirably links the journal with the tradition of radical politics and *avant-garde* literature represented by a series of little magazines in the United States. But despite the many virtues of Gilbert's book—especially its scholarly accuracy—Gilbert fails to root the ethos of the second *Partisan Review* sufficiently in the milieu of anti-Stalinist radical New York intellectuals who had coalesced into a significant force by the mid-1930s. Many of these became contributors to the magazine—James T. Farrell, Louis Hacker, Lionel Abel, Lionel Trilling, Herbert Solow, Eleanor Clark, James Burnham, Delmore Schwartz, John Dos Passos, Harold Rosenberg, and Clement Greenberg. In his 1973 interview, Dupee drew special attention to two figures "who played very key roles in our circle. Sidney Hook . . . was once a tremendous figure of inspiration to the radical and revolutionary intellectuals. Also, to all the anti-Stalinist writers in New York, Meyer Schapiro was an oracle. People like Hook and Schapiro were real guiding lights for the *Partisan Review*."[20]

While Hook has steadily gained national prominence and notoriety over the years—partly due to his numerous books and partly due to the aggres-

siveness with which he has defended his increasingly conservative views—
Schapiro has remained a somewhat obscure figure in the public eye,
although his brilliance as a teacher and art historian is legendary at Columbia University and among the New York intelligentsia. But Schapiro
was in many respects the kind of intellectual whose artistic and political
tastes the new *Partisan Review* aspired to please.

Schapiro was born in Shavly, Lithuania, on 23 September 1904 and came
to the United States in 1907. His father had an orthodox Jewish upbringing
but broke with religion when quite young and became interested in science
and socialist ideas while still in Russia. The son attended public schools in
Brooklyn and then studied at Columbia College from 1920 to 1924, where
he majored in philosophy and the history of art. He earned his doctorate in
1929 from Columbia University, where, a year earlier, he started teaching
courses in early Christian and medieval art, modern art, and the theory of
art, in the graduate school.[21]

In the 1920s Schapiro followed the activities of the American Communist
movement and was friends with Whittaker Chambers, who became a
member. But Schapiro always retained his independence of mind and in
the 1930s he was among the first of the party's intellectual supporters to
break with it in public when he saw that Stalinist politics and practice were
having a detrimental effect on the revolutionary movement. Afterwards, he
participated in attempts to coalesce an anti-Stalinist left and he remains an
independent socialist to this day. A man of extraordinary knowledge,
cultural breadth and political integrity, Schapiro has also achieved a personal rapport with many creative artists. The spring 1978 issue of *Social
Research* features nine essays on Meyer Schapiro's work, and the initial
contribution, by Metropolitan Museum of Art official Thomas B. Hess,
begins, "Meyer Schapiro always will have a special place in the history of
art history, not only for his writings, which illuminate a field that includes
the Romanesque with the Modern, the concepts of Marx with those of
Freud, but also for the benevolent influence he has had on so many living
painters and sculptors." Schapiro also shared with the *Partisan Review*
editors an admiration for the life and writings of Leon Trotsky, of whom he
wrote in September 1940: "Morally, [Trotsky] was a giant beside all his
critics set one above the other; and it is the quality of his devotion to the
cause of socialism which shines brilliantly through his life, as it is the
quality of the half-hearted, dilettante, opportunist appropriation of socialist
ideals which clouds the lives of his radical opponents."[22]

The involvement of the *Partisan Review* editors with the exiled Leon
Trotsky, and to a lesser extent with his American followers, was largely
confined to the province of ideas. And even in regard to Trotsky's theoretical views, their admiration was tempered by substantial criticism. Rahv

and Phillips, although familiar with Trotsky's writings, were actually quite removed from contact with the Trotskyist movement. Macdonald, however, became a member of such Trotskyist organizations as the Socialist Workers party and the Workers party from 1939 to 1941, and wrote copiously for the Trotskyist theoretical magazine, *New International*. Dupee contributed a book review of Celine's *Death on the Installment Plan* to *New International*, and engaged in discussions with the Trotskyist leader James Burnham, who tried to recruit him to the movement.

For *Partisan Review*, the magnetism of Leon Trotsky sprang largely from his role in the Russian Revolution and his intellectual and literary brilliance, combined with his European cosmopolitanism. But Phillips and Rahv were also attracted by Trotsky's revolutionary purity in the face of Stalinist corruption and moral turpitude. He was an intellectual who had entered the workers' struggle and had been in the leadership of historical actions, yet he retained sufficient probity to criticize, at a great personal risk, the degeneration of the Russian Revolution. His *History of the Russian Revolution* was a genuine Marxist classic, and he analyzed current political events with sparkling eloquence in trenchant pamphlets and articles. Above all, Trotsky's views on Marxism and art, explained in *Literature and Revolution* (1923) and several essays, seemed compatible with the *Partisan Review* editors' own association of revolutionary theory with literary modernism.

Before the 1937 Writers' Congress Phillips and Rahv had not publicly revealed any association with Trotskyism. Macdonald had defended Trotsky against the charges in the Moscow trials in a letter to the *New Republic* that May; Mary McCarthy had previously become a supporter of the American Committee for the Defense of Leon Trotsky; and James T. Farrell, a friend and ally of *Partisan Review* both in the John Reed Club days and in the early years after its reorganization, was known as an intransigent believer in Trotsky's innocence.[23] Now, in articles for the new *Partisan Review*, Phillips and Rahv took up several of Trotsky's political causes (especially those involving his critique of the Soviet Union and the Communist movement), and they also discussed his contribution to Marxist literary thought.

In March 1938, Phillips attempted to clarify the historical record regarding the aesthetic views of Marx and Engels. After recapitulating their essential contributions—the description of the laws governing the cultural superstructure, their tributes to various writers, several warnings against economic determinism—Phillips cited Trotsky as the only major Marxist leader who had written authentic literary criticism. Trotsky was outstanding in that he "not only saw in literature a mirror of society but was acutely conscious of those qualities, which, taken together, make up the special vision of a work of art." Phillips then summarized and praised Trotsky's analysis of postrevolutionary Soviet culture and his explanation of how the shifting social forces were refracted through the textures of literary work. More important to Phillips, however, was Trotsky's "polemic against those critics who were impatient with history and wanted to establish by decree a proletarian art." Phillips concluded his study with tributes to Trotsky's amplitude and variety of insights. He also explained Trotsky's approach to the nature of the artistic element using Eliot as an example: "Is not the autumnal sensibility of Eliot a kind of comment on the state of society?"[24]

Rahv, too, considered Trotsky's *Literature and Revolution* when he surveyed the record of an eventful decade in the summer of 1939. But on the whole his commentary was a demonstration of how far Rahv had evolved from vivid confidence in a proletarian literary renaissance. He noted that while, in the early part of the decade, the introduction of young writers to political action had played a liberating role, now, on the eve of war, with the Communist party more patriotic than the Democrats, the political movement was retrogressing toward a New Gentility. The intellectual or artist who wished to remain faithful to truth must now stand alone with his or her conscience:

> If a sufficiently organized, active and broad revolutionary movement existed, it might assimilate the artist by opening to him its own avenue of experience; but in the absence of such a movement all he can do is utilize the possibilities of individual and group secession from, and protest against, the dominant values of our time. Needless to say this does not imply a return to a philosophy of individualism. It means that all we have left to go on now is individual integrity—the probing conscience, the will to repulse and assail the forces released by a corrupt reality.

Focusing on how to maintain the integrity of the intellectual, Rahv was clearly in the process of departing from the orthodox Marxist view of the historically determined central role of the international working class. The impact of Trotsky on Rahv was not, as it was for his political adherents, a reaffirmation of authentic Marxism-Leninism with a corresponding mandate to organize the vanguard of the proletariat for the coming struggle for power. Trotsky now seemed more important to Rahv for other kinds of insights:

> An examination of the special role and changing status of the intelligentsia is, therefore, essential to any social examination of modern literature.
> Trotsky is, I believe, the only Marxist critic who develops his analysis of writers and literary trends largely around this concept. . . . But Trotsky does not credit this factor with sufficient power.[25]

Accordingly, for a time *Partisan Review*, as its position emerged in Rahv's essays, regarded the impending war from a heterodox position. The magazine accepted classical Marxist analysis, as reaffirmed by Trotsky, in

the critique of capitalism and in the way Trotsky explained the degeneration of the Russian Revolution, and the editors even applied it to the
coming war itself: "The exigencies of imperialist rivalries makes [*sic*] a new
world war inevitable, especially since, with the degeneration of the Comintern, the threat of revolutionary action has been definitely withdrawn. . . .
The war, even if the 'democrats' win, will not solve a single fundamental
problem of society. . . . Only unalterable opposition to capitalism, only
utilization of the imperialist war for revolutionary ends, opens any prospect
to humanity and its culture."[26] Yet *Partisan Review* presented no corresponding working-class program of action against the war; its great concern
seemed to be that the interimperialist maelstrom would constitute a terrible test for the morality and culture of the intellectuals.

Several documents reveal the attitude of Leon Trotsky and his American
supporters toward the *Partisan Review* group, after the latter's public
break with the Communist party in 1937. In a letter to editorial board
member Dwight Macdonald, Trotsky expressed his fear that *Partisan
Review* was tending to hide behind the abstract banners of "independence"
and "freedom," rather than using these concepts as a stepping stone for
ideological struggle. He also suggested that, in the face of the coming social
crisis, the journal might well transform itself into a "small cultural monastery, guarding itself from the outside world by skepticism, agnosticism, and
respectability."[27]

In "Art and Politics in Our Epoch," published in *Partisan Review* only a
few months later, Trotsky offered a perspective for revolutionary artists and
writers challenged by the dual obstacles of capitalism and the Soviet
Thermidor: "Generally speaking, art is an expression of man's need for a
harmonious and complete life, that is to say, his need for those major
benefits of which a class society has deprived him. That is why a protest
against reality, either conscious or unconscious, active or passive, optimistic or pessimistic, always forms part of a really creative piece of work.
Every new tendency in art has begun with a rebellion" (p. 105). Trotsky
argued his thesis by pointing to the past pattern from aesthetic revolt to
acceptance in the bourgeois academies that was followed by classicism,
romanticism, realism, naturalism, symbolism, impressionism, cubism, and
futurism. However, continuation of this trend depended on the stability of
bourgeois society. He asserted that in its decline, capitalism was no longer
capable of absorbing the implicit rebellion of new tendencies in art:
"Hence new tendencies take on a more and more violent character, alter-
nating between hope and despair. The artistic schools of the last few
decades—cubism, futurism, dadism, surrealism—follow each other without reaching a complete development. Art, which is the most complex part
of culture, the most sensitive and at the same time the least protected,
suffers most from the decay of bourgeois society" (p. 105). Since, from the
Marxist view, art is in itself insufficient as an independent force to over-

come social crisis or even defend itself, the solution requires social transformation and "the function of art in our epoch is determined by its relation
to the revolution" (p. 106).

According to Trotsky, the mistake made by many leftist intellectuals was
that, instead of declaring their allegiance to the revolutionary international
proletariat, they supported only the victorious Soviet revolution and gave
fealty to the new privileged stratum of the Stalinist bureaucracy. Furthermore, they failed to see how the fate of Soviet art testified to the character
of art's relation to revolution. Following October 1917, Soviet art underwent a great liberation. Then, after the rise and consolidation of Stalin's
bureaucratic regime, artistic quality deteriorated. Even courtly art, Trotsky noted, though based on idealization, avoided the outright falsification
that had marred Soviet art so opprobriously—especially as exemplified by
the careers of Vsevolod Ivanov and Alexei Tolstoy, and in the falsification of
the events of the Revolution in cultural artifacts. As a contrast, Trotsky
pointed to the Mexican artist Diego Rivera, whose frescoes could still draw
inspiration from the true spirit of the October insurrection.

Now, Trotsky argued, the impending social crisis generated by the war
demanded a response from dissident artists and intellectuals. Referring to
an attack on Trotskyism in a recent letter published in *Partisan Review*, he
emphasized that one must not fear smallness and isolation, for "not a single
progressive idea has begun with a 'mass base' " (p. 112). This was the rule
for art as well as for politics. Trotsky concluded by declaring the necessity
of supporting the revolutionary vanguard of the working class (that is, the
Trotskyist Fourth International); but he simultaneously emphasized how
correct it was to oppose supervision of art by any party, either Stalinist or
Trotskyist: "The ideological base of the conflict between the Fourth and the
Third Internationals is the profound disagreement not only on the tasks of
the party but in general on the entire material and spiritual life of mankind"
(p. 144). Though society might require a new flag and revolutionary program for its rescue, only a reactionary bureaucracy like the Stalinist one
could think of leading or commanding art:

> Art, like science, not only does not seek orders, but by its very essence, cannot
> tolerate them. Artistic creation has its own laws—even when it consciously
> serves a social movement. Truly intellectual creation is incompatible with lies,
> hypocrisy and the spirit of conformity. Art can become a strong ally of revolution
> only insofar as it remains faithful to itself. Poets, painters, sculptors and musi-
> cians will themselves find their own approach and methods, if the struggle for
> freedom of oppressed classes and peoples scatters the clouds of skepticism and of
> pessimism which cover the horizon of mankind. [P. 114]

That autumn (1938) *Partisan Review* published "Manifesto: Towards a
Free Revolutionary Art," which, although signed by Rivera and the French
surrealist André Breton, was largely written by Trotsky. This declaration

repeated the sentiments expressed in "Art and Politics in Our Epoch," and emphasized that the artist is "the natural ally of revolution" (p. 118). It called for the formation of an International Federation of Independent Revolutionary Art. In the winter of 1939, *Partisan Review* also printed a letter from Trotsky to Breton, in which he traced the deterioration of Malraux's work as he changed from an adventuristic but truthful supporter of the colonial revolution to his new status as apologist for Stalinism: "The struggle for revolutionary ideas in art must begin once again with the struggle for artistic *truth*, not in terms of any single school, but in terms of *the immutable faith of the artist in his own inner self*. Without this there is no art. 'You shall not lie!'—that is the formula of salvation" (p. 124).

The purpose of the new organization of revolutionary artists, Trotsky elaborated, was not to be an aesthetic or political school, but to "oxidize the atmosphere in which artists breathe and create," for under present conditions of international social cataclysm, "truly independent creation cannot but be revolutionary by its very nature" (p. 124).

The appearance of articles and programmatic statements by Trotsky in *Partisan Review* did not by any means indicate complete agreement on the part of Phillips and Rahv. The journal, by its nature, was open to a variety of radical political opinions. Nevertheless there was a definite confluence of sentiment on many questions, and in the summer of 1939 the names of Phillips and Rahv appeared as supporters of the newly formed League for Cultural Freedom and Socialism. The views expressed in the league's programmatic statement corresponded to those in previous articles by Trotsky, Breton, and Rivera. Included among the league's sponsors were a number of intellectuals known to be members of the American Trotskyist organization: James Burnham, Dwight Macdonald (the acting secretary of the League for Cultural Freedom and Socialism), Sherry Mangan (an American poet and journalist living in Paris, who contributed the "Paris Letter" column to *Partisan Review* under the pseudonym Sean Niall), George Novack (a former Harvard philosophy student who had served as secretary of the American Committee for the Defense of Leon Trotsky), Harry Roskolenko (a New York poet and early Trotskyist), and John Wheelwright (a New England poet and architectural historian).

But a gap still remained between the orthodox Marxists and Rahv and Phillips, and it would widen considerably during the next few years. The Trotskyists themselves indicated the areas of difference quite prophetically in an editorial in their paper, *Socialist Appeal*, which greeted the newly reorganized *Partisan Review* in 1937. The editorial congratulated the magazine for its break with the Communist party, and its repudiation of Stalinist extraliterary legislation. But the Trotskyists disputed some of the formulations employed by the new journal in its first editorial (December 1937), which suggested that the editors might be overreacting against organized politics in general because of their experience with the Stalinists. The *Partisan Review*, the *Socialist Appeal* editorial noted, was calling for independence not just in art, but in politics as well. To the Trotskyists, as for all orthodox Marxists, the notion of political independence or nonpartisanship was impossible in a social environment divided by warring classes, where one's every act contains political implications and consequences, including even one's subjective desire for neutrality.

To the contrary, the *Socialist Appeal* argued, the lesson to be learned from the Stalinist experience was not that *all* relations with political parties are inherently deleterious to art, but only that certain kinds are. The negative influence of the Communist party on radical intellectuals and literature did not spring from the party's being a revolutionary Leninist vanguard, but precisely from the opposite fact—that it was a bureaucratic instrument of the Thermidorean reaction in the Soviet Union. As a corrective, the Trotskyists recommended two things: first, friendly collaboration between the revolutionary cultural journal and their revolutionary party, and second, aggressive opposition by *Partisan Review* to the Stalinists as "a pack of conscienceless scoundrels in the service of the great corrupter and destroyer of the Socialist revolution." The new *Partisan Review*, the editorial asserted, had made a good beginning; but in order to thrive as a genuine revolutionary force it must not only maintain its art as independent—it must actually link up with the working-class movement. "In avowing itself hospitable, experimental, democratic, the *Partisan Review* has set its foot on the right road. But it is not enough to have a broad circumference; it is equally necessary to have an ideological and political center from which all the rest logically radiates."[28]

The literary and political peregrination of *Partisan Review* from 1934 to 1939 shows the progressive resolution of various problems, while the magazine also abandoned other positions along the way. From the editors' original view that the aesthetic advances of the 1920s were ambiguous, Rahv had turned by 1939 to an overwhelmingly positive evaluation. Modern literature, he affirmed, is essentially a dispute with the modern world. To a large degree the modern artist's introversion and privacy are necessary for survival under capitalism, because in this way artists defy commodity fetishism and "remain the masters instead of the victims of their products." Considering the recent evolution and character of the Stalinist-liberal (Popular Front) alliance of writers and their return to literary patriotism, Rahv concluded, "In view of what has happened, is it not clear that the older tradition was a thousand times more 'progressive'—if that is to be our criterion—was infinitely more disinterested, infinitely more sensitive to the actual conditions of human existence, than the shallow political writing of our latter days?"[29]

Such a view, which flowered at the decade's end, was decidedly influ-

enced by the period of transition, 1935–37; *Partisan Review*'s break with
Stalinism implied more of a repudiation of Marxism than was immediately
visible at that time. That the Moscow trials of these years were a watershed
for the whole decade was nowhere revealed more eloquently than in Rahv's
own essay "Trials of the Mind." The trials challenged the whole significance of the Soviet experiment, which had been such a powerful factor in
motivating American writers to become part of the Communist movement.
It was also a trial and test for various components of orthodox Marxist
theory—and Leon Trotsky had arisen as the great defender of Marxism-
Leninism against the epigones in Moscow. But for Rahv it was also an issue
with special meanings for intellectuals: both the intellectuals on trial in
Moscow and the intellectuals in the United States, many of whom remained silent through a self-imposed terrorism. Rahv frankly admitted that
despite his early questioning of Communist party policy he was surprised
and shaken by the trials, this "massacre of the firstborn of the October
Revolution." And Rahv's beliefs were upset far beyond just a loss of faith in
the Soviet Union: "We were not prepared for defeat. The future had our
confidence, which we granted freely, sustained by the tradition of Marxism. In that tradition we saw the marriage of science and humanism. But
now, amidst all these ferocious surprises, who has the strength to reaffirm
his beliefs, to transcend the feeling that he has been duped? One is afraid of
one's fear. Will it soon become so precise as to exclude hope?"[30] Thus a
process of doubt and skepticism had begun: the trials had undermined the
classical model of proletarian revolution altogether for Rahv, and so his
preoccupation with the alienated literary intellectual, which had always
been present, reemerged stronger than ever. It was central in his transitional attraction to Trotsky.

Although the *Partisan Review* editors were far from being Trotskyists,
the impact of Trotsky on them was substantial. It was not a passing fad or
symbol, as one recent historian has implied.[31] In 1973 Dupee reminisced,
"There's no question that Leon Trotsky definitely influenced me politically
more than any American did. Many liberal-radical intellectuals in the 1930s
worshipped FDR, but I never did."[32] But the influence was incomplete,
and Phillips and Rahv in particular trusted their own disposition toward
independent critical thought, reinforced by the negative experience with
Stalinism, to keep their distance.

Trotsky and his ideas were a vehicle by which radical intellectuals like
Phillips and Rahv, whose primary concern was literary inquiry and not the
building of political organizations, could break with Stalinism and still
maintain themselves for a while as part of the Marxist left. Trotsky's
impressive critique of Stalinism broadened their horizons on that question
beyond their own personal experience with the Communist party's moral
bankruptcy. As they followed Trotsky's analysis of political events, their

own method and mode of thought and analysis undoubtedly were affected by his polemical sharpness and historical scale. And above all, Trotsky himself incarnated the ideal of the revolutionary intellectual in excoriating the exploitation of capitalism, warring against the tragic betrayal of the Russian Revolution, and standing before the world, defiant of the Kremlin on the prisoner's dock, alone in Coyoacan. But in the eyes of the editors of *Partisan Review*, Trotsky ultimately failed to build a viable political movement and paid the price with his life. After that, and the start of the Second World War, their journey to the cultural monastery was more direct and unimpeded.

CHAPTER 13

JAMES T. FARRELL

<hr/>

The End of a Literary Decade

This essay, "The End of a Literary Decade," was written toward the end of 1939, and published in the *American Mercury*, in December, 1939. It gives a clear sense of the Thirties, and constitutes an immediate reaction to the literary atmosphere and writings of that decade.

James T. Farrell
New York
12 July 1979

The decade of the 1930s, which comes to a close this month, witnessed many controversies among writers, some so bitter that they led to enduring hatreds. The issues that evoked these controversies were posed by the left, and in the last years of the decade they became outright political in character. The accent of politics in literature and criticism has been increasingly more pronounced in these last ten years. In these notes I shall deal mainly with these features of the decade, but the reader should be reminded that a discussion of the controversies and the role of the left in American literary and intellectual life does not exhaust the subject of the "literary thirties." Many writers continued to function without being involved in the political and politicoliterary debates of the time. Among these one can number some whose position in contemporary writing is unquestioned; there is William Faulkner, for instance.

<hr/>

This essay was originally published in *American Mercury* 48 (1939): 408–15, and contains the essence of the remarks Farrell made at the University of Alabama, Tuscaloosa, during the 1978 Alabama Symposium on English and American Literature. We gratefully acknowledge permission given by *American Mercury* and James T. Farrell to republish it. Except for minor corrections in the text and the addition of two notes, the article is reprinted as it originally appeared.—EDS.

Likewise, although much has been written concerning "social content" in literature and the portrayal of social struggles in fiction, those in no way associated with political movements have frequently been most successful in utilizing material of social struggles in works of fiction. One of the finest American first novels of many years is Robert Penn Warren's *Night Rider*, which portrays a social struggle with insight and without sacrificing individual characterization to didacticism. Yet Mr. Warren has not been associated with the political tendencies that have clashed inside the ranks of American criticism and literature. . . . In short, this article does not aim at a complete survey in any sense of the word.

When the 1930s opened, there was a growing number of writers and intellectuals who thought that a radical—yes, a revolutionary—change was necessary and on its way in our society. In the first years of the decade, criticism of the status quo sharpened. It began to be reflected in new fiction. John Chamberlain's excellent *Farewell to Reform* appeared; the very title as well as the reception the book received were symptomatic of a mood of the time. Now, as the decade draws to an end, many of the same writers and intellectuals feel that bitter reaction, fascism, is imminent. In the early 1930s there was some hope and confidence. At the end, there is anxiety, apprehension, even signs of panic. The thirties have produced a new generation of tired radicals, radicals who are perhaps even more tired than their predecessors of 1917 and 1918. Important in the experience of these many writers and intellectuals during the ten years is the Soviet Union. In 1930 the Soviets still seemed to point the way to a new and more just social order; but in 1939 the Russian Revolution has been betrayed, and the ruling regime of the Soviet Union is obviously counterrevolutionary. This is the tragedy intimately bound up with the cycle from hope to despair through which so many have passed in this decade.

Many of the younger American writers who went left in the early 1930s turned their eyes toward politics with little if any background. Some of them were then political illiterates, and some have remained precisely that. As a whole, they were practically unread in politics, political theory, economics, and history. The first stage of their politicoliterary experience was generally one of novelty. They accepted and expressed all sorts of extravagant and irrational opinions. With the arrogance of ignorance they often ventured into print on subjects of which they knew nothing. They accepted ready-made political slogans and programs from the Stalinist movement.

Time was when radicalism opened men's eyes: it attracted their attention to a wider intellectual range. But the radical movement that many writers and intellectuals came to in the 1930s closed them. It was not often a path of intellectual adventure, and frequently it was a means to intellectual suicide. The basic political and historic causes of such a development are outside the scope of this article, but some of the things that happened are not. Neither are some of the results.

We can see these results in contrasts between certain individual careers. For instance, in literary criticism, one of the exceptions to what happened to many in this decade is Edmund Wilson. In the early thirties, he joined in the spiritual and intellectual migration of writers to the left. However, he retained his judgment, perception, and independence. When new questions were posed, he investigated them in all seriousness. He did not accept ready-made slogans merely because a radical brand was put on them. The result can be seen in his work. Whatever one thinks of various of his conclusions, Wilson's literary criticism has been the finest written in the last decade. It has revealed a mind that is constantly growing, and constantly enlarging its interests. A similar example, in the case of a younger critic, is that of Philip Rahv.

There is a sharp and revealing difference between Wilson in this decade and Malcolm Cowley, his successor as literary editor of the *New Republic*. Cowley also "went left." Despite the fact that he has delivered speeches on the values of the revolutionary movement to writers, his own work shows no signs that he has gained any benefits himself. His criticism during the last decade lacks character, analytical capacity, and breadth of judgment: it is wishy-washy, replete with personal asides, and often it is no more than an oblique application of the "party line" of the moment.[1]

An even better example is Granville Hicks. Before he became a Stalinist critic and joined the Communist party, Hicks was an uninspired book reviewer and critic. After this step, he laid down the "party line" in literature. He was one of the most strident of critical sectarians. His judgments were practically always didactic. He wrote much nonsense about the class character of literature, and indulged again and again in advice-mongering to writers that was accepted only by the most mediocre. When the party line changed to that of the Popular Front policy, in 1935, the character of Mr. Hicks's judgments began to change. He started to praise writers whom he attacked brutally only shortly before. In the new period as in the old, he continued to lay down the line. But now, at the end of the decade, he resigns from the Communist party. His letter of resignation casts doubts on the leadership, and more important, asserts that he could not remain in the party while harboring doubts. In other words, he could not remain in the party and think for himself. This confession coming from him makes his literary criticism of the last ten years ridiculous. It contains its own comment, and it epitomizes much of the experience of many left writers in the thirties.

During the first years of the decade, literary controversies still related to literature—to such questions as proletarian literature, Marxism, and criticism. Briefly, they were concerned with the relationship of literature and

politics, and literature and society. The essential issue in these controversies was sometimes revealed, but not always. Essentially it was
whether literature should exist in its own right and develop according to its
own logic, or whether it should be considered mere tactics for some
"higher" purpose. The issue involved was one of literary authoritarianism
versus literary freedom. Max Eastman characterized it aptly with his
phrase "artists in uniform."

A number of books were written according to the pattern of the left
sectarians. These were hailed in their day, largely unread, and are now
forgotten. One of the last of this type of novel to appear was Edwin Seaver's
Between the Hammer and the Anvil; it elaborated the sentiment, "Don't
call me sweetheart, call me comrade." However, this kind of critical
legislation did create dilemmas for some writers, dilemmas from which
they have not always escaped. John Chamberlain has pictured this dilemma in his chapter on literature in Harold Stearns's symposium, *America
Now*. I quote him:

> The dilemma of the socially conscious writer [read "Stalinist"] is illustrated by
> a young novelist of my acquaintance who has been trying for years to finish a
> book about the San Francisco waterfront strike of 1934. He cannot finish the
> book because he is all at sea concerning the motivating philosophy behind it.
> From month to month and year to year his attitude toward the present value of
> his protagonist keeps fluctuating with the movement of radical values [read
> "party lines"] of radical morality, in a world of Moscow trials, undeclared wars,
> "Trojan horse" tactics, and political "timing" that frequently works out into
> two-timing.[2]

The value of revolutionary movements to culture is that they create a
ferment of ideas and forge new perspectives that influence the cultural
productions of the future. Such was a contribution of the French Revolution; such was the effect of the Irish national revolution; such for a few short
years was the effect of the Russian Revolution before the OGPU (Unified
State Political Administration) put a uniform on the artist. There was a
certain ferment in the early thirties, but it was canalized. And predicaments such as that of Mr. Chamberlain's friend were one of the results.

In 1935 the Communist International adopted the Popular Front line.
This was reflected in American cultural environments. A kind of literary
populism was born. The very meaning of "going left" changed. Not only
serious writers were included now in the left; the influence and orbit
stretched out until it encompassed nearly everyone *but* radicals. The new
"cultural front" hastily enlisted commercial writers, high-priced Hollywood scenarists, a motley assortment of mystery-plot mechanics, humor-
ists, newspaper columnists, stripteasers, band leaders, glamour girls,
actors, press agents, Broadway producers, aging wives with thwarted literary ambitions, and other such ornaments of American culture.

A number of famous writers, until then nonradical, were drawn into the new front. Their names were hung in the shiny bay window out front for the "cultural" customers, and under their names were slogans calling for the defense of culture and democracy, not to mention the salvation of humanity. But what went on inside was another story. Under cover of this Popular Front movement was conducted one of the most pernicious literary witch hunts in American literary history. Practically all American writers of liberal or radical persuasion who opposed the line (the Stalin murders and so on) were bitterly attacked, often slandered. Writers attacked their colleagues with manners and methods typical of ward politicians wresting the job of precinct captain from a rival. Sometimes these attacks were openly political. On other occasions, they took the form of gang-ups which pretended to be something other than what they were. The League of American Writers was one of the centers of this witch hunt. Many of its members are ornaments of present-day literature as viewed from the weekly literary supplements. And many of its members joined in the witch hunt. When those who were thus attacked tried to defend themselves, some of these ornaments would declare with sudden "objectivity" that this was all factional politics. And they would go on affirming the approved line with appropriate gentility. Some of these ornaments are now declaring with characteristic objectivity that they never were fellow-travelers. But without them, this pernicious literary witch hunt could not have been conducted with such immediate efficacy.

The decade of the 1920s produced more important works in American fiction than that of the 1930s. However, the writers who began to publish in the thirties reveal one of the most interesting of developments in American writing—interesting sociologically. Out of a welter of books, there are a few of genuine merit and value, among them Henry Roth's *Call It Sleep*, Nelson Algren's *Somebody in Boots*, Edward Dahlberg's *Bottom Dogs*, some short stories by Erskine Caldwell, Daniel Fuchs's novels, John Fante's *Wait until Spring, Bandini*, and others. But many of the works were written by flashes in the pan who didn't really flash. Yet many of the forgotten novels of the decade, when viewed together, reveal a definite current in American writing.

The dominant tradition of twentieth-century American literature is one of realism and naturalism. It has produced a literature that has told us, in concrete terms, the cost of American civilization. It has unfolded the patterns of American destiny, posed in terms of individual lives the problems and contradictions of our society, and corrected many latter-day myths. Also it has often cried out in social protest, and it has set the basis for the creation of the speech of Americans into a language of literature as well as one of life. Most of the newer writers of the 1930s, whether their works be good, bad, or indifferent, have worked in that tradition.

However, we notice increasingly a difference in the types of environment described by the younger writers, and an attempt to introduce types of character that have not hitherto been treated seriously in American fiction. The 1930s in fiction attempted, briefly, to tell the story of the actuality of the American Melting Pot. Most of the younger writers of the period come from social backgrounds new to American fiction, though not to American life. They have come from the bottom and the near-bottom of American society. Their work reflects this background. Armenians, Negroes (such as those in Richard Wright's powerful book, *Uncle Tom's Children*), Italians, Jewish soda clerks, sharecroppers, Maine Yankees, miners, Cape Cod Portuguese, poolroom habitués—such are the characters whom the newcomers to our fiction have sought to describe.

In much of their work, these writers have relied on experience *qua* experience. Often they have seemed to feel that novelty is in itself sufficient for a work of literature. In consequence, there has often been no drive, no struggle revealed to attain a way of seeing life and an orientation that would permit many of these younger writers to continue growing and expanding, to go back into their material and see in it fresh emphases and additional meanings. I have spoken already of the ferment revolutionary movements create, which in turn affects culture. In the early 1930s, there was some expectation that this would happen in America. But dogmatism is the coffin lid that closes down over ferment. In consequence, many of the writers of the 1930s have not fulfilled the promise that was claimed for them.

Such writing shades off into many directions. Some of it is serious in the sense that Matthew Arnold would have used that word in relation to literature. But this tendency has also created a new type of popular fiction, the hard-boiled novel. This type of novel relies on expressive language; it lacks any underlying structure but does fit a Hollywood pattern of action; it is swift; it has all the mannerisms and none of the substance of genuine realistic writing. Works of this character are the books of Jerome Weidman, Steinbeck's *Of Mice and Men*, James Cain's *The Postman Always Rings Twice*. These books stand in a sort of intermediate position between genuinely serious works of realistic writing, and merely popular fictional entertainment. Their spread and popularity has aided in the confusing of literary values. And they have become characteristic of the 1930s.

These are some of the developments of the decade. What of the 1940s? Prediction is useless. The generation of writers of the next decade will have to come forth at a time of profound social crisis. The air is full of propaganda, passion, and partisanship. Conditions for writing seem worse daily. The dangers of suppression hang over the writer. The interest of men is getting far from the paths and the ways of literature. The coming writer stands amidst a kind of ruin. He must kindle excitement and enthusiasm for his work, confidence in himself, and he must forget his own perspectives. There are no literary movements now. There is little criticism written that is worth the paper on which it is printed. There is more talk of defending culture with bayonets now than of producing culture and gaining from it those humanizing lessons and values that go so far to make man civilized. Thus dawn the 1940s. . . .

Notes

Introduction

1. Alfred Kazin, *On Native Grounds* (1942; reprint ed., Garden City, N.Y.: Doubleday, Anchor Books, 1956), pp. 283–84.

2. Lionel Trilling, "A Novel of the Thirties," in *The Last Decade Essays and Reviews*, by Lionel Trilling, ed. Diana Trilling (New York: Harcourt, Brace, Jovanovich, 1979), pp. 15–16.

3. Kazin, *On Native Grounds,* pp. 286–87.

4. Leslie Fiedler, *Waiting for the End* (New York: Stein and Day, 1964), p. 33.

5. Modernism and realism are more closely linked than some modernist critics might like to admit. These modes and sensibilities had for some time existed side by side, mingling and mixing in curious ways that occasionally resulted in fruitful and important cross-pollination. Can one imagine, for instance, the invention of cubist collage or Duchamp's readymades without the triumph of the nineteenth-century realist aesthetics that legitimized the appropriation of gritty facts from the world in order to convert them almost unmediated into works of art?

6. James T. Farrell to editors, dated 6 July 1978.

7. Henry Roth's debt to Joyce in *Call It Sleep* is discussed intelligently in Bonnie Lyons, *Henry Roth: The Man and His Work* (New York, 1976).

8. Walter B. Rideout, *The Radical Novel in the United States, 1900–1954* (Cambridge, Mass.: Harvard University Press, 1956). Between 1900 and 1910, twenty-four were written; between 1911 and 1919, twenty-one; between 1920 and 1929, ten (not including Dos Passos's *Manhattan Transfer*); between 1930 and 1939, seventy (including all of Farrell's work and Roth's *Call It Sleep*, but not Dos Passos's works); between 1940 and 1949, twenty-seven (including Norman Mailer's *The Naked and the Dead*).

9. Stephen Spender, *The 30's and After* (New York: Random House, 1978), p. 13.

10. Ibid., p. 14.

11. See Daniel Aaron, *Writers on the Left* (New York: Harcourt, Brace and World, 1961), chapters 8–11, for a full discussion of the (mostly) public debates.

12. See James Gilbert, "Literature and Revolution in the United States: *The Partisan Review,*" *Journal of Contemporary History* 5 (1967), reprinted in *Literature and Politics in the Twentieth Century,* ed. Walter Lacqueur and George L. Mosse (New York: Harper Torchbooks, 1967), pp. 154–55. This actually seemed to be taking place in Russia. Witness the brilliant work of the constructivist artists and architects as well as the new experiments in theater by Meyerhold and others: and most visibly, perhaps, to Americans, the inventive filmmaking of Eisenstein, Vertov, and Dovzhenko.

13. See Edmund Wilson, "The Literary Consequences of the Crash," originally published in the 23 March 1932 issue of the *New Republic.* Of the crash, Wilson says, "to the writers and artists of my generation who had grown up in the Big Business era and had always resented its barbarism, its crowding-out of everything they cared about, these years were not depressing but stimulating. One couldn't help being exhilarated at the sudden unexpected collapse of that stupid gigantic fraud. It gave us a new sense of freedom; and it gave us a new sense of power to find ourselves still carrying on while the bankers, for a change, were taking a beating" (reprinted in *The Shores of Light* [New York: Farrar, Straus and Young, 1952], pp. 498–99).

14. Wilson, "The Literary Class War," *Shores of Light,* p. 539.

15. Ibid., p. 534.

16. Ibid., p. 538.

17. The attempt to attract bourgeois intellectuals by capitalizing on their modernist alienation has already been mentioned. Subsequently, there was a switch to support for and promotion of proletarian writing. Finally, in 1935, there was the concerted effort to shift to the Popular Front view. Even during the period of ultraleftism of the intellectuals between 1929 and 1934 (according to Gilbert, "Literature and Revolution," p. 157), Communists were suspicious of the intellectuals because they were not working class. Gold thought their bourgeois consciousness could be controlled, but he was wrong.

18. See Gilbert, "Literature and Revolution." See also Christopher Lasch, "Modernism, Politics, and Philip Rahv," *Partisan Review* 47 (1980): 183–94, for a penetrating, often brilliant treatment of Rahv's attempt to reconcile modernism and Marxism.

19. Walter Lacqueur, "Literature and the Historian," in *Literature and Politics,* ed. Lacqueur and Mosse, p. 10. The same is true for visual artists. See Donald Drew Egbert, *Social Radicalism and the Arts: Western Europe* (New York: Alfred A. Knopf, 1970).

20. See Arnold Hauser, *Social History of Art,* 2 vols. (New York: Alfred A. Knopf, 1951); and Egbert, *Social Radicalism.*

21. Irving Howe, *Politics and the Novel* (New York: Horizon Press, 1957), pp. 17ff.

Chapter 3
"Friendship Won't Stand That" by Townsend Ludington

1. Lawson to Dos Passos, 24 August 1937. For permission to quote from Lawson's and Dos Passos's correspondence, I am indebted to Susan Edmond

Lawson and Amanda Lawson, Elizabeth Dos Passos, and the Alderman Library of the University of Virginia, where Dos Passos's papers are housed.

2. John Dos Passos, "A Farewell to Europe!" *Common Sense* 6 (July 1937): 10.

3. John Dos Passos, *The Fourteenth Chronicle: Letters and Diaries of John Dos Passos*, ed. Townsend Ludington (Boston: Gambit, 1973), p. 514.

4. Lawson to Dos Passos, 14 September [1937], Dos Passos Papers.

5. Lawson to Dos Passos, 14 September [1937], Dos Passos Papers. For a discussion of the Communists' maneuverings see Frank A. Warren, III, *Liberals and Communism: The Red Decade Revisited* (Bloomington: Indiana University Press, 1966), pp. 133–37.

6. Dos Passos, *Fourteenth Chronicle*, pp. 512–13. This letter belongs *after* that in *Fourteenth Chronicle*, pp. 514–15.

7. John Dos Passos, "The Communist Party and the War Spirit," *Common Sense* 6 (December 1937): 11–14.

8. Dos Passos, *Fourteenth Chronicle*, pp. 516–17.

9. Dos Passos to Lawson, postmarked 8 August 1938, Dos Passos Papers.

10. Interview with author, 17 October 1974.

11. Lawson to Dos Passos, 30 August [1939], Dos Passos Papers.

12. Dos Passos to Walter Rumsey Marvin, postmarked 3 April 1919, Dos Passos Papers.

13. Dos Passos, foreword to *Roger Bloomer*, by John Howard Lawson (New York: Thomas Seltzer, 1923), pp. v, vii.

14. Dos Passos to Arthur McComb, n.d., Dos Passos Papers.

15. John Howard Lawson, "Biographical Notes," *Zeitschrift fur Anglistik und Amerikanistik* 4, no. 1 (1956): 73; *Processional: A Jazz Symphony of American Life in Four Acts* (New York: Thomas Seltzer, 1925), pp. vii–viii; and Stark Young, "Jazzing Folly and Beauty," *New York Times*, 13 January 1925, sec. 1, p. 17.

16. *New York Sun*, 12 November 1927, cited in "Inventory: John Howard Lawson Papers," Special Collections, Southern Illinois University Library, 4 January 1971, pp. 5–6.

17. John Dos Passos, "The New Masses I'd Like," *New Masses* 1 (June 1926): 20.

18. Michael Gold, "Let It Be Really New!" *New Masses* 1 (June 1926): 20, 26.

19. John Dos Passos, *Manhattan Transfer* (New York: Harper Brothers, 1925), p. 404.

20. Michael Gold, "A Barbaric Poem of New York," *New Masses* 1 (August 1926): 25–26.

21. Stuart Chase, "A Yell from the Gallery," *New Masses* 1 (June 1926): 22; John Howard Lawson, "Debunking the Art Theatre," *New Masses* 1 (June 1926): 22, 28, 30; and Lawson, interview with author, 17 October 1974.

22. John Dos Passos, "They Are Dead Now," *New Masses* 3 (October 1927): 7; *U.S.A.: The Big Money* (Boston: Houghton Mifflin, 1963), pp. 413–14; and *In All Countries* (London: Constable, 1934), pp. 52, 66–69.

23. Lawson, "Biographical Notes," p. 74.

24. "Inventory: John Howard Lawson Papers," p. 7.

25. Lawson, interview with author, 17 October 1974; Dos Passos, *Fourteenth Chronicle*, pp. 398, 382–83, 409; and editorial, *New Masses* 10 (6 March 1934): 8–9.

26. Dos Passos, *Fourteenth Chronicle*, pp. 435–36.

27. Lawson, "Biographical Notes," p. 74; Harold Clurman, *The Fervent Years*

(New York: Hill and Wang, 1957), p. 87; John Howard Lawson, *Success Story* (New York: Farrar and Rinehart, 1932), p. 40; and Michael Gold, "A Bourgeois Hamlet of Our Time," *New Masses* 11 (10 April 1934): 29.

28. Lawson to Dos Passos, 24 January [1934], Dos Passos Papers.

29. Gold, "A Bourgeois Hamlet," pp. 28–29.

30. Lawson to Dos Passos, 9 April 1934, Dos Passos Papers.

31. John Howard Lawson, " 'Inner Conflict' and Proletarian Art: A Reply to Michael Gold," *New Masses* 11 (17 April 1934): 29–30.

32. Clurman, *The Fervent Years*, p. 125. I am indebted to Gerald Rabkin, who points out Clurman's comments, as well as much else about Lawson's career, in *Drama and Commitment: Politics in the American Theatre of the Thirties* (Bloomington: Indiana University Press, 1964), pp. 127–65.

33. Lawson, "Biographical Notes," p. 75; for an account of the second trip into the South, see his pamphlet *A Southern Welcome (In Georgia and Alabama)* (New York: National Committee for the Defense of Political Prisoners, 1934).

34. Rabkin, *Drama and Commitment*, p. 155; the New Theatre essay is quoted there.

35. Dos Passos, *Fourteenth Chronicle*, pp. 446–47.

36. Lawson to Dos Passos, n.d., Dos Passos Papers.

37. Ibid.

38. John Dos Passos, "The Writer as Technician," in *American Writers' Congress,* ed. Henry Hart (New York: International, 1935), pp. 78–82; John Howard Lawson, "Techniques and the Drama," in *American Writers' Congress*, ed. Hart, pp. 123–28.

39. John Dos Passos, *The Living Thoughts of Tom Paine* (New York: Longmans, Green, 1940), pp. 8, 12.

40. John Dos Passos, *The Ground We Stand On: Some Examples from the History of a Political Creed* (New York: Harcourt, Brace, 1941), pp. 3, 5, 6, 8.

Chapter 4
"James T. Farrell and the 1930s" by Donald Pizer

1. Robin George Collingwood, *The Idea of History* (Oxford: Clarendon Press, 1946), pp. 247–48.

2. Barry Wallenstein notes the conventional application of these labels to Farrell in his "James T. Farrell: Critic of Naturalism," in *American Literary Naturalism: A Reassessment*, ed. Yoshinobu Hakutani and Lewis Fried (Heidelberg: C. Winter, 1975), pp. 154–57.

3. The classic study of the political histories of these figures in the 1930s is Daniel Aaron's *Writers on the Left* (New York: Harcourt, Brace and World, 1961). For the first kind of criticism noted above, see Philip Rahv, "Notes on the Decline of Naturalism" (1942), in *Documents of Modern Literary Naturalism*, ed. George J. Becker (Princeton, N.J.: Princeton University Press, 1963), pp. 579–90; and Malcolm Cowley, "A Natural History of American Naturalism" (1947), in *Documents*,

ed. Becker, pp. 429–51. For the second kind, see Lionel Trilling, "Reality in America," in *The Liberal Imagination* (1950; reprint ed., Garden City, N.Y.: Doubleday, Anchor Books, 1957), pp. 1–19.

4. James T. Farrell, *A Note on Literary Criticism* (New York: Vanguard Press, 1936), p. 11; and "The Development of the American Novel" (1965), in *James T. Farrell: Literary Essays 1954–74*, ed. Jack Alan Robbins (Port Washington, N.Y.: Kennekat, 1976), pp. 139–40.

5. Edgar M. Branch, *James T. Farrell* (New York: Twayne, 1971), pp. 36–37. I am indebted to Branch's excellent study for other biographical detail about Farrell that appears in this paper.

6. See Charles C. Walcutt's *American Literary Naturalism, a Divided Stream* (Minneapolis: University of Minnesota Press, 1956), p. 241; Branch, *James T. Farrell*; Lewis Fried, "James T. Farrell: Shadow and Act," *Jahrbuch fur Amerikastudien* 17 (August 1972): 140–55; and James T. Farrell, "Farrell Looks at His Writing," *Twentieth Century Literature* 22 (February 1976): 12–13.

7. James T. Farrell, *Studs Lonigan: A Trilogy* (New York: Modern Library, 1938), pp. xi–xiv.

8. Farrell, *A Note on Literary Criticism*, p. 98.

9. James T. Farrell, *Gas-House McGinty* (1933; reprint ed., New York: World, 1942), p. 38.

10. See Farrell's undated letter to Victor Weybright, quoted by Branch, *James T. Farrell*, p. 173n1. As Farrell notes in this letter, he used in *Judgment Day* only a small portion of the lengthy death-bed fantasy he wrote for the novel.

11. James T. Farrell, "A Note on Sherwood Anderson" (1954), in *Reflections at Fifty and Other Essays*, 2d ed. (London: Vanguard Press, 1956), pp. 164–66.

12. Robert Humphrey, *Stream of Consciousness in the Modern Novel* (Berkeley: University of California Press, 1954); Melvin J. Friedman, *Stream of Consciousness: A Study in Literary Method* (New Haven, Conn.: Yale University Press, 1955); and Roy Pascal, *The Dual Voice: Free Indirect Speech and Its Functioning in the Nineteenth-Century European Novel* (Manchester: Manchester University Press, 1977), p. 137.

13. Farrell, *Young Lonigan*, p. 19. Subsequent references to this novel will be cited in the text.

14. Farrell, *Judgment Day*, p. 160. Subsequent references to this novel will be cited in the text.

15. For Farrell's use of "free association" in connection with *Studs Lonigan*, see "An In-Depth Interview with James T. Farrell," *Writer's Forum* 1 (May 1965): 34, and "James T. Farrell," in *Talks with Authors*, ed. Charles F. Madden (Carbondale: Southern Illinois University Press, 1968), p. 97. For his use of "stream of consciousness," see his 1935 essay, "Farrell's Introduction to Chilean Edition of 'Young Lonigan,'" *American Book Collector* 17 (May 1967): 8. One of the few efforts to discuss *Studs* as a stream-of-consciousness novel occurs in Ann Douglas's recent "*Studs Lonigan* and the Failure of History in Mass Society," *American Quarterly* 29 (1977): 487–505.

16. Farrell wrote in 1948: "The novel is written mainly from the standpoint of immediate experiences. By that I mean this: any event which appears in the book is presented in terms of how it immediately happens, how it registers upon the

consciousness of one or more of the characters" ("The Author as Plaintiff: Testimony in a Censorship Case," *Reflections at Fifty*, p. 191).

17. The story appeared initially in 1931 and is collected in *The Short Stories of James T. Farrell* (New York: Vanguard Press, 1937).

18. *The Young Manhood of Studs Lonigan*, p. 25. Subsequent references to this novel will be cited in the text.

Chapter 5
"Steinbeck, the People, and the Party" by Sylvia Jenkins Cook

1. Michael Gold, "Wilder: Prophet of the Genteel Christ," *New Republic* 64 (22 October 1930): 266–67; Edmund Wilson, "The Literary Class War: I," *New Republic* 70 (4 May 1932): 319–23; and Gold, "The Second American Renaissance," in *Mike Gold: A Literary Anthology*, ed. Michael Folsom (New York: International, 1972), p. 245.

2. John Steinbeck, *Steinbeck: A Life in Letters*, ed. Elaine Steinbeck and Robert Wallsten (New York: Viking, 1975), p. 76.

3. Richard Astro, *John Steinbeck and Edward F. Ricketts: The Shaping of a Novelist* (Minneapolis: University of Minnesota Press, 1973), p. 38.

4. Steinbeck, *Life in Letters*, pp. 105, 98.

5. Samuel Langhorne Clemens, *Adventures of Huckleberry Finn*, ed. Sculley Bradley, Richmond Croom Beatty, and E. Hudson Long (New York: W. W. Norton, 1961), p. 118; Steinbeck, *Life in Letters*, pp. 76, 98.

6. Samuel Levenson, "The Compassion of John Steinbeck," *Canadian Forum* 20, no. 236 (September 1940): 186.

7. Steinbeck, *In Dubious Battle* (New York: Modern Library, 1936), pp. 153, 151. Subsequent references to this edition will be made in the text.

8. Edwin Berry Burgum, "The Sensibility of John Steinbeck," in *Steinbeck and His Critics: A Record of Twenty-Five Years*, ed. Ernest W. Tedlock and C. V. Wicker (Albuquerque: University of New Mexico Press, 1957), p. 108.

9. John Steinbeck, *The Long Valley* (New York: Viking, 1956), p. 302.

10. John Steinbeck, *The Grapes of Wrath* (New York: Viking, 1939), p. 45. Subsequent references to this edition will be made in the text.

11. Astro, *Steinbeck and Ricketts*, p. 39.

12. Chester E. Eisinger, "Jeffersonian Agrarianism in *The Grapes of Wrath*," *University of Kansas City Review* 14 (Winter 1947): 149–54.

13. Steinbeck, *Life in Letters*, pp. 94, 132, 158, 159, 162, 163.

14. Antonia Seixas, "John Steinbeck and the Non-teleological Bus," in *Steinbeck and His Critics*, ed. Tedlock and Wicker, p. 275n.

15. Steinbeck, *Life in Letters*, pp. 194, 197.

16. Richard H. Pells, *Radical Visions and American Dreams* (New York: Harper and Row, 1973), p. 246.

17. "Cutting Down the Laurels," unsigned editorial, *New Republic*, 10 November 1962, p. 8.

Chapter 6
"Trouble on the Land" by Louis D. Rubin, Jr.

1. Critics such as Alfred Kazin and Malcolm Cowley who identified Caldwell as being of plebian origins are quite mistaken, by the way. Though as a young man he spent some time among the proletariat, he came from an educated family with a record of leadership in the Presbyterian church. Both his father and mother were college graduates, and the elder Caldwell was a well-known minister of the ultra-conservative Associate Reformed Presbyterian church.

2. The fictional name Agee chose for his sharecropper, Gudger, is significantly a North Carolina–Tennessee mountain name. Wolfe also uses it.

Chapter 7
"The Consciousness of Technique" by Victor A. Kramer

1. James Agee and Walker Evans, *Let Us Now Praise Famous Men* (Boston: Houghton Mifflin, 1941), p. xiv. Subsequent references to this edition will be made in the text.

2. Autograph manuscript notebook, University of Texas Library, "Let Us Now Praise Famous Men," Notes, 40 1, n.d.

3. An undergraduate story published in the *Harvard Advocate*, "They That Sow in Sorrow Shall Reap," makes this clear. Note especially pp. 82–86, reprinted in *The Collected Short Prose of James Agee* (Boston: Houghton Mifflin, 1968).

4. See J. Douglas Perry, Jr., "James Agee and the American Romantic Tradition" (Ph.D. diss., Temple University, 1968); Alfred Barson, "James Agee: A Study of Artistic Consciousness" (Ph.D. diss., University of Massachusetts, 1969); Peter H. Ohlin, *Agee* (New York: Ivan Obolensky, 1966).

5. Kenneth Seib, *James Agee: Promise and Fulfillment* (Pittsburgh: University of Pittsburgh Press, 1968).

6. William Stott, *Documentary Expression and Thirties America* (New York: Oxford University Press, 1973). See final chapters.

7. A partial carbon-copy manuscript of *Famous Men*, now owned by the library of the University of Texas, reveals that "Part One" of an unused manuscript version of "Work," from which only "selections" were taken for the text, is an elaborate attempt to suggest the reiterative qualities of all physical labor. See also Alan Holder's comments in his "Encounter in Alabama: Agee and the Tenant Farmer," *Virginia Quarterly Review* 42 (1966): 205–6.

8. James Agee, *Letters of James Agee to Father Flye*, ed. James Harold Flye (New York: George Braziller, 1962), p. 104.

9. Erik Wensberg, "Celebrating Adoration and Wonder," *Nation*, 26 November 1960, p. 418.

10. Ralph W. Emerson, "The Poet," *The Selected Writings of R. W. Emerson* (New York: Modern Library, 1951), p. 326.

11. Kenneth Burke, *Rhetoric of Motives* (New York: Prentice-Hall, 1950), p. 146; and Agee, *Letters*, pp. 114–15.

12. Kenneth Burke, *Permanence and Change* (Los Altos, Calif.: Hermes, 1954), p. 54.

13. Marie Hochmuth Nichols, *Rhetoric and Criticism* (Baton Rouge: Louisiana State University Press, 1963), p. 85; and Burke, *Rhetoric of Motives*, p. 23

14. James Agee, *Agee on Film*, vol. 1 (Boston: Beacon Press, 1964), p. 288.

Chapter 8
"The View from the Broom Closet of the Regency Hyatt"
by Jack B. Moore

1. C. Hugh Holman, *The Roots of Southern Writing* (Athens: University of Georgia Press, 1972), pp. 96–107.

2. Du Bois writes about Henry Grady throughout his "Black Flame" trilogy (1957–61), but especially in the first volume in the series, *The Ordeal of Mansart* (New York: Mainstream, 1957).

3. The following stories are included in *Eight Men* (New York: World, 1961, the most accessible edition): "The Man Who Saw The Flood" and "The Man Who Was Almost a Man." I have preferred to use the titles of these stories when originally published, "Silt," and "Almos' a Man," respectively. The following stories are included in *Uncle Tom's Children* (New York: Harper and Row, 1965, the most accessible edition): "Big Boy Leaves Home," "Fire and Cloud," "Long Black Song," "Bright and Morning Star," and "Down by the Riverside."

4. Dan McCall, *The Example of Richard Wright* (New York: Harcourt, Brace and World, 1969), p. 39.

5. McCall, *The Example of Richard Wright*, p. 26; Edward Margolies, *The Art of Richard Wright* (Carbondale: Southern Illinois University Press, 1969), p. 60.

6. Milton Rickels and Patricia Rickels, *Richard Wright* (Austin, Tex.: Stock Vaughan, 1970), p. 6.

7. Addison Gayle, "Culture Hegemony: The Southern White Writer and American Letters," *Amistad 1*, ed. John A. Williams and Charles F. Harris (New York: Random House, Vintage Books, 1971), p. 20.

8. Rickels and Rickels, *Richard Wright*, p. 8.

9. Michel Fabre, *The Unfinished Quest of Richard Wright* (New York: William Morrow, 1973).

10. A recent and interesting discussion of the black proletariat-peasantry controversy is in "Black Liberation: A Proletarian Question" (*Red Papers* 5 n.d. [1971?], pp. 25–30). Pp. 25, 26, 61 supply figures concerning mechanization in the South. *Red Papers* also contains the statements of Marx and Lenin that I quote above, on pp. 18 and 23 respectively. In *The Agony of the American Left* (New York: Random House, Vintage Books, 1969), Christopher Lasch reviews some of the literature on the topic, Is the Negro issue a class issue, a race issue, or a "national" (ethnic) issue? in his chapter "Black Power: Cultural Nationalism as Politics." Lasch is to the right of the *Red Papers'* writers.

11. Quoted in Fabre, *Unfinished Quest*, p. 122.

Chapter 9
"Starting Out in the Thirties" by Glenda Hobbs

1. For a detailed discussion of the southern poor white in fiction, see Sylvia Jenkins Cook, "The Development of the Poor White Tradition" and "The Image in the Twentieth Century," in *From Tobacco Road to Route 66: The Southern Poor White in Fiction* (Chapel Hill: University of North Carolina Press, 1976), pp. 3–39.

2. Furman's three most popular books treating this theme are *Mothering on Perilous* (1910), *The Quare Women: A Story of the Kentucky Mountains* (1923), and *The Glass Window: A Story of the Quare Women* (1925). Charles Neville Buck's best-selling *The Battle Cry* (1914) and *Mountain Justice: A Tale of the Cumberlands* (1935) similarly depict this subject.

3. In "Caldwell's Politics of the Grotesque," in *From Tobacco Road to Route 66*, pp. 64–85, Cook perceptively analyzes Caldwell's thirties fiction and discusses the response of proletarian sympathizers to his work. In "The Transformation of the Poor White in the Depression," pp. 184–89, she provides a detailed account of changes in the presentation of the poor white in the 1930s.

4. Harold Strauss to Harriette Arnow, 3 October 1935, Box 2, Harriette Arnow Special Collection, University of Kentucky Library, Lexington. All references from this collection are quoted by permission of the University of Kentucky Library.

5. Strauss to Arnow, 24 October 1935, Box 2, Arnow Special Collection.

6. Faulkner, whose work transcends his time, is an exception. *As I Lay Dying* (1930) and *Absalom, Absalom!* (1936) are not written in conventional form, with a situation, a complication, and a solution. It is noteworthy, though, that when he set out to write best-sellers, in *Sanctuary* (1931) and *Light in August* (1932), he used a conventional narrative form to convey his sensationalistic stories.

7. Alfred Kazin, "Diverse Themes in Fall Fiction," *New York Herald Tribune Books*, 6 September 1936, pp. 10, 14. Margaret Wallace, "Mountain Path and Some Other Recent Works of Fiction," *New York Times Book Review*, 30 August 1936, p. 6, also notes that Louisa's characterization, and not the feud, is the "meat of the book."

8. Arnow to Strauss, n.d., 11 pages, Box 2, Arnow Special Collection.

9. Arnow to the author, 16 March 1974, p. 1.

10. Ibid.

11. Harriette Arnow, introduction to *Mountain Path*, by Harriette Arnow (1936; reprint ed., Berea, Ky.: Council of the Southern Mountains, 1963).

12. Currie Cabot, "In the Kentucky Mountains," *Saturday Review of Literature*, 29 August 1936, p. 13, praises Louisa's sharing in the "primitive mountain life"; Margaret Wallace, review of *Mountain Path, New York Times Book Review*, 30 August 1936, p. 6, applauds Louisa for regarding the Calhouns as "human beings like herself"; the phrase "sullen dignity" is from Kazin's review "Diverse Themes"; M. W. S., "Kentucky Hill Folk," *Christian Science Monitor*, 1 September 1936, p. 16, called the Calhouns "child-like" and "strangely wise"; the last quotation is taken from "Tragic Mountain Romance," *Los Angeles Times*, 30 August 1936, sec. 3, p. 5.

13. Arnow, *Mountain Path*, p. 214. All subsequent references to this work appear parenthetically in the text.

14. Arnow to Strauss, n.d., 11 pages, Box 2, Arnow Special Collection.

15. John M. Bradbury, *Renaissance in the South: A Critical History of the Literature, 1920–1960* (Chapel Hill: University of North Carolina Press, 1963), p. 171.

16. The phrase "Shakespeare in overalls" is Daniel Aaron's, in *Writers on the Left* (New York: Harcourt, Brace and World, 1961), p. 222.

17. Arnow to Strauss, n.d., begins "I wish I could talk to you," Box 2, Arnow Special Collection. The errors in the letter are the result of Arnow's admittedly poor typing rather than misspelling.

18. Arnow to the author, 16 March 1974, p. 1.

19. Arnow to Strauss, n.d., 11 pages, Box 2, Arnow Special Collection.

20. Arnow to Strauss, n.d., begins "I wish I could talk to you," Box 2, Arnow Special Collection.

21. Quoted in Wilton Eckley, *Harriette Arnow* (New York: Twayne, 1974), p. 40.

22. Arnow to Strauss, n.d., 11 pages, Box 2, Arnow Special Collection.

23. Ibid.

24. Strauss to Arnow, 18 August 1937, Box 2, Arnow Special Collection.

25. Ibid.

26. Strauss to Arnow, 29 October 1937, Box 2, Arnow Special Collection.

27. William Suskin to Arnow, 24 August 1939, Box 2, Arnow Special Collection. The version of *Between the Flowers* in the University of Kentucky Library has strong characters, a firm plot line, and the "poetic qualities" that distinguish Arnow's writing. It is unknown whether this version was submitted to publishers.

28. Barbara L. Baer, "Harriette Arnow's Chronicles of Destruction," *Nation*, 31 January 1976, pp. 117–20.

29. Malcolm Cowley, "Naturalism: No Teacup Tragedies," in *The Literary Situation* (New York: Viking, 1947), p. 94.

Chapter 10
"Oppen, Zukofsky, and the Poem as Lens" by Hugh Kenner

1. Oppen's poems are found in George Oppen, *Collected Poems* (New York: New Directions, 1975).

2. Louis Zukofsky, *"A"* (Berkeley and Los Angeles: University of California Press, 1979). See also Louis Zukofsky, *All, 1923–58* (New York: W. W. Norton, 1965).

3. William Carlos Williams, *Autobiography* (New York: Random House, 1951), p. 264.

4. For further light, see L. S. Denbo's interviews with both poets in *Contemporary Literature* 10 (1969): 159–77, 203–19; L. S. Denbo, "The Existential World of George Oppen," *Iowa Review* 3 (Winter 1972); and special issues devoted to Oppen and Zukofsky respectively by *Ironwood* 3, no. 1 (1975) and *Maps* 5 (1973).

Chapter 11
"Edmund Wilson's Political Decade" by Daniel Aaron

1. Edmund Wilson, *The American Jitters: A Year of the Slump* (1932; reprint ed., Freeport, N.Y.: Books for Libraries Press, 1968), pp. 300, 307, 310.

2. Wilson, *American Jitters*, pp. 310–11.

3. *Times Literary Supplement*, 17 November 1978, p. 1343.

4. Edmund Wilson, *Letters on Literature and Politics, 1912–1972*, ed. Elena Wilson (New York: Farrar, Straus and Giroux, 1977), pp. 154, 193, 196, 204, 220, 227.

5. Fadiman's response to a symposium, "Whither the American Writer," *Modern Quarterly* 6 (Summer 1932): 112.

6. Edmund Wilson, "The Literary Class War: II," *New Republic*, 11 May 1932, p. 348.

7. Fadiman in *Modern Quarterly* 6:112–13.

8. Wilson, *Letters*, pp. 222–24.

9. Ibid., pp. 221–22.

10. Edmund Wilson, *The Thirties: From the Notebooks and Diaries of the Period*, ed. Leon Edel (New York: Farrar, Straus and Giroux, 1980).

11. Wilson, *Letters*, pp. 222–23.

12. Robert M. Adams, "Diffractions of a Generalist," review of *An Edmund Wilson Celebration*, ed. John Wain, *Times Literary Supplement*, 17 November 1978, p. 1343.

13. "He never ceased to show me kindnesses," wrote Edward Dahlberg, and then added that Wilson was "quite ready to help a writer provided he felt superior to him." He lumped him with "other shallow feuilletonists," called his *Classics and Commercials* "a whorehouse of stage dolts and scullion prosers," and dismissed him finally as an "inveterate opsimath" and emotionless positivist. See Edward Dahlberg, *The Confessions of Edward Dahlberg* (New York: George Braziller, 1971), pp. 245–56.

14. Wilson, *American Jitters*, pp. 37–45.

15. Ibid., pp. 10, 17, 11, 25.

16. Ibid., p. 12.

17. Edmund Wilson, *Red, Black, Blond and Orange* (New York: Oxford University Press, 1956), p. 375.

18. Wilson, *Letters*, pp. 256, 262.

19. Edmund Wilson, *Travels in Two Democracies* (New York: Harcourt, Brace, 1936).

20. From reviews of *Travels in Two Democracies*: Robert Cantwell, *New Republic*, 6 May 1936, p. 271; Malcolm Cowley, *New Republic*, 10 June 1936, p. 135; Isidor Schneider, *New Masses*, 14 April 1936, p. 23; Milton Howard, *New Masses*, 1 September 1936, p. 24.

21. Wilson, *Letters*, pp. 266, 286, 287, 288, 292, 311. The most recent comment on *Travels in Two Democracies* is in Simon Karlinsky's introduction to his edition of the Wilson-Nabokov letters. He describes Wilson's views on Russia as "an affecting mixture of his own naive expectations and the hard realities he did his best to

explain away" (*The Nabokov-Wilson Letters: Correspondence between Vladimir Nabokov and Edmund Wilson, 1940–1971*, New York: Harper and Row, 1979, p. 5).

22. Edmund Wilson, *The Triple Thinkers: Ten Essays on Literature* (New York: Harcourt, Brace, 1938), pp. 102, 114.

23. Wilson, *Letters*, p. 295.

24. Wilson, *Triple Thinkers*, p. 241.

25. Daniel Aaron, "The Treachery of Recollection: The Inner and Outer History," in *Essays on History and Literature*, ed. Robert H. Bremner (Columbus: Ohio State University Press, 1966), p. 23.

26. Edmund Wilson, *Five Plays* (New York: Farrar, Straus and Young, 1954), p. 406.

27. Edmund Wilson, *Classics and Commercials: A Literary Chronicle of the Forties* (New York: Farrar, Straus, 1950), pp. 168–70.

Chapter 12
"Revolutionary Intellectuals" by Alan Wald

1. Though other figures will be mentioned in this essay—especially Dwight Macdonald, F. W. Dupee, Mary McCarthy, and Meyer Schapiro—Phillips and Rahv were among the initiators of the first version of *Partisan Review* in 1934, and they outlasted all the others associated with it. Thus it is legitimate to accord them paramount attention. I am indebted to James Burkhart Gilbert's *Writers and Partisans: A History of Literary Radicalism in America* (New York: Wiley, 1968) for some of my informaton.

2. William Phillips, "How *Partisan Review* Began," *Commentary* 62 (December 1976): 42. See also Rahv's article on T. S. Eliot in *Fantasy* 2 (Winter 1932): 17. According to Gilbert, Phillips's first writing was a play, and he contributed criticism to *Hound and Horn*. Phillips, who often used the pen name Wallace Phelps until 1935, also wrote for *Symposium*, which was partly modeled on Eliot's *Criterion* (see Gilbert, *Writers and Partisans*, pp. 110–12). Once in the radical movement, however, Phillips wrote for the *New Masses* and *Dynamo* and Rahv for *Left*, *International Literature*, and the *Little Magazine*. These facts are mentioned in *Partisan Review* 1 (November–December 1934): 5.

3. "We propose to concentrate on creative and critical literature," states the initial editorial of *Partisan Review* 1 (November–December 1934): 2. See William Phillips and Philip Rahv, "In Retrospect: Ten Years of *Partisan Review*," in *The Partisan Reader* (New York: Dial, 1946), p. 679.

4. See *Partisan Review* 2 (April–May 1935): 16–25, and *Partisan Review and Anvil* 3 (June 1936): 11–14; Wallace Phelps [William Phillips], "Three Generations," *Partisan Review* 1 (September–October 1934): 51.

5. Both Rahv and Phillips addressed the national meeting of the John Reed clubs in Chicago, September 1934. There the danger of leftism was denounced by the Writers Commission, which also called for a "genuine aesthetic recreation of the class struggle" and warned against frightening away sympathetic fellow-travelers. This was reported in *Partisan Review* 1 (November–December 1934): 60.

6. The quotations are from an editorial by William Phillips and Philip Rahv, "Problems and Perspectives in Revolutionary Literature," *Partisan Review* 1 (June–July 1934): 4, 5.

7. Phillips and Rahv, "Problems and Perspectives," pp. 5, 6.

8. Wallace Phelps [William Phillips] and Philip Rahv, "Criticism," *Partisan Review* 2 (April–May 1935): 3.

9. Wallace Phelps [William Phillips], "Form and Content," *Partisan Review* 2 (January–February 1935): 31–39; Philip Rahv, "How the Wasteland Became a Flowergarden," *Partisan Review* 1 (September–October 1934): 37–41.

10. Phelps, "Three Generations," p. 51. In *Partisan Review* 1 (September–October 1934): 38, Rahv gave the following description of one of the Stalinists' chief antagonists: "Max Eastman, politically degenerate and steeped in venom." In the same article (p. 39), Rahv cites the following as heroes of the workers: Stalin, Dimitrov, and Thaelmann. And see Phelps and Rahv, "Problems and Perspectives" p. 3. Similar sentiments have been voiced by Rahv alone in an essay in the previous issue, "The Novelist as Partisan," *Partisan Review* 1 (April–May 1934): 50–52.

11. Malcolm Cowley, "Thirty Years Later: Memories of the First American Writers' Congress," *The American Scholar* 35 (Summer 1966): 497.

12. The merger is discussed in Mike Gold's article "Papa Anvil and Mother Partisan," *New Masses* 18 (18 February 1936): 22–23. The authoritative history of the interaction between American writers and the Communist movement is Daniel Aaron's *Writers on the Left: Episodes in American Literary Communism* (New York: Harcourt, Brace and World, 1961).

13. Philip Rahv, "Two Years of the Writers Congress," *Partisan Review* 5 (February 1938): 24.

14. Philip Rahv, "Proletarian Literature: A Political Autopsy," *Southern Review* 4 (1940): 617.

15. This incident is recorded in a number of places, but the version I have used is based on an interview with Dwight Macdonald on 4 November 1973, in Buffalo, New York.

16. Phillips, "How *Partisan Review* Began," p. 45.

17. Interview with F. W. Dupee, 21 August 1973, Carmel, California.

18. See Mary McCarthy, *The Company She Keeps* (New York: Harcourt, Brace and World, 1970), pp. 167–246, and *On the Contrary* (New York: Farrar, Straus and Cudahy, 1962), pp. 75–105.

19. Malcolm Cowley, ed., *Writers at Work* (New York: Viking, 1963), pp. 297–98.

20. Interview with F. W. Dupee, 21 August 1973.

21. Schapiro to Wald, 27 July 1974.

22. Thomas B. Hess, "On the Work of Meyer Schapiro," *Social Research* 45 (Spring 1978): 6; Schapiro to James T. Farrell, 1 September 1940.

23. For a depiction of the impact of the trials on American intellectuals see Alan Wald, "Memories of the John Dewey Commission Forty Years Later," *Antioch Review* 35 (1977): 438–51.

24. William Phillips, "The Esthetic of the Founding Fathers," *Partisan Review* 4 (March 1938): 17, 19.

25. Philip Rahv, "Twilight of the Thirties," *Partisan Review* 5 (Summer 1939): 15, 11.

26. Rahv, "Trials of the Mind," p. 10.

27. Leon Trotsky, "The Future of *Partisan Review:* A Letter to Dwight Mc-donald," in *Leon Trotsky on Literature and Art,* ed. Paul Siegel (New York: Pathfinder, 1970), pp. 101–3. Additional quotations will be cited parenthetically in the text.

28. Editorial, *Socialist Appeal,* 4 December 1937, p. 7. In an interview in San Francisco in October 1972, George Novack stated that he was the author of the editorial, which was unsigned.

29. Philip Rahv, "Twilight of the Thirties," *Partisan Review* 5 (Summer 1939): 14.

30. Rahv, "Trials of the Mind," p. 3.

31. Richard Pells, *Radical Visions and American Dreams* (New York: Harper and Row, Harper Torchbooks, 1974), p. 336.

32. Interview with F. W. Dupee, 21 August 1973.

Chapter 13
"The End of a Literary Decade" by James T. Farrell

1. See James T. Farrell, "Dos Passos and His Critics," *American Mercury* 47 (1939): 489–94.

2. John Chamberlain, "Literature," in *America Now,* ed. Harold Stearns (New York: Literary Guild, 1938), pp. 37–38.

Contributors

DANIEL AARON is currently a member of the Department of English and American Literature and Language at Harvard University. Among his numerous publications are *Writers on the Left, The Unwritten War: American Writers and the Civil War*, and more recently the introduction to Edmund Wilson's *Letters on Literature and Politics*. Presently he is engaged in writing a book on the American man of letters, a study in which Edmund Wilson will figure prominently.

RALPH F. BOGARDUS is director of the Program in American Studies at the University of Alabama. He has published articles on such American writers as Henry James, W. D. Howells, and Jacob A. Riis in scholarly journals that include *New York History, Centennial Review*, and *American Literary Realism, 1870–1910*. He is currently working on a study of the collaboration between Henry James and photographer Alvin Langdon Coburn on the New York edition frontispieces.

SYLVIA JENKINS COOK is a member of the English Department at the University of Missouri–St. Louis. She is the author of *From Tobacco Road to Route 66: The Southern Poor White in Fiction*, as well as of a number of articles dealing with politics, feminism, and literature in the 1930s. She is now working on a study of Erskine Caldwell.

JAMES T. FARRELL (1904–1979) published over fifty books of fiction and nonfiction during his lifetime. Best known for his *Studs Lonigan* trilogy of the 1930s, he continued to create fiction of extraordinary power, chronicling the psychological price so many people pay by living in a mass American culture. His other works include the Danny O'Neill pentalogy, the *Bernard Clare* trilogy, and more recent works, *The Silence of History* (1963), *What Time Collects* (1964), and *Lonely for the Future* (1974).

JOSEPHINE HERBST (1897–1969) was a novelist, essayist, and journalist who was involved with the literary left during the 1920s and 1930s. Though neglected, she continued to write for the remainder of her life. Her works include a trilogy of novels, *Pity Is Not Enough* (1933), *The Executioner Waits* (1934), and *Rope of Gold* (1939). During the last two decades of her life, she was at work on her memoirs: "A Year of Disgrace," published in *Noble Savage* 3 (1961); "The Starched Blue Sky of Spain," in *Noble Savage* 1 (1960); and "Yesterday's Road," appearing in this volume. She also wrote a novella called *Hunter of Doves*, which was published in *Botteghe Oscura* 13 (1954).

GLENDA HOBBS is associate director of the Writer Development Department at the Mark Taper Forum in Los Angeles. Her essays on Harriette Arnow and Sarah Orne Jewett have appeared in the *Kate Chopin Newsletter*, *Studies in Short Fiction*, and the *Georgia Review*. She is currently editing a collection of Harriette Arnow's short stories. Her entry on Harriette Arnow in the *Dictionary of Literary Biography: American Novelists since World War II*, second series, has also recently appeared.

FRED HOBSON teaches American literature at the University of Alabama in Tuscaloosa. He has published articles and essays on southern writers in the *Virginia Quarterly Review, Sewanee Review, Southern Literary Journal*, and *Mississippi Quarterly*. He is author of *Serpent in Eden: H. L. Mencken and the South*, and he is currently completing a study of self-exploration by southern writers from Edmund Ruffin to W. J. Cash.

IRVING HOWE is Distinguished Professor of English at the Graduate Center of the City University of New York and is editor of *Dissent*. He has published numerous essays and books during his extraordinary career. His work includes *Literature and Politics, Leon Trotsky*, and book-length literary studies of William Faulkner, Sherwood Anderson, and Thomas Hardy. His best-known book, *World of Our Fathers*, won a National Book Award in 1976.

HUGH KENNER is professor of English and American literature and chairman of the English department at the Johns Hopkins University. He is a highly respected critic whose many books include the definitive work *The Pound Era* and *A Homemade World: The American Modernist Writers*, as well as studies of Joyce, Beckett, Eliot, and Wyndham Lewis. He has also written brilliantly on nonliterary subjects as disparate as Buckminster Fuller, Buster Keaton, and Andy Warhol.

VICTOR A. KRAMER teaches English and American literature at Georgia State University in Atlanta. He has written *James Agee* (for the Twayne series), and numerous articles on American writers. He has also coedited the *Olmstead South* and is currently completing a study of Thomas Merton for Twayne.

TOWNSEND LUDINGTON is a professor in the English department at the University of North Carolina in Chapel Hill. He has edited *The Fourteenth Chronicle: Letters and Diaries of John Dos Passos* and is the author of the recent biographical study, *John Dos Passos: Twentieth Century Odyssey*. He has also written a number of articles and essays on American writers that have appeared in the *New Republic* and other periodicals.

JACK B. MOORE chairs the Program in American Studies at the University of South Florida in Tampa. He has written extensively on black American literary figures such as Wright, and he has recently completed a study of W. E. B. Du Bois.

DONALD PIZER is Pierce Butler Professor of English at Tulane University. He has been a Fulbright lecturer at the University of Hamburg, and he held the Andrew W. Mellon Professorship in the Humanities at Tulane during 1977–78. He has published numerous articles and books on American literary subjects, including *Realism and Naturalism in Nineteenth-Century American Literature, The Novels of Frank Norris*, and *The Novels of Theodore Dreiser*.

LOUIS D. RUBIN, JR., is University Distinguished Professor of English at the University of North Carolina in Chapel Hill. His many articles, essays, editions, and book-length studies are well known and highly regarded. His recent publications include *The Writer in the South, William Elliott Shoots a Bear: Essays on the Southern Literary Imagination*, and *The Wary Fugitives*.

ALAN WALD is associate professor of English and American studies at the University of Michigan. He is the author of a number of articles and essays on 1930s American writers and has published *James T. Farrell: The Revolutionary Socialist Years*. He has recently completed a book about Harvard poets John Wheelwright and Sherry Mangan.

Index